Praise for *Foundations of Scalable Systems*

Building scalable distributed systems is hard. This book just made it easier. With topics ranging from concurrency and load balancing to caching and database scaling, you'll learn the skills necessary to make your systems scale to meet the demands of today's modern world.

—*Mark Richards, Software Architect, Founder of DeveloperToArchitect.com*

Through lively examples and a no-nonsense style, Professor Gorton presents and discusses the principles, architectures, and technologies foundational to scalable distributed systems design. This book serves as an essential modern text for students and practitioners alike.

—*Anna Liu, Senior Manager, Amazon Web Services*

The technology in this space is changing all the time, and there is a lot of hype and buzzwords out there. Ian Gorton cuts through that and explains the principles and trade-offs you need to understand to successfully design large-scale software systems.

—*John Klein, Carnegie Mellon University Software Engineering Institute*

Scalability is a serious topic in software design, and this book provides a great overview of the many aspects that need to be considered by architects and software engineers. Ian Gorton succeeds in striking an excellent balance between theory and practice, presenting his real-life experience in a way that is immediately useful. His lighthearted writing style makes for an enjoyable and easy read, with the occasional sidetrack to explain things like the link between software architecture and Italian-inspired cuisine.

—*Eltjo Poort, Architect, CGI*

Foundations of Scalable Systems
Designing Distributed Architectures

Ian Gorton

Beijing · Boston · Farnham · Sebastopol · Tokyo

Foundations of Scalable Systems

by Ian Gorton

Published by O'Reilly Media, Inc., 1005 Gravenstein Highway North, Sebastopol, CA 95472.

O'Reilly books may be purchased for educational, business, or sales promotional use. Online editions are also available for most titles (*http://oreilly.com*). For more information, contact our corporate/institutional sales department: 800-998-9938 or *corporate@oreilly.com*.

Acquisitions Editor: Melissa Duffield	**Indexer:** nSight, Inc.
Development Editor: Virginia Wilson	**Interior Designer:** David Futato
Production Editor: Jonathon Owen	**Cover Designer:** Karen Montgomery
Copyeditor: Justin Billing	**Illustrator:** Kate Dullea
Proofreader: nSight, Inc.	

July 2022:   First Edition

Revision History for the First Edition
2022-06-29:   First Release
2023-03-17:   Second Release

See *https://oreil.ly/scal-sys* for release details.

978-1-098-10606-5

[LSI]

Table of Contents

Part IV. Event and Stream Processing

Preface

This book is built around the thesis that the ability of software systems to operate at scale is increasingly a key factor that defines success. As our world becomes more interconnected, this characteristic will only become more prevalent. Hence, the goal of this book is to provide the reader with the core knowledge of distributed and concurrent systems. It also introduces a collection of software architecture approaches and distributed technologies that can be used to build scalable systems.

Why Scalability?

The pace of change in our world is daunting. Innovations appear daily, creating new capabilities for us all to interact, conduct business, entertain ourselves...even end pandemics. The fuel for much of this innovation is software, written by veritable armies of developers in major internet companies, crack small teams in startups, and all shapes and sizes of teams in between.

Delivering software systems that are responsive to user needs is difficult enough, but it becomes an order of magnitude more difficult to do for systems at scale. We all know of systems that fail suddenly when exposed to unexpected high loads—such situations are (in the best cases) bad publicity for organizations, and at worst can result in lost jobs or destroyed companies.

Software is unlike physical systems in that it's amorphous—its physical form (1s and 0s) bears no resemblance to its actual capabilities. We'd never expect to transform a small village of 500 people into a city of 10 million overnight. But we sometimes expect our software systems to suddenly handle one thousand times the number of requests they were designed for. Unsurprisingly, the outcomes are rarely pretty.

Who This Book Is For

The major target audience for this book is software engineers and architects who have zero or limited experience with distributed, concurrent systems. They need to deepen both their theoretical and practical design knowledge in order to meet the challenges of building larger-scale, typically internet-facing applications.

What You Will Learn

This book covers the landscape of concurrent and distributed systems through the lens of scalability. While it's impossible to totally divorce scalability from other architectural qualities, scalability is the main focus of discussion. Of course, other qualities necessarily come into play, with performance, availability, and consistency regularly raising their heads.

Building distributed systems requires some fundamental understanding of distribution and concurrency—this knowledge is a recurrent theme throughout this book. It's needed because of the two essential problems in distributed systems that make them complex, as I describe below.

First, although systems as a whole operate perfectly correctly nearly all the time, an individual part of the system may fail at any time. When a component fails (whether due to a hardware crash, network outage, bug in a server, etc.), we have to employ techniques that enable the system as a whole to continue operations and recover from failures. Every distributed system will experience component failure, often in weird, mysterious, and unanticipated ways.

Second, creating a scalable distributed system requires the coordination of multiple moving parts. Each component of the system needs to keep its part of the bargain and process requests as quickly as possible. If just one component causes requests to be delayed, the whole system may perform poorly and even eventually crash.

There is a rich body of literature available to help you deal with these problems. Luckily for us engineers, there's also an extensive collection of technologies that are designed to help us build distributed systems that are tolerant to failure and scalable. These technologies embody theoretical approaches and complex algorithms that are incredibly hard to build correctly. Using these platform-level, widely applicable technologies, our applications can stand on the shoulders of giants, enabling us to build sophisticated business solutions.

Specifically, readers of this book will learn:

- The fundamental characteristics of distributed systems, including state management, time coordination, concurrency, communications, and coordination

- Architectural approaches and supporting technologies for building scalable, robust services

- How distributed databases operate and can be used to build scalable distributed systems

- Architectures and technologies such as Apache Kafka and Flink for building streaming, event-based systems

Note for Educators

Much of the content of this book has been developed in the context of an advanced undergraduate/graduate course at Northeastern University. It has proven a very popular and effective approach for equipping students with the knowledge and skills needed to launch their careers with major internet companies. Additional materials on the book website (*https://oreil.ly/fss-git-repo*) are available to support educators who wish to use the book for their course.

Conventions Used in This Book

The following typographical conventions are used in this book:

Italic
    Indicates new terms, URLs, email addresses, filenames, and file extensions.

`Constant width`
    Used for program listings, as well as within paragraphs to refer to program elements such as variable or function names, databases, data types, environment variables, statements, and keywords.

`Constant width bold`
    Shows commands or other text that should be typed literally by the user.

`Constant width italic`
    Shows text that should be replaced with user-supplied values or by values determined by context.

 This element signifies a general note.

This element indicates a warning or caution.

Using Code Examples

Supplemental material (code examples, exercises, etc.) is available for download at *https://oreil.ly/fss-git-repo*.

If you have a technical question or a problem using the code examples, please send email to *bookquestions@oreilly.com*.

This book is here to help you get your job done. In general, if example code is offered with this book, you may use it in your programs and documentation. You do not need to contact us for permission unless you're reproducing a significant portion of the code. For example, writing a program that uses several chunks of code from this book does not require permission. Selling or distributing examples from O'Reilly books does require permission. Answering a question by citing this book and quoting example code does not require permission. Incorporating a significant amount of example code from this book into your product's documentation does require permission.

We appreciate, but generally do not require, attribution. An attribution usually includes the title, author, publisher, and ISBN. For example: "*Foundations of Scalable Solutions* by Ian Gorton (O'Reilly). Copyright 2022 Ian Gorton, 978-1-098-10606-5."

If you feel your use of code examples falls outside fair use or the permission given above, feel free to contact us at *permissions@oreilly.com*.

O'Reilly Online Learning

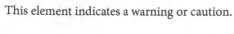 For more than 40 years, *O'Reilly Media* has provided technology and business training, knowledge, and insight to help companies succeed.

Our unique network of experts and innovators share their knowledge and expertise through books, articles, and our online learning platform. O'Reilly's online learning platform gives you on-demand access to live training courses, in-depth learning paths, interactive coding environments, and a vast collection of text and video from O'Reilly and 200+ other publishers. For more information, visit *https://oreilly.com*.

How to Contact Us

Please address comments and questions concerning this book to the publisher:

> O'Reilly Media, Inc.
> 1005 Gravenstein Highway North
> Sebastopol, CA 95472
> 800-998-9938 (in the United States or Canada)
> 707-829-0515 (international or local)
> 707-829-0104 (fax)

We have a web page for this book, where we list errata, examples, and any additional information. You can access this page at *https://oreil.ly/scal-sys*.

Email *bookquestions@oreilly.com* to comment or ask technical questions about this book.

For news and information about our books and courses, visit *https://oreilly.com*.

Find us on LinkedIn: *https://linkedin.com/company/oreilly-media*

Follow us on Twitter: *https://twitter.com/oreillymedia*

Watch us on YouTube: *https://www.youtube.com/oreillymedia*

Acknowledgments

None of this work would ever have happened without the inspiration afforded to me by my graduate school advisor, Professor Jon Kerridge. His boundless enthusiasm has fueled me in this work for three decades.

Matt Bass and John Klein from Carnegie Mellon University were invaluable resources in the early stages of this project. I thank them for the great discussions about the whole spectrum of scalable software architectures.

My reviewers have been excellent—diligent and insightful—and have kept me on the right track. Eternal gratitude is due to Mark Richards, Matt Stine, Thiyagu Palanisamy, Jess Males, Orkhan Huseynli, Adnan Rashid, and Nirav Aga. And many thanks to Virginia Wilson for fixing my wonky words!

I'd also like to thank all my students, and especially Ruijie Xiao, in the CS6650 Building Scalable Distributed Systems course at Northeastern University in Seattle. You've provided me with invaluable feedback on how best to communicate the many complex concepts covered in this book. You are the best guinea pigs ever!

PART I
The Basics

The first four chapters in Part I of this book advocate the need for scalability as a key architectural attribute in modern software systems. These chapters provide broad coverage of the basic mechanisms for achieving scalability, the fundamental characteristics of distributed systems, and an introduction to concurrent programming. This knowledge lays the foundation for what follows, and if you are new to the areas of distributed, concurrent systems, you'll need to spend some time on these chapters. They will make the rest of the book much easier to digest.

CHAPTER 1

Introduction to Scalable Systems

The last 20 years have seen unprecedented growth in the size, complexity, and capacity of software systems. This rate of growth is hardly likely to slow in the next 20 years—what future systems will look like is close to unimaginable right now. However, one thing we can guarantee is that more and more software systems will need to be built with constant growth—more requests, more data, and more analysis—as a primary design driver.

Scalable is the term used in software engineering to describe software systems that can accommodate growth. In this chapter I'll explore what precisely is meant by the ability to scale, known (not surprisingly) as *scalability*. I'll also describe a few examples that put hard numbers on the capabilities and characteristics of contemporary applications and give a brief history of the origins of the massive systems we routinely build today. Finally, I'll describe two general principles for achieving scalability, replication and optimization, which will recur in various forms throughout the rest of this book, and examine the indelible link between scalability and other software architecture quality attributes.

What Is Scalability?

Intuitively, scalability is a pretty straightforward concept. If we ask Wikipedia for a definition (*https://oreil.ly/JsYXf*), it tells us, "Scalability is the property of a system to handle a growing amount of work by adding resources to the system." We all know how we scale a highway system—we add more traffic lanes so it can handle a greater number of vehicles. Some of my favorite people know how to scale beer production—they add more capacity in terms of the number and size of brewing vessels, the number of staff to perform and manage the brewing process, and the number of kegs they can fill with fresh, tasty brews. Think of any physical system—a transit system, an airport, elevators in a building—and how we increase capacity is pretty obvious.

Unlike physical systems, software systems are somewhat amorphous. They are not something you can point at, see, touch, feel, and get a sense of how it behaves internally from external observation. A software system is a digital artifact. At its core, the stream of 1s and 0s that make up executable code and data are hard for anyone to tell apart. So, what does scalability mean in terms of a software system?

Put very simply, and without getting into definition wars, scalability defines a software system's capability to handle growth in some dimension of its operations. Examples of operational dimensions are:

- The number of simultaneous user or external (e.g., sensor) requests a system can process
- The amount of data a system can effectively process and manage
- The value that can be derived from the data a system stores through predictive analytics
- The ability to maintain a stable, consistent response time as the request load grows

For example, imagine a major supermarket chain is rapidly opening new stores and increasing the number of self-checkout kiosks in every store. This requires the core supermarket software systems to perform the following functions:

- Handle increased volume from item scanning without decreased response time. Instantaneous responses to item scans are necessary to keep customers happy.
- Process and store the greater data volumes generated from increased sales. This data is needed for inventory management, accounting, planning, and likely many other functions.
- Derive "real-time" (e.g., hourly) sales data summaries from each store, region, and country and compare to historical trends. This trend data can help highlight unusual events in regions (unexpected weather conditions, large crowds at events, etc.) and help affected stores to quickly respond.
- Evolve the stock ordering prediction subsystem to be able to correctly anticipate sales (and hence the need for stock reordering) as the number of stores and customers grow.

These dimensions are effectively the scalability requirements of the system. If, over a year, the supermarket chain opens 100 new stores and grows sales by 400 times (some of the new stores are big!), then the software system needs to scale to provide the necessary processing capacity to enable the supermarket to operate efficiently. If the systems don't scale, we could lose sales when customers become unhappy. We might hold stock that will not be sold quickly, increasing costs. We might miss opportunities to increase sales by responding to local circumstances with special offerings. All these factors reduce customer satisfaction and profits. None are good for business.

Successfully scaling is therefore crucial for our imaginary supermarket's business growth, and likewise is in fact the lifeblood of many modern internet applications. But for most business and government systems, scalability is not a primary quality requirement in the early stages of development and deployment. New features to enhance usability and utility become the drivers of our development cycles. As long as performance is adequate under normal loads, we keep adding user-facing features to enhance the system's business value. In fact, introducing some of the sophisticated distributed technologies I'll describe in this book before there is a clear requirement can actually be deleterious to a project, with the additional complexity causing development inertia.

Still, it's not uncommon for systems to evolve into a state where enhanced performance and scalability become a matter of urgency, or even survival. Attractive features and high utility breed success, which brings more requests to handle and more data to manage. This often heralds a tipping point, wherein design decisions that made sense under light loads suddenly become technical debt.[1] External trigger events often cause these tipping points: look in the March/April 2020 media for the many reports of government unemployment and supermarket online ordering sites crashing under demand caused by the coronavirus pandemic.

Increasing a system's capacity in some dimension by increasing resources is called *scaling up* or *scaling out*—I'll explore the difference between these later. In addition, unlike physical systems, it is often equally important to be able to *scale down* the capacity of a system to reduce costs.

The canonical example of this is Netflix, which has a predictable regional diurnal load that it needs to process. Simply, a lot more people are watching Netflix in any geographical region at 9 p.m. than are at 5 a.m. This enables Netflix to reduce its processing resources during times of lower load. This saves the cost of running the processing nodes that are used in the Amazon cloud, as well as societally worthy things such as reducing data center power consumption. Compare this to a highway. At night when few cars are on the road, we don't retract lanes (except to make repairs). The full road capacity is available for the few drivers to go as fast as they like. In software systems, we can expand and contract our processing capacity in a matter of seconds to meet instantaneous load. Compared to physical systems, the strategies we deploy are vastly different.

---

1 Neil Ernst et al., *Technical Debt in Practice: How to Find It and Fix It* (MIT Press, 2021).

There's a lot more to consider about scalability in software systems, but let's come back to these issues after examining the scale of some contemporary software systems circa 2021.

Examples of System Scale in the Early 2000s

Looking ahead in this technology game is always fraught with danger. In 2008 I wrote:

> "While petabyte datasets and gigabit data streams are today's frontiers for data-intensive applications, no doubt 10 years from now we'll fondly reminisce about problems of this scale and be worrying about the difficulties that looming exascale applications are posing."[2]

Reasonable sentiments, it is true, but exascale? That's almost commonplace in today's world. Google reported multiple exabytes of Gmail in 2014 (*https://oreil.ly/vQ7M3*), and by now, do all Google services manage a yottabyte or more? I don't know. I'm not even sure I know what a yottabyte is! Google won't tell us about their storage, but I wouldn't bet against it. Similarly, how much data does Amazon store in the various AWS data stores for their clients? And how many requests does, say, DynamoDB process per second, collectively, for all supported client applications? Think about these things for too long and your head will explode.

A great source of information that sometimes gives insights into contemporary operational scales are the major internet companies' technical blogs. There are also websites analyzing internet traffic that are highly illustrative of traffic volumes. Let's take a couple of point-in-time examples to illustrate a few things we do know today. Bear in mind these will look almost quaint in a year or four:

- Facebook's engineering blog describes Scribe (*https://oreil.ly/omAo8*), their solution for collecting, aggregating, and delivering petabytes of log data per hour, with low latency and high throughput. Facebook's computing infrastructure comprises millions of machines, each of which generates log files that capture important events relating to system and application health. Processing these log files, for example from a web server, can give development teams insights into their application's behavior and performance, and support faultfinding. Scribe is a custom buffered queuing solution that can transport logs from servers at a rate of several terabytes per second and deliver them to downstream analysis and data warehousing systems. That, my friends, is a lot of data!

- You can see live internet traffic for numerous services at Internet Live Stats (*https://oreil.ly/9Acav*). Dig around and you'll find some staggering statistics; for

---

2 Ian Gorton et al., "Data-Intensive Computing in the 21st Century," *Computer* 41, no. 4 (April 2008): 30–32.

example, Google handles around 3.5 billion search requests per day, Instagram users upload about 65 million photos per day, and there are something like 1.7 billion websites. It is a fun site with lots of information. Note that the data is not real, but rather estimates based on statistical analyses of multiple data sources.

- In 2016, Google published a paper describing the characteristics of its codebase (*https://oreil.ly/hyMgl*). Among the many startling facts reported is the fact that "The repository contains 86 TBs of data, including approximately two billion lines of code in nine million unique source files." Remember, this was 2016.[3]

Still, real, concrete data on the scale of the services provided by major internet sites remain shrouded in commercial-in-confidence secrecy. Luckily, we can get some deep insights into the request and data volumes handled at internet scale through the annual usage report from one tech company. Beware though, as it is from Pornhub.[4] You can browse their incredibly detailed usage statistics from 2019 (*https://oreil.ly/hOxsP*) here. It's a fascinating glimpse into the capabilities of massive-scale systems.

How Did We Get Here? A Brief History of System Growth

I am sure many readers will have trouble believing there was civilized life before internet searching, YouTube, and social media. In fact, the first video upload to YouTube (*https://oreil.ly/a8i1b*) occurred in 2005. Yep, it is hard even for me to believe. So, let's take a brief look back in time at how we arrived at the scale of today's systems. Below are some historical milestones of note:

1980s

An age dominated by time-shared mainframes and minicomputers. PCs emerged in the early 1980s but were rarely networked. By the end of the 1980s, development labs, universities, and (increasingly) businesses had email and access to primitive internet resources.

1990–95

Networks became more pervasive, creating an environment ripe for the creation of the World Wide Web (WWW) with HTTP/HTML technology that had been pioneered at CERN by Tim Berners-Lee (*https://oreil.ly/IULsL*) during the 1980s. By 1995, the number of websites was tiny, but the seeds of the future were planted with companies like Yahoo! in 1994 and Amazon and eBay in 1995.

---

3 Rachel Potvin and Josh Levenberg, "Why Google Stores Billions of Lines of Code in a Single Repository," *Communications of the ACM* 59, 7 (July 2016): 78–87.

4 The report is not for the squeamish. Here's one illustrative PG-13 data point—the site had 42 billion visits in 2019! Some of the statistics will definitely make your eyes bulge.

1996–2000

The number of websites grew from around 10,000 to 10 million (*https://oreil.ly/ikPrg*), a truly explosive growth period. Networking bandwidth and access also grew rapidly. Companies like Amazon, eBay, Google, and Yahoo! were pioneering many of the design principles and early versions of advanced technologies for highly scalable systems that we know and use today. Everyday businesses rushed to exploit the new opportunities that e-business offered, and this brought system scalability to prominence, as explained in the sidebar "How Scale Impacted Business Systems".

2000–2006

The number of websites grew from around 10 million to 80 million during this period, and new service and business models emerged. In 2005, YouTube was launched. 2006 saw Facebook become available to the public. In the same year, Amazon Web Services (AWS), which had low-key beginnings in 2004, relaunched with its S3 and EC2 services.

2007–today

We now live in a world with around 2 billion websites, of which about 20% are active. There are something like 4 billion internet users (*https://oreil.ly/LEU3c*). Huge data centers operated by public cloud operators like AWS, Google Cloud Platform (GCP), and Microsoft Azure, along with a myriad of private data centers, for example, Twitter's operational infrastructure (*https://oreil.ly/lUXMu*), are scattered around the planet. Clouds host millions of applications, with engineers provisioning and operating their computational and data storage systems using sophisticated cloud management portals. Powerful cloud services make it possible for us to build, deploy, and scale our systems literally with a few clicks of a mouse. All companies have to do is pay their cloud provider bill at the end of the month.

This is the world that this book targets. A world where our applications need to exploit the key principles for building scalable systems and leverage highly scalable infrastructure platforms. Bear in mind, in modern applications, most of the code executed is not written by your organization. It is part of the containers, databases, messaging systems, and other components that you compose into your application through API calls and build directives. This makes the selection and use of these components at least as important as the design and development of your own business logic. They are architectural decisions that are not easy to change.

How Scale Impacted Business Systems

The surge of users with internet access in the 1990s brought new online moneymaking opportunities for businesses. There was a huge rush to expose business functions (sales, services, etc.) to users through a web browser. This heralded a profound change in how we had to think about building systems.

Take, for example, a retail bank. Before providing online services, it was possible to accurately predict the loads the bank's business systems would experience. We knew how many people worked in the bank and used the internal systems, how many terminals/PCs were connected to the bank's networks, how many ATMs you had to support, and the number and nature of connections to other financial institutions. Armed with this knowledge, we could build systems that support, say, a maximum of 3,000 concurrent users, safe in the knowledge that this number could not be exceeded. Growth would also be relatively slow, and most of the time (i.e., outside business hours) the load would be a lot less than the peak. This made our software design decisions and hardware provisioning a lot easier.

Now, imagine our retail bank decides to let all customers have internet banking access and the bank has five million customers. What is the maximum load now? How will load be dispersed during a business day? When are the peak periods? What happens if we run a limited time promotion to try and sign up new customers? Suddenly, our relatively simple and constrained business systems environment is disrupted by the higher average and peak loads and unpredictability you see from internet-based user populations.

Scalability Basic Design Principles

The basic aim of scaling a system is to increase its capacity in some application-specific dimension. A common dimension is increasing the number of requests that a system can process in a given time period. This is known as the system's throughput. Let's use an analogy to explore two basic principles we have available to us for scaling our systems and increasing throughput: replication and optimization.

In 1932, one of the world's iconic wonders of engineering, the Sydney Harbour Bridge (*https://oreil.ly/u7bOH*), was opened. Now, it is a fairly safe assumption that traffic volumes in 2021 are somewhat higher than in 1932. If by any chance you have driven over the bridge at peak hour in the last 30 years, then you know that its capacity is exceeded considerably every day. So how do we increase throughput on physical infrastructures such as bridges?

This issue became very prominent in Sydney in the 1980s, when it was realized that the capacity of the harbor crossing had to be increased. The solution was the rather less iconic Sydney Harbour Tunnel (*https://oreil.ly/1VWm7*), which essentially follows the same route underneath the harbor. This provides four additional lanes of traffic and hence added roughly one-third more capacity to harbor crossings. In not-too-far-away Auckland, their harbor bridge (*https://oreil.ly/E7yJz*) also had a capacity problem as it was built in 1959 with only four lanes. In essence, they adopted the same solution as Sydney, namely, to increase capacity. But rather than build a tunnel, they ingeniously doubled the number of lanes by expanding the bridge with the hilariously named "Nippon clip-ons" (*https://oreil.ly/g7QBu*), which widened the bridge on each side.

These examples illustrate the first strategy we have in software systems to increase capacity. We basically replicate the software processing resources to provide more capacity to handle requests and thus increase throughput, as shown in Figure 1-1. These replicated processing resources are analogous to the traffic lanes on bridges, providing a mostly independent processing pathway for a stream of arriving requests.

Luckily, in cloud-based software systems, replication can be achieved at the click of a mouse, and we can effectively replicate our processing resources thousands of times. We have it a lot easier than bridge builders in that respect. Still, we need to take care to replicate resources in order to alleviate real bottlenecks. Adding capacity to processing paths that are not overwhelmed will add needless costs without providing scalability benefit.

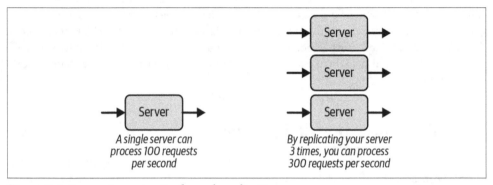

Figure 1-1. Increasing capacity through replication

The second strategy for scalability can also be illustrated with our bridge example. In Sydney, some observant person realized that in the mornings a lot more vehicles cross the bridge from north to south, and in the afternoon we see the reverse pattern. A smart solution was therefore devised—allocate more of the lanes to the high-demand direction in the morning, and sometime in the afternoon, switch this around. This effectively increased the capacity of the bridge without allocating any new resources—we *optimized* the resources we already had available.

We can follow this same approach in software to scale our systems. If we can somehow optimize our processing by using more efficient algorithms, adding extra indexes in our databases to speed up queries, or even rewriting our server in a faster programming language, we can increase our capacity without increasing our resources. The canonical example of this is Facebook's creation of (the now discontinued) HipHop for PHP (*https://oreil.ly/d2JFX*), which increased the speed of Facebook's web page generation by up to six times by compiling PHP code to C++.

I'll revisit these two design principles—namely replication and optimization— throughout this book. You will see that there are many complex implications of adopting these principles, arising from the fact that we are building distributed systems. Distributed systems have properties that make building scalable systems *interesting*, which in this context has both positive and negative connotations.

Scalability and Costs

Let's take a trivial hypothetical example to examine the relationship between scalability and costs. Assume we have a web-based (e.g., web server and database) system that can service a load of 100 concurrent requests with a mean response time of 1 second. We get a business requirement to scale up this system to handle 1,000 concurrent requests with the same response time. Without making any changes, a simple load test of this system reveals the performance shown in Figure 1-2 (left). As the request load increases, we see the mean response time steadily grow to 10 seconds with the projected load. Clearly this does not satisfy our requirements in its current deployment configuration. The system doesn't scale.

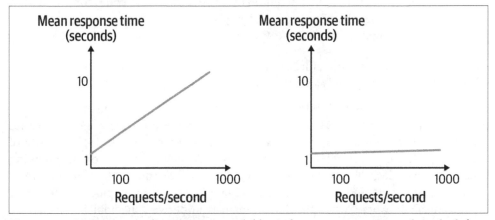

Figure 1-2. Scaling an application; non-scalable performance is represented on the left, and scalable performance on the right

Some engineering effort is needed in order to achieve the required performance. Figure 1-2 (right) shows the system's performance after this effort has been modified. It now provides the specified response time with 1,000 concurrent requests. And so, we have successfully scaled the system. Party time!

A major question looms, however. Namely, how much effort and resources were required to achieve this performance? Perhaps it was simply a case of running the web server on a more powerful (virtual) machine. Performing such reprovisioning on a cloud might take 30 minutes at most. Slightly more complex would be reconfiguring the system to run multiple instances of the web server to increase capacity. Again, this should be a simple, low-cost configuration change for the application, with no code changes needed. These would be excellent outcomes.

However, scaling a system isn't always so easy. The reasons for this are many and varied, but here are some possibilities:

- The database becomes less responsive with 1,000 requests per second, requiring an upgrade to a new machine.
- The web server generates a lot of content dynamically and this reduces response time under load. A possible solution is to alter the code to more efficiently generate the content, thus reducing processing time per request.
- The request load creates hotspots in the database when many requests try to access and update the same records simultaneously. This requires a schema redesign and subsequent reloading of the database, as well as code changes to the data access layer.
- The web server framework that was selected emphasized ease of development over scalability. The model it enforces means that the code simply cannot be scaled to meet the requested load requirements, and a complete rewrite is required. Use another framework? Use another programming language even?

There's a myriad of other potential causes, but hopefully these illustrate the increasing effort that might be required as we move from possibility (1) to possibility (4).

Now let's assume option (1), upgrading the database server, requires 15 hours of effort and a thousand dollars in extra cloud costs per month for a more powerful server. This is not prohibitively expensive. And let's assume option (4), a rewrite of the web application layer, requires 10,000 hours of development due to implementing a new language (e.g., Java instead of Ruby). Options (2) and (3) fall somewhere in between options (1) and (4). The cost of 10,000 hours of development is seriously significant. Even worse, while the development is underway, the application may be losing market share and hence money due to its inability to satisfy client requests' loads. These kinds of situations can cause systems and businesses to fail.

This simple scenario illustrates how the dimensions of resource and effort costs are inextricably tied to scalability. If a system is not designed intrinsically to scale, then the downstream costs and resources of increasing its capacity to meet requirements may be massive. For some applications, such as HealthCare.gov (*https://oreil.ly/ P7nyc*), these (more than $2 billion) costs are borne and the system is modified to eventually meet business needs. For others, such as Oregon's health care exchange (*https://oreil.ly/fTDcc*), an inability to scale rapidly at low cost can be an expensive ($303 million, in Oregon's case) death knell.

We would never expect someone would attempt to scale up the capacity of a suburban home to become a 50-floor office building. The home doesn't have the architecture, materials, and foundations for this to be even a remote possibility without being completely demolished and rebuilt. Similarly, we shouldn't expect software systems that do not employ scalable architectures, mechanisms, and technologies to be quickly evolved to meet greater capacity needs. The foundations of scale need to be built in from the beginning, with the recognition that the components will evolve over time. By employing design and development principles that promote scalability, we can more rapidly and cheaply scale up systems to meet rapidly growing demands. I'll explain these principles in Part II of this book.

Software systems that can be scaled exponentially while costs grow linearly are known as hyperscale systems, which I define as follows: "Hyper scalable systems exhibit exponential growth in computational and storage capabilities while exhibiting linear growth rates in the costs of resources required to build, operate, support, and evolve the required software and hardware resources." You can read more about hyperscale systems in this article (*https://oreil.ly/WwHqX*).

Scalability and Architecture Trade-Offs

Scalability is just one of the many quality attributes, or nonfunctional requirements, that are the lingua franca of the discipline of software architecture. One of the enduring complexities of software architecture is the necessity of quality attribute trade-offs. Basically, a design that favors one quality attribute may negatively or positively affect others. For example, we may want to write log messages when certain events occur in our services so we can do forensics and support debugging of our code. We need to be careful, however, how many events we capture, because logging introduces overheads and negatively affects performance and cost.

Experienced software architects constantly tread a fine line, crafting their designs to satisfy high-priority quality attributes, while minimizing the negative effects on other quality attributes.

Scalability is no different. When we point the spotlight at the ability of a system to scale, we have to carefully consider how our design influences other highly desirable properties such as performance, availability, security, and the oft overlooked manageability. I'll briefly discuss some of these inherent trade-offs in the following sections.

Performance

There's a simple way to think about the difference between performance and scalability. When we target performance, we attempt to satisfy some desired metrics for individual requests. This might be a mean response time of less than 2 seconds, or a worst-case performance target such as the 99th percentile response time less than 3 seconds.

Improving performance is in general a good thing for scalability. If we improve the performance of individual requests, we create more capacity in our system, which helps us with scalability as we can use the unused capacity to process more requests.

However, it's not always that simple. We may reduce response times in a number of ways. We might carefully optimize our code by, for example, removing unnecessary object copying, using a faster JSON serialization library, or even completely rewriting code in a faster programming language. These approaches optimize performance without increasing resource usage.

An alternative approach might be to optimize individual requests by keeping commonly accessed state in memory rather than writing to the database on each request. Eliminating a database access nearly always speeds things up. However, if our system maintains large amounts of state in memory for prolonged periods, we may (and in a heavily loaded system, will) have to carefully manage the number of requests our system can handle. This will likely reduce scalability as our optimization approach for individual requests uses more resources (in this case, memory) than the original solution, and thus reduces system capacity.

We'll see this tension between performance and scalability reappear throughout this book. In fact, it's sometimes judicious to make individual requests slightly slower so we can utilize additional system capacity. A great example of this is described when I discuss load balancing in the next chapter.

Availability

Availability and scalability are in general highly compatible partners. As we scale our systems through replicating resources, we create multiple instances of services that can be used to handle requests from any users. If one of our instances fails, the others remain available. The system just suffers from reduced capacity due to a failed, unavailable resource. Similar thinking holds for replicating network links, network routers, disks, and pretty much any resource in a computing system.

Things get complicated with scalability and availability when state is involved. Think of a database. If our single database server becomes overloaded, we can replicate it and send requests to either instance. This also increases availability as we can tolerate the failure of one instance. This scheme works great if our databases are read only. But as soon as we update one instance, we somehow have to figure out how and when to update the other instance. This is where the issue of replica consistency raises its ugly head.

In fact, whenever state is replicated for scalability and availability, we have to deal with consistency. This will be a major topic when I discuss distributed databases in Part III of this book.

Security

Security is a complex, highly technical topic worthy of its own book. No one wants to use an insecure system, and systems that are hacked and compromise user data cause CTOs to resign, and in extreme cases, companies to fail.

The basic elements of a secure system are authentication, authorization, and integrity. We need to ensure data cannot be intercepted in transit over networks, and data at rest (persistent store) cannot be accessed by anyone who does not have permission to access that data. Basically, I don't want anyone seeing my credit card number as it is communicated between systems or stored in a company's database.

Hence, security is a necessary quality attribute for any internet-facing systems. The costs of building secure systems cannot be avoided, so let's briefly examine how these affect performance and scalability.

At the network level, systems routinely exploit the Transport Layer Security (TLS) protocol (*https://oreil.ly/pG2eg*), which runs on top of TCP/IP (see Chapter 3). TLS provides encryption, authentication, and integrity using asymmetric cryptography (*https://oreil.ly/FqPSm*). This has a performance cost for establishing a secure connection as both parties need to generate and exchange keys. TLS connection establishment also includes an exchange of certificates to verify the identity of the server (and optionally client), and the selection of an algorithm to check that the data is not tampered with in transit. Once a connection is established, in-flight data is encrypted using symmetric cryptography, which has a negligible performance penalty as modern CPUs have dedicated encryption hardware. Connection establishment usually requires two message exchanges between client and server, and is thus comparatively slow. Reusing connections as much as possible minimizes these performance overheads.

There are multiple options for protecting data at rest. Popular database engines such as SQL Server and Oracle have features such as transparent data encryption (TDE) that provides efficient file-level encryption. Finer-grain encryption mechanisms, down to field level, are increasingly required in regulated industries such as finance. Cloud providers offer various features too, ensuring data stored in cloud-based data stores is secure. The overheads of secure data at rest are simply costs that must be borne to achieve security—studies suggest the overheads are in the 5–10% range.

Another perspective on security is the CIA triad (*https://oreil.ly/building-secure*), which stands for *confidentiality*, *integrity*, and *availability*. The first two are pretty much what I have described above. Availability refers to a system's ability to operate reliably under attack from adversaries. Such attacks might be attempts to exploit a system design weakness to bring the system down. Another attack is the classic distributed denial-of-service (DDoS), in which an adversary gains control over multitudes of systems and devices and coordinates a flood of requests that effectively make a system unavailable.

In general, security and scalability are opposing forces. Security necessarily introduces performance degradation. The more layers of security a system encompasses, then a greater burden is placed on performance, and hence scalability. This eventually affects the bottom line—more powerful and expensive resources are required to achieve a system's performance and scalability requirements.

Manageability

As the systems we build become more distributed and complex in their interactions, their management and operations come to the fore. We need to pay attention to ensuring every component is operating as expected, and the performance is continuing to meet expectations.

The platforms and technologies we use to build our systems provide a multitude of standards-based and proprietary monitoring tools that can be used for these purposes. Monitoring dashboards can be used to check the ongoing health and behavior of each system component. These dashboards, built using highly customizable and open tools such as Grafana (*https://oreil.ly/PNaBs*), can display system metrics and send alerts when various thresholds or events occur that need operator attention. The term used for this sophisticated monitoring capability is *observability* (*https://oreil.ly/xcuLd*).

There are various APIs such as Java's MBeans (*https://oreil.ly/vtTUT*), AWS Cloud-Watch (*https://oreil.ly/cvviZ*) and Python's AppMetrics (*https://oreil.ly/oa9MT*) that engineers can utilize to capture custom metrics for their systems—a typical example is request response times. Using these APIs, monitoring dashboards can be tailored to provide live charts and graphs that give deep insights into a system's behavior. Such insights are invaluable to ensure ongoing operations and highlight parts of the system that may need optimization or replication.

Scaling a system invariably means adding new system components—hardware and software. As the number of components grows, we have more moving parts to monitor and manage. This is never effort-free. It adds complexity to the operations of the system and costs in terms of monitoring code that requires developing and observability platform evolution.

The only way to control the costs and complexity of manageability as we scale is through automation. This is where the world of DevOps enters the scene. *DevOps* (*https://oreil.ly/effective-devops*) is a set of practices and tooling that combine software development and system operations. DevOps reduces the development lifecycle for new features and automates ongoing test, deployment, management, upgrade, and monitoring of the system. It's an integral part of any successful scalable system.

Summary and Further Reading

The ability to scale an application quickly and cost-effectively should be a defining quality of the software architecture of contemporary internet-facing applications. We have two basic ways to achieve scalability, namely increasing system capacity, typically through replication, and performance optimization of system components.

Like any software architecture quality attribute, scalability cannot be achieved in isolation. It inevitably involves complex trade-offs that need to be tuned to an application's requirements. I'll be discussing these fundamental trade-offs throughout the remainder of this book, starting in the next chapter when I describe concrete architecture approaches to achieve scalability.

CHAPTER 2

Distributed Systems Architectures: An Introduction

In this chapter, I'll broadly cover some of the fundamental approaches to scaling a software system. You can regard this as a 30,000-foot view of the content that is covered in Part II, Part III, and Part IV of this book. I'll take you on a tour of the main architectural approaches used for scaling a system, and give pointers to later chapters where these issues are dealt with in depth. You can think of this as an overview of why we need these architectural tactics, with the remainder of the book explaining the how.

The type of systems this book is oriented toward are the internet-facing systems we all utilize every day. I'll let you name your favorite. These systems accept requests from users through web and mobile interfaces, store and retrieve data based on user requests or events (e.g., a GPS-based system), and have some *intelligent* features such as providing recommendations or notifications based on previous user interactions.

I'll start with a simple system design and show how it can be scaled. In the process, I'll introduce several concepts that will be covered in much more detail later in this book. This chapter just gives a broad overview of these concepts and how they aid in scalability—truly a whirlwind tour!

Basic System Architecture

Virtually all massive-scale systems start off small and grow due to their success. It's common, and sensible, to start with a development framework such as Ruby on Rails, Django, or equivalent, which promotes rapid development to get a system quickly up and running. A typical very simple software architecture for "starter" systems, which closely resembles what you get with rapid development frameworks, is shown in Figure 2-1. This comprises a client tier, application service tier, and a database tier. If you use Rails or equivalent, you also get a framework which hardwires a model–view–controller (MVC) pattern for web application processing and an object–relational mapper (ORM) that generates SQL queries.

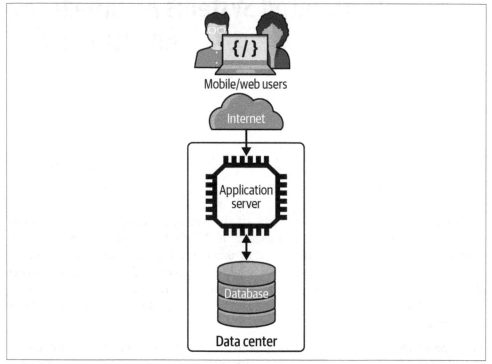

Figure 2-1. Basic multitier distributed systems architecture

With this architecture, users submit requests to the application from their mobile app or web browser. The magic of internet networking (see Chapter 3) delivers these requests to the application service which is running on a machine hosted in some corporate or commercial cloud data center. Communications uses a standard application-level network protocol, typically HTTP.

The application service runs code supporting an API that clients use to send HTTP requests. Upon receipt of a request, the service executes the code associated with the requested API. In the process, it may read from or write to a database or some other external system, depending on the semantics of the API. When the request is complete, the service sends the results to the client to display in their app or browser.

Many, if not most systems conceptually look exactly like this. The application service code exploits a server execution environment that enables multiple requests from multiple users to be processed simultaneously. There's a myriad of these application server technologies—for example, Java EE and the Spring Framework for Java, Flask (*https://oreil.ly/8FYu5*) for Python—that are widely used in this scenario.

This approach leads to what is generally known as a monolithic architecture.[1] Monoliths tend to grow in complexity as the application becomes more feature-rich. All API handlers are built into the same server code body. This eventually makes it hard to modify and test rapidly, and the execution footprint can become extremely heavyweight as all the API implementations run in the same application service.

Still, if request loads stay relatively low, this application architecture can suffice. The service has the capacity to process requests with consistently low latency. But if request loads keep growing, this means latencies will increase as the service has insufficient CPU/memory capacity for the concurrent request volume and therefore requests will take longer to process. In these circumstances, our single server is overloaded and has become a bottleneck.

In this case, the first strategy for scaling is usually to "scale up" the application service hardware. For example, if your application is running on AWS, you might upgrade your server from a modest t3.xlarge instance with four (virtual) CPUs and 16 GB of memory to a t3.2xlarge instance, which doubles the number of CPUs and memory available for the application.[2]

Scaling up is simple. It gets many real-world applications a long way to supporting larger workloads. It obviously costs more money for hardware, but that's scaling for you.

It's inevitable, however, that for many applications the load will grow to a level which will swamp a single server node, no matter how many CPUs and how much memory you have. That's when you need a new strategy—namely, scaling out, or horizontal scaling, which I touched on in Chapter 1.

Scale Out

Scaling out relies on the ability to replicate a service in the architecture and run multiple copies on multiple server nodes. Requests from clients are distributed across the replicas so that in theory, if we have N replicas and R requests, each server node processes R/N requests. This simple strategy increases an application's capacity and hence scalability.

To successfully scale out an application, you need two fundamental elements in your design. As illustrated in Figure 2-2, these are:

---

1 Mark Richards and Neal Ford. *Fundamentals of Software Architecture: An Engineering Approach* (O'Reilly Media, 2020).

2 See Amazon EC2 Instance Types (*https://oreil.ly/rtYaJ*) for a description of AWS instances.

A load balancer

All user requests are sent to a load balancer, which chooses a service replica target to process the request. Various strategies exist for choosing a target service, all with the core aim of keeping each resource equally busy. The load balancer also relays the responses from the service back to the client. Most load balancers belong to a class of internet components known as reverse proxies (*https://oreil.ly/78lLN*). These control access to server resources for client requests. As an intermediary, reverse proxies add an extra network hop for a request; they need to be extremely low latency to minimize the overheads they introduce. There are many off-the-shelf load balancing solutions as well as cloud provider–specific ones, and I'll cover the general characteristics of these in much more detail in Chapter 5.

Stateless services

For load balancing to be effective and share requests evenly, the load balancer must be free to send consecutive requests from the same client to different service instances for processing. This means the API implementations in the services must retain no knowledge, or state, associated with an individual client's session. When a user accesses an application, a user session is created by the service and a unique session is managed internally to identify the sequence of user interactions and track session state. A classic example of session state is a shopping cart. To use a load balancer effectively, the data representing the current contents of a user's cart must be stored somewhere—typically a data store—such that any service replica can access this state when it receives a request as part of a user session. In Figure 2-2, this is labeled as a "Session store."

Scaling out is attractive as, in theory, you can keep adding new (virtual) hardware and services to handle increased request loads and keep request latencies consistent and low. As soon as you see latencies rising, you deploy another server instance. This requires no code changes with stateless services and is relatively cheap as a result—you just pay for the hardware you deploy.

Scaling out has another highly attractive feature. If one of the services fails, the requests it is processing will be lost. But as the failed service manages no session state, these requests can be simply reissued by the client and sent to another service instance for processing. This means the application is resilient to failures in the service software and hardware, thus enhancing the application's availability.

Unfortunately, as with any engineering solution, simple scaling out has limits. As you add new service instances, the request processing capacity grows, potentially infinitely. At some stage, however, reality will bite and the capability of your single database to provide low-latency query responses will diminish. Slow queries will mean longer response times for clients. If requests keep arriving faster than they are being processed, some system components will become overloaded and fail due to resource exhaustion, and clients will see exceptions and request timeouts. Essentially, your database becomes a bottleneck that you must engineer away in order to scale your application further.

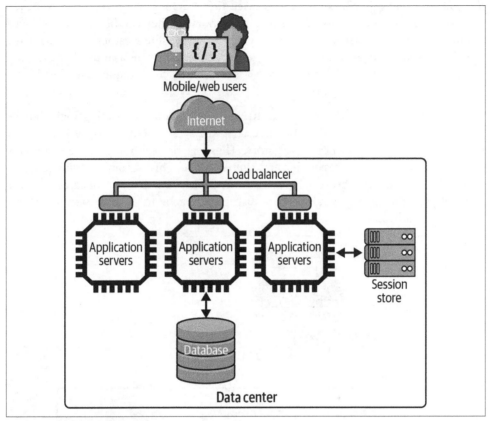

Figure 2-2. Scale-out architecture

Scaling the Database with Caching

Scaling up by increasing the number of CPUs, memory, and disks in a database server can go a long way to scaling a system. For example, at the time of writing, GCP can provision a SQL database on a db-n1-highmem-96 node, which has 96 virtual CPUs (vCPUs), 624 GB of memory, 30 TB of disk, and can support 4,000 connections. This will cost somewhere between $6K and $16K per year, which sounds like a good deal to me! Scaling up is a common database scalability strategy.

Large databases need constant care and attention from highly skilled database administrators to keep them tuned and running fast. There's a lot of wizardry in this job—e.g., query tuning, disk partitioning, indexing, on-node caching, and so on—and hence database administrators are valuable people you want to be very nice to. They can make your application services highly responsive.

In conjunction with scaling up, a highly effective approach is querying the database as infrequently as possible from your services. This can be achieved by employing *distributed caching* in the scaled-out service tier. Caching stores recently retrieved and commonly accessed database results in memory so they can be quickly retrieved without placing a burden on the database. For example, the weather forecast for the next hour won't change, but may be queried by hundreds or thousands of clients. You can use a cache to store the forecast once it is issued. All client requests will read from the cache until the forecast expires.

For data that is frequently read and changes rarely, your processing logic can be modified to first check a distributed cache, such as a Redis (*https://redis.io*) or memcached (*https://memcached.org*) store. These cache technologies are essentially distributed key-value stores with very simple APIs. This scheme is illustrated in Figure 2-3. Note that the session store from Figure 2-2 has disappeared. This is because you can use a general-purpose distributed cache to store session identifiers along with application data.

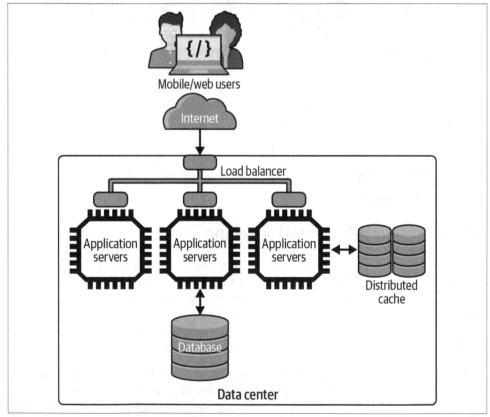

Figure 2-3. Introducing distributed caching

Accessing the cache requires a remote call from your service. If the data you need is in the cache, on a fast network you can expect submillisecond cache reads. This is far less expensive than querying the shared database instance, and also doesn't require a query to contend for typically scarce database connections.

Introducing a caching layer also requires your processing logic to be modified to check for cached data. If what you want is not in the cache, your code must still query the database and load the results into the cache as well as return it to the caller. You also need to decide when to remove, or invalidate, cached results—your course of action depends on the nature of your data (e.g., weather forecasts expire naturally) and your application's tolerance to serving out-of-date—also known as *stale*—results to clients.

A well-designed caching scheme can be invaluable in scaling a system. Caching works great for data that rarely changes and is accessed frequently, such as inventory catalogs, event information, and contact data. If you can handle a large percentage, say, 80% or more, of read requests from your cache, then you effectively buy extra capacity at your databases as they never see a large proportion of requests.

Still, many systems need to rapidly access terabytes and larger data stores that make a single database effectively prohibitive. In these systems, a distributed database is needed.

Distributing the Database

There are more distributed database technologies around in 2022 than you probably want to imagine. It's a complex area, and one I'll cover extensively in Part III. In very general terms, there are two major categories:

Distributed SQL stores
> These enable organizations to scale out their SQL database relatively seamlessly by storing the data across multiple disks that are queried by multiple database engine replicas. These multiple engines logically appear to the application as a single database, hence minimizing code changes. There is also a class of "born distributed" SQL databases that are commonly known as NewSQL stores that fit in this category.

Distributed so-called "NoSQL" stores (from a whole array of vendors)
> These products use a variety of data models and query languages to distribute data across multiple nodes running the database engine, each with their own locally attached storage. Again, the location of the data is transparent to the application, and typically controlled by the design of the data model using hashing functions on database keys. Leading products in this category are Cassandra, MongoDB, and Neo4j.

Figure 2-4 shows how our architecture incorporates a distributed database. As the data volumes grow, a distributed database can increase the number of storage nodes. As nodes are added (or removed), the data managed across all nodes is rebalanced to attempt to ensure the processing and storage capacity of each node is equally utilized.

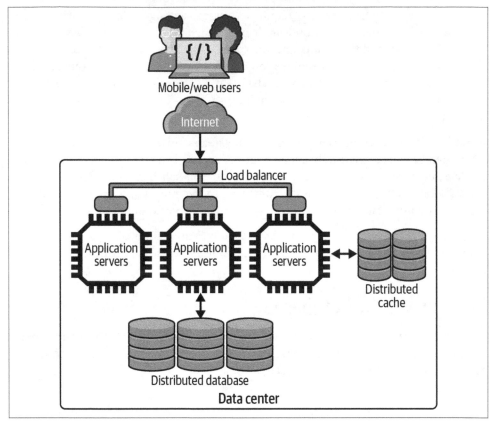

Figure 2-4. Scaling the data tier using a distributed database

Distributed databases also promote availability. They support replicating each data storage node so if one fails or cannot be accessed due to network problems, another copy of the data is available. The models utilized for replication and the trade-offs these require (spoiler alert: consistency) are covered in later chapters.

If you are utilizing a major cloud provider, there are also two deployment choices for your data tier. You can deploy your own virtual resources and build, configure, and administer your own distributed database servers. Alternatively, you can utilize cloud-hosted databases. The latter simplifies the administrative effort associated with managing, monitoring, and scaling the database, as many of these tasks essentially become the responsibility of the cloud provider you choose. As usual, the no free lunch principle applies. You always pay, whichever approach you choose.

Multiple Processing Tiers

Any realistic system that you need to scale will have many different services that interact to process a request. For example, accessing a web page on Amazon.com can require in excess of 100 different services being called before a response is returned to the user.[3]

The beauty of the stateless, load-balanced, cached architecture I am elaborating in this chapter is that it's possible to extend the core design principles and build a multitiered application. In fulfilling a request, a service can call one or more dependent services, which in turn are replicated and load-balanced. A simple example is shown in Figure 2-5. There are many nuances in how the services interact, and how applications ensure rapid responses from dependent services. Again, I'll cover these in detail in later chapters.

---

3 Werner Vogels, "Modern Applications at AWS," All Things Distributed, 28 Aug. 2019, *https://oreil.ly/FXOep*.

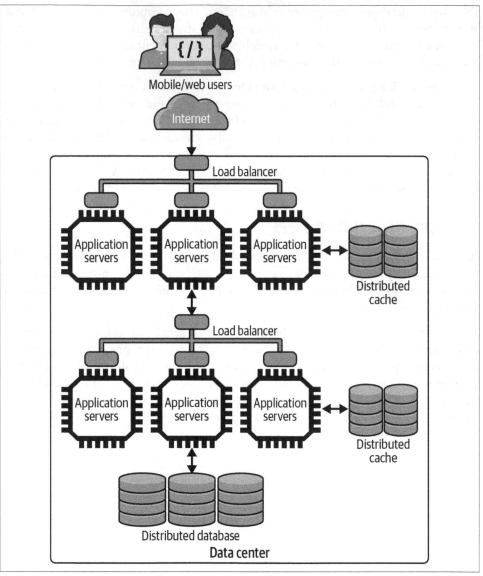

Figure 2-5. Scaling processing capacity with multiple tiers

This design also promotes having different, load-balanced services at each tier in the architecture. For example, Figure 2-6 illustrates two replicated internet-facing services that both utilized a core service that provides database access. Each service is load balanced and employs caching to provide high performance and availability. This design is often used to provide a service for web clients and a service for mobile clients, each of which can be scaled independently based on the load they experience. It's commonly called the Backend for Frontend (BFF) pattern.[4]

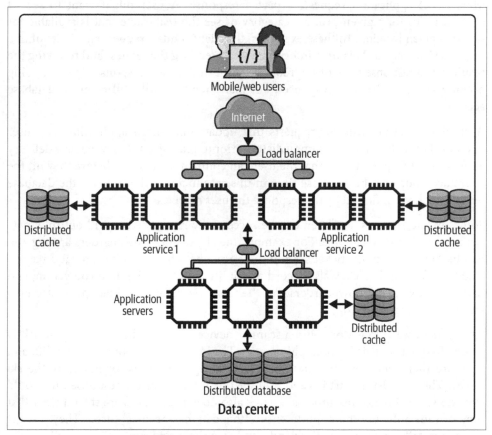

Figure 2-6. Scalable architecture with multiple services

In addition, by breaking the application into multiple independent services, you can scale each based on the service demand. If, for example, you see an increasing volume of requests from mobile users and decreasing volumes from web users, it's possible to provision different numbers of instances for each service to satisfy demand. This is a major advantage of refactoring monolithic applications into multiple independent services, which can be separately built, tested, deployed, and scaled. I'll explore some of the major issues in designing systems based on such services, known as microservices, in Chapter 9.

---

4 Sam Newman, "Pattern: Backends For Frontends," Sam Newman & Associates, November 18, 2015. *https://oreil.ly/1KR1z*.

Increasing Responsiveness

Most client application requests expect a response. A user might want to see all auction items for a given product category or see the real estate that is available for sale in a given location. In these examples, the client sends a request and waits until a response is received. This time interval between sending the request and receiving the result is the response time of the request. You can decrease response times by using caching and precalculated responses, but many requests will still result in database accesses.

A similar scenario exists for requests that update data in an application. If a user updates their delivery address immediately prior to placing an order, the new delivery address must be persisted so that the user can confirm the address before they hit the "purchase" button. The response time in this case includes the time for the database write, which is confirmed by the response the user receives.

Some update requests, however, can be successfully responded to without fully persisting the data in a database. For example, the skiers and snowboarders among you will be familiar with lift ticket scanning systems that check you have a valid pass to ride the lifts that day. They also record which lifts you take, the time you get on, and so on. Nerdy skiers/snowboarders can then use the resort's mobile app to see how many lifts they ride in a day.

As a person waits to get on a lift, a scanner device validates the pass using an RFID (radio-frequency identification) chip reader. The information about the rider, lift, and time are then sent over the internet to a data capture service operated by the ski resort. The lift rider doesn't have to wait for this to occur, as the response time could slow down the lift-loading process. There's also no expectation from the lift rider that they can instantly use their app to ensure this data has been captured. They just get on the lift, talk smack with their friends, and plan their next run.

Service implementations can exploit this type of scenario to improve responsiveness. The data about the event is sent to the service, which acknowledges receipt and concurrently stores the data in a remote queue for subsequent writing to the database. Distributed queueing platforms can be used to reliably send data from one service to another, typically but not always in a first-in, first-out (FIFO) manner.

Writing a message to a queue is typically much faster than writing to a database, and this enables the request to be successfully acknowledged much more quickly. Another service is deployed to read messages from the queue and write the data to the database. When a skier checks their lift rides—maybe three hours or three days later—the data has been persisted successfully in the database.

The basic architecture to implement this approach is illustrated in Figure 2-7.

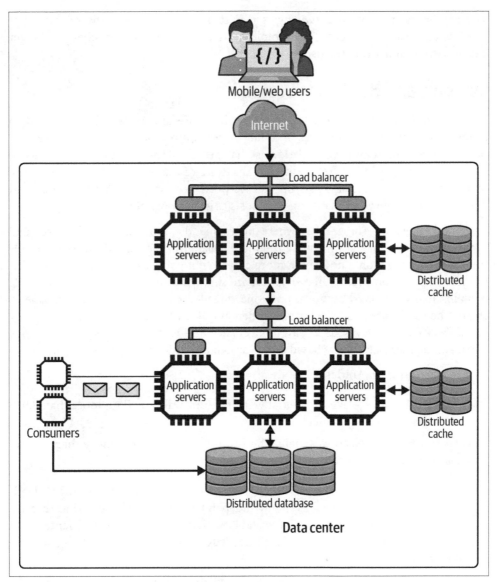

Figure 2-7. Increasing responsiveness with queueing

Whenever the results of a write operation are not immediately needed, an application can use this approach to improve responsiveness and, as a result, scalability. Many queueing technologies exist that applications can utilize, and I'll discuss how these operate in Chapter 7. These queueing platforms all provide asynchronous communications. A *producer* service writes to the queue, which acts as temporary storage, while another *consumer* service removes messages from the queue and makes the necessary updates to, in our example, a database that stores skier lift ride details.

The key is that the data *eventually* gets persisted. Eventually typically means a few seconds at most but use cases that employ this design should be resilient to longer delays without impacting the user experience.

Systems and Hardware Scalability

Even the most carefully crafted software architecture and code will be limited in terms of scalability if the services and data stores run on inadequate hardware. The open source and commercial platforms that are commonly deployed in scalable systems are designed to utilize additional hardware resources in terms of CPU cores, memory, and disks. It's a balancing act between achieving the performance and scalability you require, and keeping your costs as low as possible.

That said, there are some cases where upgrading the number of CPU cores and available memory is not going to buy you more scalability. For example, if code is single threaded, running it on a node with more cores is not going to improve performance. It'll just use one core at any time. The rest are simply not used. If multithreaded code contains many serialized sections, only one threaded core can proceed at a time to ensure the results are correct. This phenomenon is described by Amdahl's law (*https://oreil.ly/w8Z5l*). This gives us a way to calculate the theoretical acceleration of code when adding more CPU cores based on the amount of code that executes serially.

Two data points from Amdahl's law are:

- If only 5% of a code executes serially, the rest in parallel, adding more than 2,048 cores has essentially no effect.
- If 50% of a code executes serially, the rest in parallel, adding more than 8 cores has essentially no effect.

This demonstrates why efficient, multithreaded code is essential to achieving scalability. If your code is not running as highly independent tasks implemented as threads, then not even money will buy you scalability. That's why I devote Chapter 4 to the topic of multithreading—it's a core knowledge component for building scalable distributed systems.

To illustrate the effect of upgrading hardware, Figure 2-8 shows how the throughput of a benchmark system improves as the database is deployed on more powerful (and expensive) hardware.[5] The benchmark employs a Java service that accepts requests from a load generating client, queries a database, and returns the results to the client. The client, service, and database run on different hardware resources deployed in the same regions in the AWS cloud.

---

5 Results are courtesy of Ruijie Xiao from Northeastern University, Seattle.

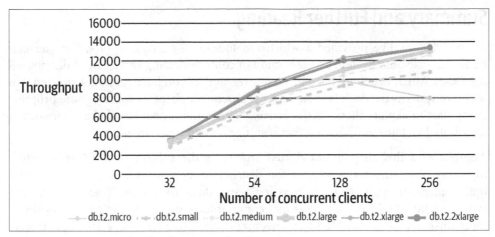

Figure 2-8. An example of scaling up a database server

In the tests, the number of concurrent requests grows from 32 to 256 (*x*-axis) and each line represents the system throughput (*y*-axis) for a different hardware configuration on the AWS EC2's Relational Database Service (RDS). The different configurations are listed at the bottom of the chart, with the least powerful on the left and most powerful on the right. Each client sends a fixed number of requests synchronously over HTTP, with no pause between receiving results from one request and sending the next. This consequently exerts a high request load on the server.

From this chart, it's possible to make some straightforward observations:

- In general, the more powerful the hardware selected for the database, the higher the throughput. That is good.

- The difference between the db.t2.xlarge and db.t2.2xlarge instances in terms of throughput is minimal. This could be because the service tier is becoming a bottleneck, or our database model and queries are not exploiting the additional resources of the db.t2.2xlarge RDS instance. Regardless—more bucks, no bang.

- The two least powerful instances perform pretty well until the request load is increased to 256 concurrent clients. The dip in throughput for these two instances indicates they are overloaded and things will only get worse if the request load increases.

Hopefully, this simple example illustrates why scaling through simple upgrading of hardware needs to be approached carefully. Adding more hardware always increases costs, but may not always give the performance improvement you expect. Running simple experiments and taking measurements is essential for assessing the effects of hardware upgrades. It gives you solid data to guide your design and justify costs to stakeholders.

Summary and Further Reading

In this chapter I've provided a whirlwind tour of the major approaches you can utilize to scale out a system as a collection of communicating services and distributed databases. Much detail has been brushed over, and as you have no doubt realized—in software systems the devil is in the detail. Subsequent chapters will therefore progressively start to explore these details, starting with some fundamental characteristics of distributed systems in Chapter 3 that everyone should be aware of.

Another area this chapter has skirted around is the subject of software architecture. I've used the term *services* for distributed components in an architecture that implement application business logic and database access. These services are independently deployed processes that communicate using remote communications mechanisms such as HTTP. In architectural terms, these services are most closely mirrored by those in the service-oriented architecture (SOA) pattern, an established architectural approach for building distributed systems. A more modern evolution of this approach revolves around microservices. These tend to be more cohesive, encapsulated services that promote continuous development and deployment.

If you'd like a much more in-depth discussion of these issues, and software architecture concepts in general, then Mark Richards' and Neal Ford's book *Fundamentals of Software Architecture: An Engineering Approach* (*https://oreil.ly/soft-arch*) (O'Reilly, 2020) is an excellent place to start.

Finally, there's a class of *big data* software architectures that address some of the issues that come to the fore with very large data collections. One of the most prominent is data reprocessing. This occurs when data that has already been stored and analyzed needs to be reanalyzed due to code or business rule changes. This reprocessing may occur due to software fixes, or the introduction of new algorithms that can derive more insights from the original raw data. There's a good discussion of the Lambda and Kappa architectures, both of which are prominent in this space, in Jay Krepps' 2014 article "Questioning the Lambda Architecture" (*https://oreil.ly/zkUBT*) on the O'Reilly Radar blog.

CHAPTER 3

Distributed Systems Essentials

As I described in Chapter 2, scaling a system naturally involves adding multiple independently moving parts. We run our software components on multiple machines and our databases across multiple storage nodes, all in the quest of adding more processing capacity. Consequently, our solutions are distributed across multiple machines in multiple locations, with each machine processing events concurrently, and exchanging messages over a network.

This fundamental nature of distributed systems has some profound implications on the way we design, build, and operate our solutions. This chapter provides the basic information you need to know to appreciate the issues and complexities of distributed software systems. I'll briefly cover communications networks hardware and software, remote method invocation, how to deal with the implications of communications failures, distributed coordination, and the thorny issue of time in distributed systems.

Communications Basics

Every distributed system has software components that communicate over a network. If a mobile banking app requests the user's current bank account balance, a (very simplified) sequence of communications occurs along the lines of:

1. The mobile banking app sends a request over the cellular network addressed to the bank to retrieve the user's bank balance.

2. The request is routed across the internet to where the bank's web servers are located.

3. The bank's web server authenticates the request (confirms that it originated from the supposed user) and sends a request to a database server for the account balance.

4. The database server reads the account balance from disk and returns it to the web server.

5. The web server sends the balance in a reply message addressed to the app, which is routed over the internet and the cellular network until the balance magically appears on the screen of the mobile device.

It almost sounds simple when you read the above, but in reality, there's a huge amount of complexity hidden beneath this sequence of communications. Let's examine some of these complexities in the following sections.

Communications Hardware

The bank balance request example above will inevitably traverse multiple different networking technologies and devices. The global internet is a heterogeneous machine, comprising different types of network communications channels and devices that shuttle many millions of messages per second across networks to their intended destinations.

Different types of communications channels exist. The most obvious categorization is wired versus wireless. For each category there are multiple network transmission hardware technologies that can ship bits from one machine to another. Each technology has different characteristics, and the ones we typically care about are speed and range.

For physically wired networks, the two most common types are local area networks (LANs) and wide area networks (WANs). LANs are networks that can connect devices at "building scale," being able to transmit data over a small number (e.g., 1–2) of kilometers. Contemporary LANs in data centers can transport between 10 and 100 gigabits per second (Gbps). This is known as the network's bandwidth, or capacity. The time taken to transmit a message across a LAN—the network's latency —is submillisecond with modern LAN technologies.

WANs are networks that traverse the globe and make up what we collectively call the internet. These long-distance connections are the high speed data pipelines connecting cities, countries, and continents with fiber optic cables. These cables support a networking technology known as wavelength division multiplexing (*https://oreil.ly/ H7uwR*) which makes it possible to transmit up to 171 Gbps over 400 different channels, giving more than 70 terabits per second (Tbps) of total bandwidth for a single fiber link. The fiber cables that span the world normally comprise four or more strands of fiber, giving bandwidth capacity of hundreds of Tbps for each cable.

Latency is more complicated with WANs, however. WANs transmit data over hundreds and thousands of kilometers, and the maximum speed that the data can travel in fiber optic cables is the theoretical speed of light. In reality, these cables can't reach the speed of light, but do get pretty close to it, as shown in Table 3-1.

Table 3-1. WAN speeds

Path	Distance	Travel time (speed of light)	Travel time (fiber optic cable)
New York to San Francisco	4,148 km	14 ms	21 ms
New York to London	5,585 km	19 ms	28 ms
New York to Sydney	15,993 km	53 ms	80 ms

Actual times will be slower than the fiber optic travel times in Table 3-1 as the data needs to pass through networking equipment known as routers (*https://oreil.ly/ t7I0Y*). The global internet has a complex hub-and-spoke topology with many potential paths between nodes in the network. Routers are therefore responsible for transmitting data on the physical network connections to ensure data is transmitted across the internet from source to destination.

Routers are specialized, high-speed devices that can handle several hundred Gbps of network traffic, pulling data off incoming connections and sending the data out to different outgoing network connections based on their destination. Routers at the core of the internet comprise racks of these devices and can process tens to hundreds of Tbps. This is how you and thousands of your friends get to watch a steady video stream on Netflix at the same time.

Wireless technologies have different range and bandwidth characteristics. WiFi routers that we are all familiar with in our homes and offices are wireless Ethernet networks and use 802.11 protocols to send and receive data. The most widely used WiFi protocol, 802.11ac, allows for maximum (theoretical) data rates of up to 5,400 Mbps. The most recent 802.11ax protocol, also known as WiFi 6, is an evolution of 802.11ac technology that promises increased throughput speeds of up to 9.6 Gbps. The range of WiFi routers is of the order of tens of meters and of course is affected by physical impediments like walls and floors.

Cellular wireless technology uses radio waves to send data from our phones to routers mounted on cell towers, which are generally connected by wires to the core internet for message routing. Each cellular technology introduces improved bandwidth and other dimensions of performance. The most common technology at the time of writing is 4G LTE wireless broadband. 4G LTE is around 10 times faster than the older 3G, able to handle sustained download speeds around 10 Mbps (peak download speeds are nearer 50 Mbps) and upload speeds between 2 and 5 Mbps.

Emerging 5G cellular networks promise 10x bandwidth improvements over existing 4G, with 1–2 millisecond latencies between devices and cell towers. This is a great improvement over 4G latencies, which are in the 20–40 millisecond range. The trade-off is range. 5G base station range operates at about 500 meters maximum, whereas 4G provides reliable reception at distances of 10–15 km.

This whole collection of different hardware types for networking comes together in the global internet. The internet is a heterogeneous network, with many different operators around the world and every type of hardware imaginable. Figure 3-1 shows a simplified view of the major components that comprise the internet. Tier 1 networks are the global high-speed internet backbone. There are around 20 Tier 1 internet service providers (ISPs) who manage and control global traffic. Tier 2 ISPs are typically regional (e.g., one country), have lower bandwidth than Tier 1 ISPs, and deliver content to customers through Tier 3 ISPs. Tier 3 ISPs are the ones that charge you exorbitant fees for your home internet every month.

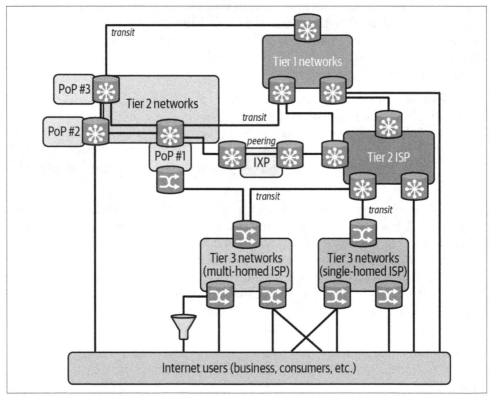

Figure 3-1. Simplified view of the internet

There's a lot more complexity to how the internet works than described here. That level of networking and protocol complexity is beyond the scope of this chapter. From a distributed systems software perspective, we need to understand more about the "magic" that enables all this hardware to route messages from, say, my cell phone to my bank and back. This is where the *Internet Protocol (IP)* comes in.

Communications Software

Software systems on the internet communicate using the Internet Protocol (IP) suite (*https://oreil.ly/DJf0L*). The IP suite specifies host addressing, data transmission formats, message routing, and delivery characteristics. There are four abstract layers, which contain related protocols that support the functionality required at that layer. These are, from lowest to highest:

1. The data link layer, specifying communication methods for data across a single network segment. This is implemented by the device drivers and network cards that live inside your devices.

2. The internet layer specifies addressing and routing protocols that make it possible for traffic to traverse the independently managed and controlled networks that comprise the internet. This is the IP layer in the internet protocol suite.

3. The transport layer, specifying protocols for reliable and best-effort, host-to-host communications. This is where the well-known Transmission Control Protocol (TCP) and User Datagram Protocol (UDP) live.

4. The application layer, which comprises several application-level protocols such as HTTP and the secure copy protocol (SCP).

Each of the higher-layer protocols builds on the features of the lower layers. In the following section, I'll briefly cover IP for host discovery and message routing, and TCP and UDP that can be utilized by distributed applications.

Internet Protocol (IP)

IP defines how hosts are assigned addresses on the internet and how messages are transmitted between two hosts who know each other's addresses.

Every device on the internet has its own address. These are known as Internet Protocol (IP) addresses. The location of an IP address can be found using an internet-wide directory service known as Domain Name System (DNS). DNS is a widely distributed, hierarchical database that acts as the address book of the internet.

The technology currently used to assign IP addresses, known as Internet Protocol version 4 (IPv4), will eventually be replaced by its successor, IPv6. IPv4 is a 32-bit addressing scheme that before long will run out of addresses due to the number of devices connecting to the internet. IPv6 is a 128-bit scheme that will offer an (almost) infinite number of IP addresses. As an indicator, in July 2020 about 33% of the traffic processed by Google.com (*https://oreil.ly/3ix6W*) is IPv6.

DNS servers are organized hierarchically. A small number of root DNS servers, which are highly replicated, are the starting point for resolving an IP address. When an internet browser tries to find a website, a network host known as the local DNS server (managed by your employer or ISP) will contact a root DNS server with the requested hostname. The root server replies with a referral to a so-called *authoritative* DNS server that manages name resolution for, in our banking example, *.com* addresses. There is an authoritative name server for each top-level internet domain (*.com*, *.org*, *.net*, etc.).

Next, the local DNS server will query the *.com* DNS server, which will reply with the address of the DNS server that knows about all the IP addresses managed by *igbank.com*. This DNS is queried, and it returns the actual IP address we need to communicate with the application. The overall scheme is illustrated in Figure 3-2.

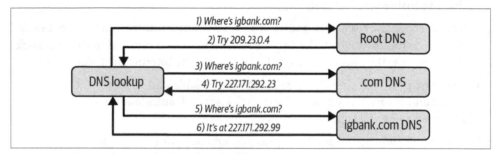

Figure 3-2. Example DNS lookup for igbank.com

The whole DNS database is highly geographically replicated so there are no single points of failure, and requests are spread across multiple physical servers. Local DNS servers also remember the IP addresses of recently contacted hosts, which is possible as IP addresses don't change very often. This means the complete name resolution process doesn't occur for every site we contact.

Armed with a destination IP address, a host can start sending data across the network as a series of IP data packets. IP delivers data from the source to the destination host based on the IP addresses in the packet headers. IP defines a packet structure that contains the data to be delivered, along with header data including source and destination IP addresses. Data sent by an application is broken up into a series of packets which are independently transmitted across the internet.

IP is known as a best-effort delivery protocol. This means it does not attempt to compensate for the various error conditions that can occur during packet transmission. Possible transmission errors include data corruption, packet loss, and duplication. In addition, every packet is routed across the internet from source to destination independently. Treating every packet independently is known as packet switching. This allows the network to dynamically respond to conditions such as network link failure and congestion, and hence is a defining characteristic of the internet. This does mean, however, that different packets may be delivered to the same destination via different network paths, resulting in out-of-order delivery to the receiver.

Because of this design, the IP is unreliable. If two hosts require reliable data transmission, they need to add additional features to make this occur. This is where the next layer in the IP protocol suite, the transport layer, enters the scene.

Transmission Control Protocol (TCP)

Once an application or browser has discovered the IP address of the server it wishes to communicate with, it can send messages using a transport protocol API. This is achieved using TCP or UDP, which are the popular standard transport protocols for the IP network stack.

Distributed applications can choose which of these protocols to use. Implementations are widely available in mainstream programming languages such as Java, Python, and C++. In reality, use of these APIs is not common as higher-level programming abstractions hide the details from most applications. In fact, the IP protocol suite application layer contains several of these application-level APIs, including HTTP, which is very widely used in mainstream distributed systems.

Still, it's important to understand TCP, UDP, and their differences. Most requests on the internet are sent using TCP. TCP is:

- Connection-oriented
- Stream-oriented
- Reliable

I'll explain each of these qualities, and why they matter, below.

TCP is known as a connection-oriented protocol. Before any messages are exchanged between applications, TCP uses a three-step handshake to establish a two-way connection between the client and server applications. The connection stays open until the TCP client calls close() to terminate the connection with the TCP server. The server responds by acknowledging the close() request before the connection is dropped.

Once a connection is established, a client sends a sequence of requests to the server as a data stream. When a data stream is sent over TCP, it is broken up into individual network packets, with a maximum packet size of 65,535 bytes. Each packet contains a source and destination address, which is used by the underlying IP protocol to route the messages across the network.

The internet is a packet switched network, which means every packet is individually routed across the network. The route each packet traverses can vary dynamically based on the conditions in the network, such as link congestion or failure. This means the packets may not arrive at the server in the same order they are sent from the client. To solve this problem, a TCP sender includes a sequence number in each packet so the receiver can reassemble packets into a stream that is identical to the order they were sent.

Reliability is needed as network packets can be lost or delayed during transmission between sender and receiver. To achieve reliable packet delivery, TCP uses a cumulative acknowledgment mechanism. This means a receiver will periodically send an acknowledgment packet that contains the highest sequence number of the packets received without gaps in the packet stream. This implicitly acknowledges all packets sent with a lower sequence number, meaning all have been successfully received. If a sender doesn't receive an acknowledgment within a timeout period, the packet is resent.

TCP has many other features, such as checksums to check packet integrity, and dynamic flow control to ensure a sender doesn't overwhelm a slow receiver by sending data too quickly. Along with connection establishment and acknowledgments, this makes TCP a relatively heavyweight protocol, which trades off reliability over efficiency.

This is where UDP comes into the picture. UDP is a simple, connectionless protocol, which exposes the user's program to any unreliability of the underlying network. There is no guarantee that delivery will occur in a prescribed order, or that it will happen at all. It can be thought of as a thin veneer (layer) on top of the underlying IP protocol, and deliberately trades off raw performance over reliability.

This, however, is highly appropriate for many modern applications where the odd lost packet has very little effect. Think streaming movies, video conferencing, and gaming, where one lost packet is unlikely to be perceptible by a user.

Figure 3-3 depicts some of the major differences between TCP and UDP. TCP incorporates a connection establishment three-packet handshake (SYN, SYN ACK, ACK), and piggybacks acknowledgments (ACK) of packets so that any packet loss can be handled by the protocol. There's also a TCP connection close phase involving a four-way handshake that is not shown in the diagram. UDP dispenses with connection establishment, tear down, acknowledgments, and retries. Therefore, applications using UDP need to be tolerant of packet loss and client or server failures (and behave accordingly).

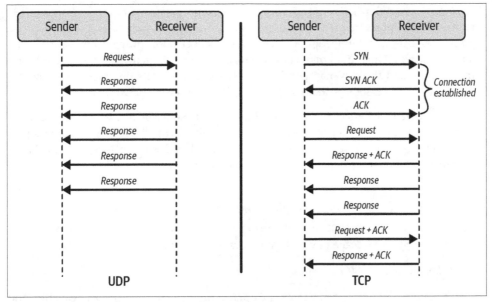

Figure 3-3. Comparing TCP and UDP

Remote Method Invocation

It's perfectly feasible to write our distributed applications using low-level APIs that interact directly with the transport layer protocols TCP and UDP. The most common approach is the standardized sockets library—see the brief overview in the sidebar. This is something you'll hopefully never need to do, as sockets are complex and error prone. Essentially, sockets create a bidirectional pipe between two nodes that you can use to send streams of data. There are (luckily) much better ways to build distributed communications, as I'll describe in this section. These approaches abstract away much of the complexity of using sockets. However, sockets still lurk underneath, so some knowledge is necessary.

An Overview of Sockets

A socket is one endpoint of a two-way network connection between a client and a server. Sockets are identified by a combination of the node's IP address and an abstraction known as a *port*. A port is a unique numeric identifier, which allows a node to support communications for multiple applications running on the node.

Each IP address can support 65,535 TCP ports and another 65,535 UDP ports. On a server, each *{<IP Address>, <port>}* combination can be associated with an application. This combination forms a unique endpoint that the transport layer uses to deliver data to the desired server.

A socket connection is identified by a unique combination of client and server IP addresses and ports, namely <*client IP address, client port, server IP address, server port*>. Each unique connection also allocates a socket descriptor on both the client and the server. Once the connection is created, the client sends data to the server in a stream, and the server responds with results. The sockets library supports both protocols, with the SOCK_STREAM option for TCP, and the SOCK_DGRAM for UDP.

You can write distributed applications directly to the sockets API, which is an operating system core component. Socket APIs are available in all mainstream programming languages. However, the sockets library is a low-level, hard-to-use API. You should avoid it unless you have a real need to write system-level code.

In our mobile banking example, the client might request a balance for the user's checking account using sockets. Ignoring specific language issues (and security!), the client could send a message payload as follows over a connection to the server:

{*"balance"*, *"000169990"*}

In this message, "balance" represents the operation we want the server to execute, and "000169990" is the bank account number.

In the server, we need to know that the first string in the message is the operation identifier, and based on this value being "balance", the second is the bank account number. The server then uses these values to presumably query a database, retrieve the balance, and send back the results, perhaps as a message formatted with the account number and current balance, as below:

{*"000169990"*, *"220.77"*}

In any complex system, the server will support many operations. In *igbank.com*, there might be for example "login", "transfer", "address", "statement", "transactions", and so on. Each will be followed by different message payloads that the server needs to interpret correctly to fulfill the client's request.

What we are defining here is an application-specific protocol. As long as we send the necessary values in the correct order for each operation, the server will be able to respond correctly. If we have an erroneous client that doesn't adhere to our application protocol, well, our server needs to do thorough error checking. The socket library provides a primitive, low-level method for client/server communications. It provides highly efficient communications but is difficult to correctly implement and evolve the application protocol to handle all possibilities. There are better mechanisms.

Stepping back, if we were defining the *igbank.com* server interface in an object-oriented language such as Java, we would have each operation it can process as a method. Each method is passed an appropriate parameter list for that operation, as shown in this example code:

```
// Simple igbank.com server interface
public interface IGBank {
    public float balance  (String accNo);
    public boolean  statement(String month) ;
    // other operations
}
```

There are several advantages of having such an interface, namely:

- Calls from the client to the server can be statically checked by the compiler to ensure they are of the correct format and argument types.

- Changes in the server interface (e.g., adding a new parameter) force changes in the client code to adhere to the new method signature.

- The interface is clearly defined by the class definition and thus straightforward for a client programmer to understand and utilize.

These benefits of an explicit interface are of course well known in software engineering. The whole discipline of object-oriented design is pretty much based upon these foundations, where an interface defines a contract between the caller and callee. Compared to the implicit application protocol we need to follow with sockets, the advantages are significant.

This fact was recognized reasonably early in the creation of distributed systems. Since the early 1990s, we have seen an evolution of technologies that enable us to define explicit server interfaces and call these across the network using essentially the same syntax as we would in a sequential program. A summary of the major approaches is given in Table 3-2. Collectively, they are known as Remote Procedure Call (RPC), or Remote Method Invocation (RMI) technologies.

Table 3-2. Summary of major RPC/RMI technologies

Technology	Date	Main features
Distributed Computing Environment (DCE) (*https://oreil.ly/bvbR3*)	Early 1990s	DCE RPC provides a standardized approach for client/server systems. Primary languages were C/C++.
Common Object Request Broker Architecture (CORBA) (*https://oreil.ly/IO9qD*)	Early 1990s	Facilitates language-neutral client/server communications based on an object-oriented interface definition language (IDL). Primary language support in C/C++, Java, Python, and Ada.
Java Remote Method Invocation (RMI) (*https://oreil.ly/1fvGm*)	Late 1990s	A pure Java-based remote method invocation that facilitates distributed client/server systems with the same semantics as Java objects.
XML web services	2000	Supports client/server communications based on HTTP and XML. Servers define their remote interface in the Web Services Description Language (WSDL).
gRPC	2015	Open source, based on HTTP/2 for transport, and uses Protocol Buffers (Protobuf) (*https://oreil.ly/ytHhl*) as the interface description language

While the syntax and semantics of these RPC/RMI technologies vary, the essence of how each operates is the same. Let's continue with our Java example of *igbank.com* to examine the whole class of approaches. Java offers a Remote Method Invocation (RMI) API for building client/server applications.

Using Java RMI, we can trivially make our `IGBank` interface example from above into a remote interface, as illustrated in the following code:

```
import java.rmi.*;
// Simple igbank.com server interface
public interface IGBank extends Remote{
    public float balance  (String accNo)
        throws RemoteException;
    public boolean  statement(String month)
        throws RemoteException ;
    // other operations
}
```

The `java.rmi.Remote` interface serves as a marker to inform the Java compiler we are creating an RMI server. In addition, each method must throw `java.rmi.RemoteEx ception`. These exceptions represent errors that can occur when a distributed call between two objects is invoked over a network. The most common reasons for such an exception would be a communications failure or the server object having crashed.

We then must provide a class that implements this remote interface. The sample code below shows an extract of the server implementation:

```
public class IGBankServer extends UnicastRemoteObject
                        implements IGBank  {
    // constructor/method implementations omitted
    public static void main(String args[]){
        try{
          IGBankServer server=new IGBankServer();
          // create a registry in local JVM on default port
          Registry registry = LocateRegistry.createRegistry(1099);
          registry.bind("IGBankServer", server);
          System.out.println("server ready");
        }catch(Exception e){
                // code omitted for brevity}
        }
    }
```

Points to note are:

- The server extends the `UnicastRemoteObject` class. This essentially provides the functionality to instantiate a remotely callable object.

- Once the server object is constructed, its availability must be advertised to remote clients. This is achieved by storing a reference to the object in a system service known as the *RMI registry*, and associating a logical name with it—in this example, "*IGBankServer*." The registry is a simple directory service that enables clients to look up the location (network address and object reference) of and obtain a reference to an RMI server by simply supplying the logical name it is associated with in the registry.

An extract from the client code to connect to the server is shown in the following example. It obtains a reference to the remote object by performing a lookup operation in the RMI registry and specifying the logical name that identifies the server. The reference returned by the lookup operation can then be used to call the server object in the same manner as a local object. However, there is a difference—the client must be ready to catch a RemoteException that will be thrown by the Java runtime when the server object cannot be reached:

```
// obtain a remote reference to the server
IGBank bankServer=
       (IGBank)Naming.lookup("rmi://localhost:1099/IGBankServer");
//now we can call the server
System.out.println(bankServer.balance("00169990"));
```

Figure 3-4 depicts the call sequence among the components that comprise an RMI system. The Stub and Skeleton are objects generated by the compiler from the RMI interface definition, and these facilitate the actual remote communications. The skeleton is in fact a TCP network endpoint (*host, port*) that listens for calls to the associated server.

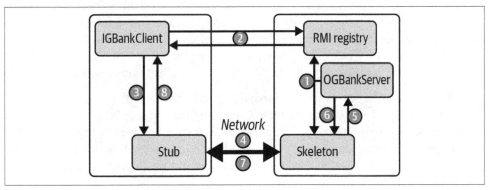

Figure 3-4. Schematic depicting the call sequence for establishing a connection and making a call to an RMI server object

The sequence of operations is as follows:

1. When the server starts, its logical reference is stored in the RMI registry. This entry contains the Java client stub that can be used to make remote calls to the server.

2. The client queries the registry, and the stub for the server is returned.

3. The client stub accepts a method call to the server interface from the Java client implementation.

4. The stub transforms the request into one or more network packets that are sent to the server host. This transformation process is known as marshalling.

5. The skeleton accepts network requests from the client, and unmarshalls the network packet data into a valid call to the RMI server object implementation. Unmarshalling is the opposite of marshalling—it takes a sequence of network packets and transforms them into a call to an object.

6. The skeleton waits for the method to return a response.

7. The skeleton marshalls the method results into a network reply packet that is returned to the client.

8. The stub unmarshalls the data and passes the result to the Java client call site.

This Java RMI example illustrates the basics that are used for implementing any RPC/RMI mechanism, even in modern languages like Erlang (*https://oreil.ly/D5biM*) and Go (*https://oreil.ly/zD8dS*). You are most likely to encounter Java RMI when using the Java Enterprise JavaBeans (EJB) technology. EJBs are a server-side component model built on RMI, which have seen wide usage in the last 20 or so years in enterprise systems.

Regardless of the precise implementation, the basic attraction of RPC/RMI approaches is to provide an abstract calling mechanism that supports *location transparency* for clients making remote server calls. Location transparency is provided by the registry, or in general any mechanism that enables a client to locate a server through a directory service. This means it is possible for the server to update its network location in the directory without affecting the client implementation.

RPC/RMI is not without its flaws. Marshalling and unmarshalling can become inefficient for complex object parameters. Cross-language marshalling—client in one language, server in another—can cause problems due to types being represented differently in different languages, causing subtle incompatibilities. And if a remote method signature changes, all clients need to obtain a new compatible stub, which can be cumbersome in large deployments.

For these reasons, most modern systems are built around simpler protocols based on HTTP and using JSON for parameter representation. Instead of operation names, HTTP verbs (PUT, GET, POST, etc.) have associated semantics that are mapped to a specific URL. This approach originated in the work by Roy Fielding on the REST approach.[1] REST has a set of semantics that comprise a *RESTful* architecture style,

---

1 Roy T. Fielding, "Architectural Styles and the Design of Network-Based Software Architectures." Dissertation, University of California, Irvine, 2000.

and in reality most systems do not adhere to these. We'll discuss REST and HTTP API mechanisms in Chapter 5.

Partial Failures

The components of distributed systems communicate over a network. In communications technology terminology, the shared local and wide area networks that our systems communicate over are known as *asynchronous* networks.

With asynchronous networks:

- Nodes can choose to send data to other nodes at any time.

- The network is *half-duplex*, meaning that one node sends a request and must wait for a response from the other. These are two separate communications.

- The time for data to be communicated between nodes is variable, due to reasons like network congestion, dynamic packet routing, and transient network connection failures.

- The receiving node may not be available due to a software or machine crash.

- Data can be lost. In wireless networks, packets can be corrupted and hence dropped due to weak signals or interference. Internet routers can drop packets during congestion.

- Nodes do not have identical internal clocks; hence they are not synchronized.

> This is in contrast with synchronous networks, which essentially are full duplex, transmitting data in both directions at the same time with each node having an identical clock for synchronization (*https://oreil.ly/SEPCs*).

What does this mean for our applications? Well, put simply, when a client sends a request to a server, how long does it wait until it receives a reply? Is the server node just being slow? Is the network congested and the packet has been dropped by a router? If the client doesn't get a reply, what should it do?

Let's explore these scenarios in detail. The core problem here, namely whether and when a response is received, is known as handling partial failures, and the general situation is depicted in Figure 3-5.

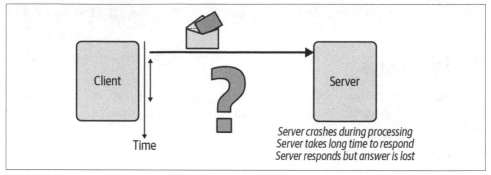

Figure 3-5. Handling partial failures

When a client wishes to connect to a server and exchanges messages, the following outcomes may occur:

- The request succeeds and a rapid response is received. All is well. (In reality, this outcome occurs for almost every request. *Almost* is the operative word here.)

- The destination IP address lookup may fail. In this case, the client rapidly receives an error message and can act accordingly.

- The IP address is valid but the destination node or target server process has failed. The sender will receive a timeout error message and can inform the user.

- The request is received by the target server, which fails while processing the request and no response is ever sent.

- The request is received by the target server, which is heavily loaded. It processes the request but takes a long time (e.g., 34 seconds) to respond.

- The request is received by the target server and a response is sent. However, the response is not received by the client due to a network failure.

The first three points are easy for the client to handle, as a response is received rapidly. A result from the server or an error message—either allows the client to proceed. Failures that can be detected quickly are easy to deal with.

The rest of the outcomes pose a problem for the client. They do not provide any insight into the reason why a response has not been received. From the client's perspective, these three outcomes look exactly the same. The client cannot know without waiting (potentially forever) whether the response will arrive eventually or never arrive; waiting forever doesn't get much work done.

More insidiously, the client cannot know if the operation succeeded and a server or network failure caused the result to never arrive, or if the request is on its way—delayed simply due to congestion in the network/server. These faults are collectively known as *crash faults* (*https://oreil.ly/AAc9M*).

The typical solution that clients adopt to handle crash faults is to resend the request after a configured timeout period. However, this is fraught with danger, as Figure 3-6 illustrates. The client sends a request to the server to deposit money in a bank account. When it receives no response after a timeout period, it resends the request. What is the resulting balance? The server may have applied the deposit, or it may not, depending on the partial failure scenario.

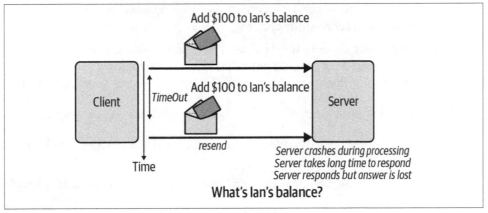

Figure 3-6. Client retries a request after timeout

The chance that the deposit may occur twice is a fine outcome for the customer, but the bank is unlikely to be amused by this possibility. Therefore, we need a way to ensure in our server operations implementation that retried, duplicate requests from clients only result in the request being applied once. This is necessary to maintain correct application semantics.

This property is known as *idempotence*. Idempotent operations can be applied multiple times without changing the result beyond the initial application. This means that for the example in Figure 3-6, the client can retry the request as many times as it likes, and the account will only be increased by $100.

Requests that make no persistent state changes are naturally idempotent. This means all read requests are inherently safe and no extra work is needed on the server. Updates are a different matter. The system needs to devise a mechanism such that duplicate client requests do not cause any state changes and can be detected by the server. In API terms, these endpoints cause mutation of the server state and must therefore be idempotent.

The general approach to building idempotent operations is as follows:

- Clients include a unique *idempotency key* in all requests that mutate state. The key identifies a single operation from the specific client or event source. It is usually a composite of a user identifier, such as the session key, and a unique value such as a local timestamp, UUID, or a sequence number.

- When the server receives a request, it checks to see if it has previously seen the idempotency key value by reading from a database that is uniquely designed for implementing idempotence. If the key is not in the database, this is a new request. The server therefore performs the business logic to update the application state. It also stores the idempotency key in a database to indicate that the operation has been successfully applied.

- If the idempotency key is in the database, this indicates that this request is a retry from the client and hence should not be processed. In this case the server returns a valid response for the operation so that (hopefully) the client won't retry again.

The database used to store idempotency keys can be implemented in, for example:

- A separate database table or collection in the transactional database used for the application data

- A dedicated database that provides very low latency lookups, such as a simple key-value store

Unlike application data, idempotency keys don't have to be retained forever. Once a client receives an acknowledgment of a success for an individual operation, the idempotency key can be discarded. The simplest way to achieve this is to automatically remove idempotency keys from the store after a specific time period, such as 60 minutes or 24 hours, depending on application needs and request volumes.

In addition, an idempotent API implementation must ensure that the application state is modified *and* the idempotency key is stored. Both must occur for success. If the application state is modified and, due to some failure, the idempotent key is not stored, then a retry will cause the operation to be applied twice. If the idempotency key is stored but for some reason the application state is not modified, then the operation has not been applied. If a retry arrives, it will be filtered out as duplicate as the idempotency key already exists, and the update will be lost.

The implication here is that the updates to the application state and idempotency key store must *both* occur, or *neither* must occur. If you know your databases, you'll recognize this as a requirement for transactional semantics. We'll discuss how distributed transactions are achieved in Chapter 12. Essentially, transactions ensure *exactly-once semantics for operations*, which guarantees that all messages will always be processed exactly once—precisely what we need for idempotence.

Exactly once does not mean that there are no message transmission failures, retries, and application crashes. These are all inevitable. The important thing is that the retries eventually succeed and the result is always the same.

We'll return to the issue of communications delivery guarantees in later chapters. As Figure 3-7 illustrates, there's a spectrum of semantics, each with different guarantees and performance characteristics. *At-most-once* delivery is fast and unreliable—this is what the UDP protocol provides. *At-least-once* delivery is the guarantee provided by TCP/IP, meaning duplicates are inevitable. *Exactly-once* delivery, as we've discussed here, requires guarding against duplicates and hence trades off reliability against slower performance.

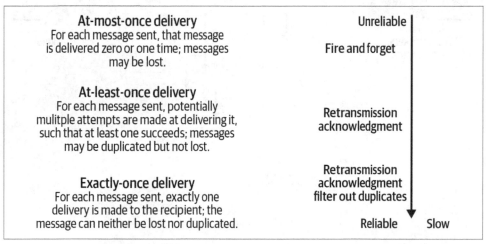

Figure 3-7. Communications delivery guarantees

As we'll see, some advanced communications mechanisms can provide our applications with exactly-once semantics. However, these don't operate at internet scale because of the performance implications. That is why, as our applications are built on the at-least-once semantics of TCP/IP, we must implement exactly-once semantics in our APIs that cause state mutation.

Consensus in Distributed Systems

Crash faults have another implication for the way we build distributed systems. This is best illustrated by the Two Generals' Problem (*https://oreil.ly/ap5eq*), which is depicted in Figure 3-8.

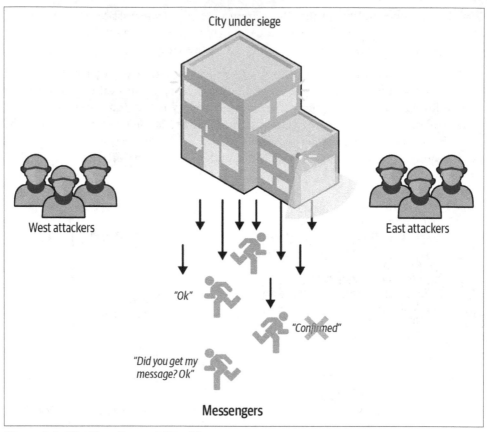

Figure 3-8. The Two Generals' Problem

Imagine a city under siege by two armies. The armies lie on opposite sides of the city, and the terrain surrounding the city is difficult to travel through and visible to snipers in the city. In order to overwhelm the city, it's crucial that both armies attack at the same time. This will stretch the city's defenses and make victory more likely for the attackers. If only one army attacks, then they will likely be repelled.

Given these constraints, how can the two generals reach agreement on the exact time to attack, such that both generals know for certain that agreement has been reached? They both need certainty that the other army will attack at the agreed time, or disaster will ensue.

To coordinate an attack, the first general sends a messenger to the other, with instructions to attack at a specific time. As the messenger may be captured or killed by snipers, the sending general cannot be certain the message has arrived unless they get an acknowledgment messenger from the second general. Of course, the acknowledgment messenger may be captured or killed, so even if the original messenger does get through, the first general may never know. And even if the acknowledgment message arrives, how does the second general know this, unless they get an acknowledgment from the first general?

Hopefully the problem is apparent. With messengers being randomly captured or extinguished, there is no guarantee the two generals will ever reach consensus on the attack time. In fact, it can be proven that it is not possible to *guarantee* agreement will be reached. There are solutions that increase the likelihood of reaching consensus. For example, *Game of Thrones* style, each general may send 100 different messengers every time, and even if most are killed, this increases the probability that at least one will make the perilous journey to the other friendly army and successfully deliver the message.

The Two Generals' Problem is analogous to two nodes in a distributed system wishing to reach agreement on some state, such as the value of a data item that can be updated at either. Partial failures are analogous to losing messages and acknowledgments. Messages may be lost or delayed for an indeterminate period of time—the characteristics of asynchronous networks, as I described earlier in this chapter.

In fact it can be demonstrated that consensus on an asynchronous network in the presence of crash faults, where messages can be delayed but not lost, is impossible to achieve within bounded time. This is known as the FLP Impossibility Theorem.[2]

Luckily, this is only a theoretical limitation, demonstrating it's not possible to *guarantee* consensus will be reached with unbounded message delays on an asynchronous network. In reality, distributed systems reach consensus all the time. This is possible because while our networks are asynchronous, we can establish sensible practical bounds on message delays and retry after a timeout period. FLP is therefore a worst-case scenario, and as such I'll discuss algorithms for establishing consensus in distributed databases in Chapter 12.

Finally, we should note the issue of Byzantine failures. Imagine extending the Two Generals' Problem to N generals who need to agree on a time to attack. However, in this scenario, traitorous messengers may change the value of the time of the attack, or a traitorous general may send false information to other generals.

This class of *malicious* failures are known as Byzantine faults and are particularly sinister in distributed systems. Luckily, the systems we discuss in this book typically live behind well-protected, secure enterprise networks and administrative environments. This means we can in practice exclude handling Byzantine faults. Algorithms that do address such malicious behaviors exist, and if you are interested in a practical

---

2 Michael J. Fischer et al., "Impossibility of Distributed Consensus with One Faulty Process," *Journal of the ACM* 32, no. 2 (1985): 374–82. *https://doi.org/10.1145/3149.214121*.

example, take a look at blockchain consensus mechanisms (*https://oreil.ly/r3vQT*) and Bitcoin (*https://oreil.ly/IPohu*).

Time in Distributed Systems

Every node in a distributed system has its own internal clock. If all the clocks on every machine were perfectly synchronized, we could always simply compare the timestamps on events across nodes to determine the precise order they occurred in. If this were reality, many of the problems I'll discuss with distributed systems would pretty much go away.

Unfortunately, this is not the case. Clocks on individual nodes *drift* due to environmental conditions like changes in temperature or voltage. The amount of drift varies on every machine, but values such as 10–20 seconds per day are not uncommon. (Or with my current coffee machine at home, about 5 minutes per day!)

If left unchecked, clock drift would render the time on a node meaningless—like the time on my coffee machine if I don't correct it every few days. To address this problem, a number of *time services* exist. A time service represents an accurate time source, such as a GPS or atomic clock, which can be used to periodically reset the clock on a node to correct for drift on packet-switched, variable-latency data networks.

The most widely used time service is Network Time Protocol (NTP) (*http://www.ntp.org*), which provides a hierarchically organized collection of time servers spanning the globe. The root servers, of which there are around 300 worldwide, are the most accurate. Time servers in the next level of the hierarchy (approximately 20,000) synchronize to within a few milliseconds of the root server periodically, and so on throughout the hierarchy, with a maximum of 15 levels. Globally, there are more than 175,000 NTP servers.

Using the NTP protocol, a node in an application running an NTP client can synchronize to an NTP server. The time on a node is set by a UDP message exchange with one or more NTP servers. Messages are time stamped, and through the message exchange the time taken for message transit is estimated. This becomes a factor in the algorithm used by NTP to establish what the time on the client should be reset to. A simple NTP configuration is shown in Figure 3-9. On a LAN, machines can synchronize to an NTP server within a small number of milliseconds accuracy.

One interesting effect of NTP synchronization for our applications is that the resetting of the clock can move the local node time forward or backward. This means that if our application is measuring the time taken for events to occur (e.g., to calculate event response times), it is possible that the end time of the event may be earlier than the start time if the NTP protocol has set the local time backward.

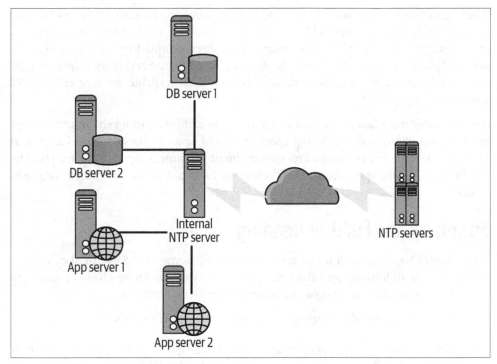

Figure 3-9. Illustrating using the NTP service

In fact, a compute node has two clocks. These are:

Time of day clock

> This represents the number of milliseconds since midnight, January 1st 1970. In Java, you can get the current time using `System.currentTimeMillis()`. This is the clock that can be reset by NTP, and hence may jump forward or backward if it is a long way behind or ahead of NTP time.

Monotonic clock

> This represents the amount of time (in seconds and nanoseconds) since an unspecified point in the past, such as the last time the system was restarted. It will only ever move forward; however, it again may not be a totally accurate measure of elapsed time because it stalls during an event such as virtual machine suspension. In Java, you can get the current monotonic clock time using `System.nanoTime()`.

Applications can use an NTP service to ensure the clocks on every node in the system are closely synchronized. It's typical for an application to resynchronize clocks on anything from a one hour to one day time interval. This ensures the clocks remain close in value. Still, if an application really needs to precisely know the order of events that occur on different nodes, clock drift is going to make this fraught with danger.

There are other time services that provide higher accuracy than NTP. Chrony (*https://oreil.ly/ylrw3*) supports the NTP protocol but provides much higher accuracy and greater scalability than NTP—the reason it has been adopted by Facebook (*https://oreil.ly/JqKHP*). Amazon has built the Amazon Time Sync Service by installing GPS and atomic clocks in its data centers. This service is available for free to all AWS customers.

The takeaway from this discussion is that our applications cannot rely on timestamps of events on different nodes to represent the actual order of these events. Clock drift even by a second or two makes cross-node timestamps meaningless to compare. The implications of this will become clear when we start to discuss distributed databases in detail.

Summary and Further Reading

This chapter has covered a lot of ground to explain some of the essential characteristics of communications and time in distributed systems. These characteristics are important for application designers and developers to understand.

The key issues that should resonate from this chapter are as follows:

1. Communications in distributed systems can transparently traverse many different types of underlying physical networks, including WiFi, wireless, WANs, and LANs. Communication latencies are hence highly variable, and influenced by the physical distance between nodes, physical network properties, and transient network congestion. At large scale, latencies between application components are something that should be minimized as much as possible (within the laws of physics, of course).

2. The Internet Protocol stack ensures reliable communications across heterogeneous networks through a combination of the IP and TCP protocols. Communications can fail due to network communications fabric and router failures that make nodes unavailable, as well as individual node failure. Your code will experience various TCP/IP overheads, for example, for connection establishment, and errors when network failures occur. Hence, understanding the basics of the IP suite is important for design and debugging.

3. RMI/RPC technologies build the TCP/IP layer to provide abstractions for client/server communications that mirror making local method/procedure calls. However, these more abstract programming approaches still need to be resilient to network issues such as failures and retransmissions. This is most apparent in application APIs that mutate state on the server, and must be designed to be idempotent.

4. Achieving agreement, or consensus on state across multiple nodes in the presence of crash faults is not possible in bounded time on asynchronous networks.

Luckily, real networks, especially LANs, are fast and mostly reliable, meaning we can devise algorithms that achieve consensus in practice. I'll cover these in Part III of the book when we discuss distributed databases.

5. There is no reliable global time source that nodes in an application can rely upon to synchronize their behavior. Clocks on individual nodes vary and cannot be used for meaningful comparisons. This means applications cannot meaningfully compare clocks on different nodes to determine the order of events.

These issues will pervade the discussions in the rest of this book. Many of the unique problems and solutions that are adopted in distributed systems stem from these fundamentals. There's no escaping them!

An excellent source for more detailed, more theoretical coverage of all aspects of distributed systems is George Coulouris et al., *Distributed Systems: Concepts and Design*, 5th ed. (Pearson, 2001).

Likewise for computer networking, you'll find out all you wanted to know and no doubt more in James Kurose and Keith Ross's *Computer Networking: A Top-Down Approach*, 7th ed. (Pearson, 2017).

CHAPTER 4

An Overview of Concurrent Systems

Distributed systems comprise multiple independent pieces of code executing in parallel, or concurrently, on many processing nodes across multiple locations. Any distributed system is hence by definition a concurrent system, even if each node is processing events one at a time. The behavior of the various nodes must of course be coordinated in order to make the application behave as desired.

As I described in Chapter 3, coordinating nodes in a distributed system is fraught with danger. Luckily, our industry has matured sufficiently to provide complex, powerful software frameworks that hide many of these distributed system perils from our applications (most of the time, anyway). The majority of this book focuses on describing how we can utilize these frameworks to build scalable distributed systems.

This chapter, however, is concerned with concurrent behavior in our systems on a single node. By explicitly writing our software to perform multiple actions concurrently, we can optimize the processing and resource utilization on a single node, and hence increase our processing capacity both locally and system-wide.

I'll use the Java 7.0 concurrency capabilities for examples, as these are at a lower level of abstraction than those introduced in Java 8.0. Knowing how concurrent systems operate "closer to the machine" is essential foundational knowledge when building concurrent and distributed systems. Once you understand the lower-level mechanisms for building concurrent systems, the more abstract approaches are easier to optimally exploit. And while this chapter is Java-specific, the fundamental problems of concurrent systems don't change when you write systems in other languages. Mechanisms for handling concurrency exist in all mainstream programming languages. "Concurrency Models" on page 63 gives some more details on alternative approaches and how they are implemented in modern languages.

One final point. This chapter is a concurrency *primer*. It won't teach you everything you need to know to build complex, high-performance concurrent systems. It will also be useful if your experience writing concurrent programs is rusty, or you have some exposure to concurrent code in another programming language. The further reading section at the end of the chapter points to more comprehensive coverage of this topic for those who wish to delve deeper.

Why Concurrency?

Think of a busy coffee shop. If everyone orders a simple coffee, then the barista can quickly and consistently deliver each drink. Suddenly, the person in front of you orders a soy, vanilla, no sugar, quadruple-shot iced brew. Everyone in line sighs and starts reading their social media. In two minutes the line is out of the door.

Processing requests in web applications is analogous to our coffee example. In a coffee shop, we enlist the help of a new barista to simultaneously make coffees on a different machine to keep the line length in control and serve customers quickly. In software, to make applications responsive, we need to somehow process requests in our server in an overlapping manner, handling requests concurrently.

In the good old days of computing, each CPU was only able to execute a single machine instruction at any instant. If our server application runs on such a CPU, why do we need to structure our software systems to potentially execute multiple instructions concurrently? It all seems slightly pointless.

There is actually a very good reason. Virtually every program does more than just execute machine instructions. For example, when a program attempts to read from a file or send a message on the network, it must interact with the hardware subsystem (disk, network card) that is peripheral to the CPU. Reading data from a magnetic hard disk takes around 10 milliseconds (ms). During this time, the program must wait for the data to be available for processing.

Now, even an ancient CPU such as a 1988 Intel 80386 (*https://oreil.ly/NK6NC*) can execute more than 10 million instructions per second (mips) (*https://oreil.ly/8jWH5*). 10 ms is one hundredth of a second. How many instructions could our 80386 execute in a hundredth second? Do the math. (Hint—it's a lot!) A lot of wasted processing capacity, in fact.

This is how operating systems such as Linux can run multiple programs on a single CPU. While one program is waiting for an I/O event, the operating system schedules another program to execute. By explicitly structuring our software to have multiple activities that can be executed in parallel, the operating system can schedule tasks that have work to do while others wait for I/O. We'll see in more detail how this works with Java later in this chapter.

In 2001, IBM introduced the world's first multicore processor, a chip with two CPUs—see Figure 4-1 for a simplified illustration. Today, even my laptop has 16 CPUs, or "cores," as they are commonly known. With a multicore chip, a software system that is structured to have multiple parallel activities can be executed concurrently on each core, up to the number of available cores. In this way, we can fully utilize the processing resources on a multicore chip, and thus increase our application's processing capacity.

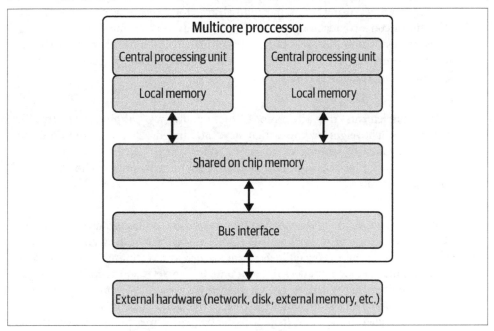

Figure 4-1. Simplified view of a multicore processor

The primary way to structure a software system as concurrent activities is to use *threads*. Virtually every programming language has its own threading mechanism. The underlying semantics of all these mechanisms are similar—there are only a few primary threading models in mainstream use—but obviously the syntax varies by language. In the following sections, I'll explain how threads are supported in Java, and how we need to design our programs to be safe (i.e., correct) and efficient when executing in parallel. Armed with this knowledge, leaping into the concurrency features supported in other languages shouldn't be too arduous.

Concurrency Models

This chapter describes one model for concurrent systems, based on independently executing threads using locks to operate on shared, mutable resources. Concurrency models have been a much studied and explored topic in computer science for roughly the last 50 years. Many theoretical proposals have been put forward, and some of these are implemented in modern programming languages. These models provide alternative approaches for structuring and coordinating concurrent activities in programs. Here's a sampler that you might well encounter in your work:

Go

> The communicating sequential processes (CSP) model forms the basis of Go's concurrency features (*https://oreil.ly/29b49*). In CSP, processes synchronize by sending messages using communication abstractions known as channels. In Go, the unit of concurrency is a goroutine, and goroutines communicate by sending messages using unbuffered or buffered channels. Unbuffered channels are used to synchronize senders and receivers, as communications only occur when both goroutines are ready to exchange data.

Erlang

> Erlang implements the actor model of concurrency (*https://oreil.ly/TcoyK*). Actors are lightweight processes that have no shared state, and communicate by asynchronously sending messages to other actors. Actors use a mailbox, or queue, to buffer messages and can use pattern matching to choose which messages to process.

Node.js

> Node.js eschews anything resembling multiple threads and instead utilizes a single-threaded nonblocking (*https://oreil.ly/xaQB2*) model managed by an event loop. This means when an I/O operation is required, such as accessing a database, Node.js instigates the operation but does not wait until it completes. Operations are delegated to the operating system to execute asynchronously, and upon completion the results are placed on the main thread's stack as callbacks. These callbacks are subsequently executed in the event loop. This model works well for codes performing frequent I/O requests, as it avoids the overheads associated with thread creation and management. However, if your code needs to perform a CPU-intensive operation, such as sorting a large list, you only have one thread. This will therefore block all other requests until the sort is complete. Rarely an ideal situation.

Hopefully this gives you a feel for the diversity of concurrency models and primitives in modern programming languages. Luckily, when you know the fundamentals and one model, the rest are straightforward to learn.

Threads

Every software process has a single thread of execution by default. This is the thread that the operating system manages when it schedules the process for execution. In Java, for example, the main() function you specify as the entry point to your code defines the behavior of this thread. This single thread has access to the program's environment and resources such as open file handles and network connections. As the program calls methods in objects instantiated in the code, the program's runtime stack is used to pass parameters and manage variable scopes. Standard programming language runtime stuff, that we all know and love. This is a sequential process.

In your systems, you can use programming language features to create and execute additional threads. Each thread is an independent sequence of execution and has its own runtime stack to manage local object creation and method calls. Each thread also has access to the process' global data and environment. A simple depiction of this scheme is shown in Figure 4-2.

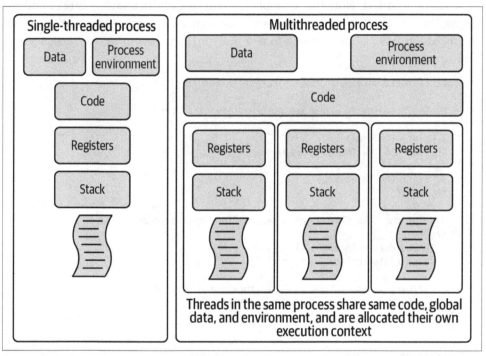

Figure 4-2. Comparing a single-threaded and multithreaded process

In Java, we can define a thread using a class that implements the Runnable interface and defines the run() method. Let's look at a simple example:

```
class NamingThread implements Runnable {

private String name;

public NamingThread(String threadName) {
    name = threadName ;
        System.out.println("Constructor called: " + threadName) ;
    }

    public void run() {
```

```
        //Display info about this  thread
            System.out.println("Run called : " + name);
            System.out.println(name + " : " + Thread.currentThread());
            // and now terminate  ....
    }
}
```

To execute the thread, we need to construct a `Thread` object using an instance of our `Runnable` and call the `start()` method to invoke the code in its own execution context. This is shown in the next code example, along with the output of running the code in bold text. Note this example has two threads: the `main()` thread and the `NamingThread`. The main thread starts the `NamingThread`, which executes asynchronously, and then waits for 1 second to give our `run()` method in `NamingThread` ample time to complete:

```
public static void main(String[] args) {

    NamingThread name0 = new NamingThread("My first thread");

    //Create the thread
    Thread t0 = new Thread (name0);

    // start the threads
    t0.start();

    //delay the main thread for a second (1000 milliseconds)
    try {
        Thread.currentThread().sleep(1000);
    } catch (InterruptedException e) {}

        //Display info about the main thread and terminate
        System.out.println(Thread.currentThread());

}

===EXECUTION OUTPUT===
Constructor called: My first thread
Run called : My first thread
My first thread : Thread[Thread-0,5,main]
Thread[main,5,main]
```

For illustration, we also call the static `currentThread()` method, which returns a string containing:

- The system-generated thread identifier.

- The thread priority, which by default is 5 for all threads. We'll cover thread priorities later.

- The identifier of the parent thread—in this example both parent threads are the `main` thread.

Note that to instantiate a thread, we call the `start()` method, not the `run()` method we define in the `Runnable`. The `start()` method contains the internal system magic to create the execution context for a separate thread to execute. If we call `run()` directly, the code will execute, but no new thread will be created. The `run()` method will execute as part of the `main` thread, just like any other Java method invocation that you know and love. You will still have a single-threaded code.

In the example, we use `sleep()` to pause the execution of the `main` thread and make sure it does not terminate before the `NamimgThread`. This approach, namely coordinating two threads by delaying for an absolute time period (1 second in the example) is not a very robust mechanism. What if for some reason—a slower CPU, a long delay reading disk, additional complex logic in the method—our thread doesn't terminate in the expected timeframe? In this case, `main` will terminate first—this is not what we intend. In general, if you are using absolute times for thread coordination, you are doing it wrong. Almost always. Like 99.99999% of the time.

A simple and robust mechanism for one thread to wait until another has completed its work is to use the `join()` method. We could replace the `try-catch` block in the above example with:

```
t0.join();
```

This method causes the calling thread (in this case, `main`) to block until the thread referenced by `t0` terminates. If the referenced thread has terminated before the call to `join()`, then the method call returns immediately. In this way we can coordinate, or synchronize, the behavior of multiple threads. Synchronization of multiple threads is in fact the major focus of the rest of this chapter.

Order of Thread Execution

The system scheduler (in Java, this lives in the Java virtual machine [JVM]) controls the order of thread execution. From the programmer's perspective, the order of execution is *nondeterministic*. Get used to that term, I'll use it a lot. The concept of nondeterminism is fundamental to understanding multithreaded code.

I'll illustrate this by building on the earlier `NamingThread` example. Instead of creating a single `NamingThread`, I'll create and start up a few. Three, in fact, as shown in the following code example. Again, sample output from running the code is in bold text beneath the code itself:

```
NamingThread name0 = new NamingThread("thread0");
NamingThread name1 = new NamingThread("thread1");
NamingThread name2 = new NamingThread("thread2");

//Create the threads
Thread t0 = new Thread (name0);
```

```
        Thread t1 = new Thread (name1);
        Thread t2 = new Thread (name2);

        // start the threads
        t0.start();  ❶
        t1.start();  ❶
        t2.start();  ❶

===EXECUTION OUTPUT===
Run called : thread0
thread0 : Thread[Thread-0,5,main]  ❷
Run called : thread2  ❸
Run called : thread1
thread1 : Thread[Thread-1,5,main]  ❹
thread2 : Thread[Thread-2,5,main]
Thread[main,5,main]
```

The output shown is a sample from just one execution. You can see the code starts three threads sequentially, namely *t0*, *t1*, and *t2* (see ❶). Looking at the output, we see thread *t0* completes (see ❷) before the others start. Next *t2*'s run() method is called (see ❸) followed by *t1*'s run() method, even though *t1* was started before *t2*. Thread *t1* then runs to completion (see ❹) before *t2*, and eventually the *main* thread and the program terminate.

This is just one possible order of execution. If we run this program again, we will almost certainly see a different execution trace. This is because the JVM scheduler is deciding which thread to execute, and for how long. Put very simply, once the scheduler has given a thread an execution time slot on a CPU, it can interrupt the thread after a specified time period and schedule another one to run. This interruption is known as preemption. Preemption ensures each thread is given an opportunity to make progress. Hence the threads run independently and asynchronously until completion, and the scheduler decides which thread runs when based on a scheduling algorithm.

There's more to thread scheduling than this, and I'll explain the basic scheduling algorithm used later in this chapter. For now, there is a major implication for programmers; regardless of the order of thread execution—which you don't control—your code should produce correct results. Sounds easy? Read on.

Problems with Threads

The basic problem in concurrent programming is coordinating the execution of multiple threads so that whatever order they are executed in, they produce the correct answer. Given that threads can be started and preempted nondeterministically, any moderately complex program will have essentially an infinite number of possible orders of execution. These systems aren't easy to test.

There are two fundamental problems that all concurrent programs need to avoid. These are race conditions and deadlocks, and these topics are covered in the next two subsections.

Race Conditions

Nondeterministic execution of threads implies that the code statements that comprise the threads:

- Will execute sequentially as defined within each thread.
- Can be overlapped in any order across threads. This is because the number of statements that are executed for each thread execution slot is determined by the scheduler.

Hence, when many threads are executed on a single processor, their execution is *interleaved*. The CPU executes some steps from one thread, then performs some steps from another, and so on. If we are executing on a multicore CPU, then we can execute one thread per core. The statements of each thread execution are still however interleaved in a nondeterministic manner.

Now, if every thread simply does its own thing and is completely independent, this is not a problem. Each thread executes until it terminates, as in our trivial Naming Thread example. This stuff is a piece of cake! Why are these thread things meant to be complex?

Unfortunately, totally independent threads are not how most multithreaded systems behave. If you refer back to Figure 4-2, you will see that multiple threads share the global data within a process. In Java this is both global and static data.

Threads can use shared data structures to coordinate their work and communicate status across threads. For example, we may have threads handling requests from web clients, one thread per request. We also want to keep a running total of how many requests we process each day. When a thread completes a request, it increments a global RequestCounter object that all threads share and update after each request. At the end of the day, we know how many requests were processed. A simple and elegant solution indeed. Well, maybe?

The code below shows a very simple implementation that mimics the request counter example scenario. It creates 50,000 threads to update a shared counter. Note we use a lambda function for brevity to create the threads, and a (really bad idea) 5-second delay in main to allow the threads to finish:[1]

---

1 The correct way to handle these problems, namely barrier synchronization, is covered later in this chapter.

```
public class RequestCounter {
  final static private int NUMTHREADS = 50000;
  private int count = 0;

  public  void inc() {
    count++;
  }

  public int getVal() {
    return this.count;
  }

  public static void main(String[] args) throws InterruptedException {
    final RequestCounter counter = new RequestCounter();

    for (int i = 0; i < NUMTHREADS; i++) {
      // lambda runnable creation
      Runnable thread = () -> {counter.inc(); };
        new Thread(thread).start();
    }

    Thread.sleep(5000);
    System.out.println("Value should be " + NUMTHREADS + "It is: " +
counter.getVal());
  }
}
```

What you can do at home is clone this code from the book's GitHub repo (*https://oreil.ly/fss-git-repo*), run this code a few times, and see what results you get. In 10 executions my mean was 49,995. I didn't once get the correct answer of 50,000. Weird.

Why?

The answer lies in how abstract, high-level programming language statements, in Java in this case, are executed on a machine. In this example, to perform an increment of a counter, the CPU must:

- Load the current value into a register.
- Increment the register value.
- Write the results back to the original memory location.

This simple increment is actually a sequence of three machine-level operations.

As Figure 4-3 shows, at the machine level these three operations are independent and not treated as a single *atomic* operation. By atomic, we mean an operation that cannot be interrupted and hence once started will run to completion.

As the increment operation is not atomic at the machine level, one thread can load the counter value into a CPU register from memory, but before it writes the incremented value back, the scheduler preempts the thread and allows another thread to start. This thread loads the old value of the counter from memory and writes back the incremented value. Eventually the original thread executes again and writes back its incremented value, which just happens to be the same as what is already in memory.

This means we've lost an update. From our 10 tests of the counter code above, we see this is happening on average 5 times in 50,000 increments. Hence such events are rare, but even if it happens 1 time in 10 million, you still have an incorrect result.

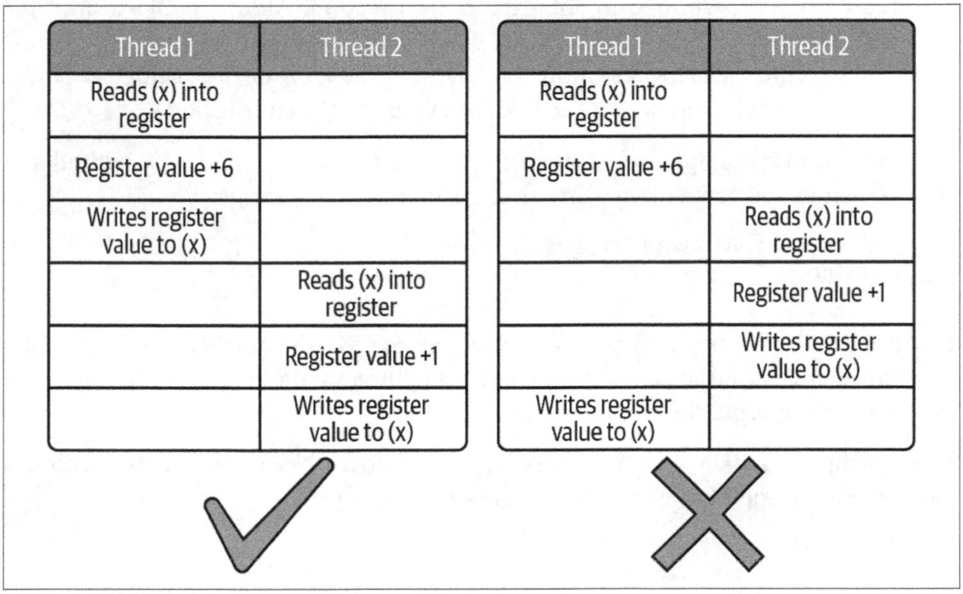

Thread 1	Thread 2	Thread 1	Thread 2
Reads (x) into register		Reads (x) into register	
Register value +6		Register value +6	
Writes register value to (x)			Reads (x) into register
	Reads (x) into register		Register value +1
	Register value +1		Writes register value to (x)
	Writes register value to (x)	Writes register value to (x)	

Figure 4-3. Increments are not atomic at the machine level

When we lose updates in this manner, it is called a race condition. Race conditions can occur whenever multiple threads make changes to some shared state, in this case a simple counter. Essentially, different interleavings of the threads can produce different results.

Race conditions are insidious, evil errors, because their occurrence is typically rare, and they can be hard to detect as most of the time the answer will be correct. Try running the multithreaded counter code example with 1,000 threads instead of 50,000, and you will see this in action. I got the correct answer nine times out of ten.

So, this situation can be summarized as "same code, occasionally different results." Like I said, race conditions are evil! Luckily, eradicating them is straightforward if you take a few precautions.

The key is to identify and protect *critical sections*. A critical section is a section of code that updates shared data structures and hence must be executed atomically if accessed by multiple threads. The example of incrementing a shared counter is an example of a critical section. Another is removing an item from a list. We need to delete the head node of the list and move the reference to the head of the list from the removed node to the next node in the list. Both operations must be performed atomically to maintain the integrity of the list. This is a critical section.

In Java, the `synchronized` keyword defines a critical section. If used to decorate a method, then when multiple threads attempt to call that method on the same shared object, only one is permitted to enter the critical section. All others block until the thread exits the synchronized method, at which point the scheduler chooses the next thread to execute the critical section. We say the execution of the critical section is serialized, as only one thread at a time can be executing the code inside it.

To fix the counterexample, you therefore just need to identify the `inc()` method as a critical section and make it a synchronized method, i.e.:

```
synchronized public void inc() {
    count++;
}
```

Test it out as many times as you like. You'll always get the correct answer. Slightly more formally, this means any interleaving of the threads that the scheduler throws at us will always produce the correct results.

The `synchronized` keyword can also be applied to blocks of statements within a method. For example, we could rewrite the above example as:

```
public void inc() {
        synchronized(this){
            count++;
        }
}
```

Underneath the covers, every Java object has a *monitor lock*, sometimes known as an intrinsic lock, as part of its runtime representation. The monitor is like the bathroom on a long-distance bus—only one person is allowed to (and should!) enter at once, and the door lock stops others from entering when in use.

In our totally sanitary Java runtime environment, a thread must acquire the monitor lock to enter a synchronized method or synchronized block of statements. Only one thread can own the lock at any time, and hence execution is serialized. This, very basically, is how Java and similar languages implement critical sections.

As a rule of thumb, you should keep critical sections as small as possible so that the serialized code is minimized. This can have positive impacts on performance and hence scalability. I'll return to this topic later, but I'm really talking about Amdahl's law (*https://oreil.ly/kLFs1*) again, as introduced in Chapter 2. Synchronized blocks are the serialized parts of a system as described by Amdahl, and the longer they execute for, then the less potential we have for system scalability.

Deadlocks

To ensure correct results in multithreaded code, I explained that we have to restrict the inherent nondeterminism to serialize access to critical sections. This avoids race conditions. However, if we are not careful, we can write code that restricts nondeterminism so much that our program stops. And never continues. This is formally known as a deadlock.

A deadlock occurs when two or more threads are blocked forever, and none can proceed. This happens when threads need exclusive access to a shared set of resources and the threads acquire locks in different orders. This is illustrated in the example below in which two threads need exclusive access to critical sections A and B. Thread 1 acquires the lock for critical section A, and thread 2 acquires the lock for critical section B. Both then block forever as they cannot acquire the locks they need to continue.

Two threads sharing access to two shared variables via synchronized blocks:

- Thread 1: enters critical section A.
- Thread 2: enters critical section B.
- Thread 1: blocks on entry to critical section B.
- Thread 2: blocks on entry to critical section A.
- Both threads wait forever.

A deadlock, also known as a deadly embrace, causes a program to stop. It doesn't take a vivid imagination to realize that this can cause all sorts of undesirable outcomes. I'm happily texting away while my autonomous vehicle drives me to the bar. Suddenly, the vehicle code deadlocks. It won't end well.

Deadlocks occur in more subtle circumstances than the simple example above. The classic example is the dining philosophers problem. The story goes like this.

Five philosophers sit around a shared table. Being philosophers, they spend a lot of time thinking deeply. In between bouts of deep thinking, they replenish their brain function by eating from a plate of food that sits in front of them. Hence a philosopher is either eating or thinking or transitioning between these two states.

In addition, the philosophers must all be physically very close, highly dexterous, and COVID-19 vaccinated friends, as they share chopsticks to eat. Only five chopsticks are on the table, placed between each philosopher. When one philosopher wishes to eat, they follow a protocol of picking up their left chopstick first, then their right chopstick. Once they are ready to think again, they first return the right chopstick, then the left.

Figure 4-4 depicts our philosophers, each identified by a unique number. As each is either concurrently eating or thinking, we can model each philosopher as a thread.

Figure 4-4. The dining philosophers problem

The code is shown in Example 4-1. The shared chopsticks are represented by instances of the Java `Object` class. As only one object can hold the monitor lock on an object at any time, they are used as entry conditions to the critical sections in which the philosophers acquire the chopsticks they need to eat. After eating, the chopsticks are returned to the table and the lock is released on each so that neighboring philosophers can eat whenever they are ready.

Example 4-1. The philosopher thread

```java
public class Philosopher implements Runnable {

  private final Object leftChopStick;
  private final Object rightChopStick;

  Philosopher(Object leftChopStick, Object rightChopStick) {
    this.leftChopStick = leftChopStick;
    this.rightChopStick = rightChopStick;
  }
  private void LogEvent(String event) throws InterruptedException {
    System.out.println(Thread.currentThread()
                               .getName() + " " + event);
    Thread.sleep(1000);
  }

  public void run() {
    try {
      while (true) {
        LogEvent(": Thinking deeply");
        synchronized (leftChopStick) {
          LogEvent( ": Picked up left chopstick");
          synchronized (rightChopStick) {
            LogEvent(": Picked up right chopstick - eating");
            LogEvent(": Put down right chopstick");
          }
          LogEvent(": Put down left chopstick. Ate too much");
        }
      } // end while
    } catch (InterruptedException e) {
      Thread.currentThread().interrupt();
    }
  }
}
```

To bring the philosophers described in Example 4-1 to life, we must instantiate a thread for each and give each philosopher access to their neighboring chopsticks. This is done through the thread constructor call at ❶ in Example 4-2. In the for loop we create five philosophers and start these as independent threads, where each chopstick is accessible to two threads, one as a left chopstick, and one as a right.

Example 4-2. Dining philosophers—deadlocked version

```java
private final static int NUMCHOPSTICKS = 5 ;
private final static int NUMPHILOSOPHERS = 5;
public static void main(String[] args) throws Exception {

  final Philosopher[] ph = new Philosopher[NUMPHILOSOPHERS];
  Object[] chopSticks = new Object[NUMCHOPSTICKS];
```

```
    for (int i = 0; i < NUMCHOPSTICKS; i++) {
      chopSticks[i] = new Object();
    }

    for (int i = 0; i < NUMPHILOSOPHERS; i++) {
      Object leftChopStick = chopSticks[i];
      Object rightChopStick = chopSticks[(i + 1) % chopSticks.length];

      ph[i] = new Philosopher(leftChopStick, rightChopStick);  ❶

      Thread th = new Thread(ph[i], "Philosopher " + i);
      th.start();
    }
  }
```

Running this code produces the following output on my first attempt. If you run the code you will almost certainly see different outputs, but the final outcome will be the same:

```
Philosopher 3 : Thinking deeply
Philosopher 4 : Thinking deeply
Philosopher 0 : Thinking deeply
Philosopher 1 : Thinking deeply
Philosopher 2 : Thinking deeply
Philosopher 3 : Picked up left chopstick
Philosopher 0 : Picked up left chopstick
Philosopher 2 : Picked up left chopstick
Philosopher 4 : Picked up left chopstick
Philosopher 1 : Picked up left chopstick
```

Ten lines of output, then…nothing! We have a deadlock. This is a classic circular waiting deadlock. Imagine the following scenario:

- Each philosopher indulges in a long thinking session.

- Simultaneously, they all decide they are hungry and reach for their left chopstick.

- No philosopher can eat (proceed) as none can pick up their right chopstick.

Real philosophers in this situation would figure out some way to proceed by putting down a chopstick or two until one or more of their colleagues can eat. We can sometimes do this in our software by using timeouts on blocking operations. When the timeout expires, a thread releases the critical section and retries, allowing other blocked threads a chance to proceed. This is not optimal though, as blocked threads hurt performance and setting timeout values is an inexact science.

It is much better, therefore, to design a solution to be deadlock-free. This means that one or more threads will always be able to make progress. With circular wait deadlocks, this can be achieved by imposing a resource allocation protocol on the shared resources, so that threads will not always request resources in the same order.

In the dining philosophers problem, we can do this by making sure one of our philosophers picks up their right chopstick first. Let's assume we instruct Philosopher 4 to do this. This leads to a possible sequence of operations such as below:

- Philosopher 0 picks up left chopstick (chopStick[0]) then right (chopStick[1])
- Philosopher 1 picks up left chopstick (chopStick[1]) then right (chopStick[2])
- Philosopher 2 picks up left chopstick (chopStick[2]) then right (chopStick[3])
- Philosopher 3 picks up left chopstick (chopStick[3]) then right (chopStick[4])
- Philosopher 4 picks up right chopstick (chopStick[0]) then left (chopStick[4])

In this example, Philosopher 4 must block, as Philosopher 0 already has acquired access to chopstick[0]. With Philosopher 4 blocked, Philosopher 3 is assured access to chopstick[4] and can then proceed to satisfy their appetite.

The fix for the dining philosophers solution is shown in Example 4-3.

Example 4-3. Solving the dining philosophers deadlock

```
if (i == NUMPHILOSOPHERS - 1) {
  // The last philosopher picks up the right chopstick first
  ph[i] = new Philosopher(rightChopStick, leftChopStick);
} else {
  // all others pick up the left chopstick first
  ph[i] = new Philosopher(leftChopStick, rightChopStick);
}
```

More formally we are imposing an ordering on the acquisition of shared resources, such that:

chopStick[0] < chopStick[1] < chopStick[2] < chopStick[3] < chopStick[4]

This means each thread will always attempt to acquire chopstick[0] before chop stick[1], and chopstick[1] before chopstick[2], and so on. For Philosopher 4, this means they will attempt to acquire chopstick[0] before chopstick[4], thus breaking the potential for a circular wait deadlock.

Deadlocks are a complicated topic and this section has just scratched the surface. You'll see deadlocks in many distributed systems. For example, a user request acquires a lock on some data in a *Students* database table, and must then update rows in the *Classes* table to reflect student attendance. Simultaneously another user request acquires locks on the *Classes* table, and next must update some information in the *Students* table. If these requests interleave such that each request acquires locks in an overlapping fashion, we have a deadlock.

Thread States

Multithreaded systems have a system scheduler that decides which threads to run when. In Java, the scheduler is known as a preemptive, priority-based scheduler. In short, this means it chooses to execute the highest priority thread which wishes to run.

Every thread has a priority (by default 5, range 0 to 10). A thread inherits its priority from its parent thread. Higher priority threads get scheduled more frequently than lower priority threads, but in most applications having all threads as the default priority suffices.

The scheduler cycles threads through four distinct states, based on their behavior. These are:

Created
> A thread object has been created but its `start()` method has not been invoked. Once `start()` is invoked, the thread enters the runnable state.

Runnable
> A thread is able to run. The scheduler will choose which thread(s) to execute in a first-in, first-out (FIFO) manner—one thread can be allocated at any time to each core in the node. Threads then execute until they block (e.g., on a `synchron ized` statement), execute a `yield()`, `suspend()`, or `sleep()` statement, the `run()` method terminates, or they are preempted by the scheduler. Preemption occurs when a higher priority thread becomes runnable, or when a system-specific time period, known as a time slice, expires. Preemption based on time slicing allows the scheduler to ensure that all threads eventually get a chance to execute—no execution-hungry threads can hog the CPU.

Blocked
> A thread is blocked if it is waiting for a lock, a notification event to occur (e.g., sleep timer to expire, `resume()` method executed), or is waiting for a network or disk request to complete. When the specific event a blocked thread is waiting for occurs, it moves back to the runnable state.

Terminated
> A thread's `run()` method has completed or it has called the `stop()` method. The thread will no longer be scheduled.

An illustration of this scheme is in Figure 4-5. The scheduler effectively maintains FIFO queue in the runnable state for each thread priority. High-priority threads are typically used to respond to events (e.g., an emergency timer) and execute for a short period of time. Low-priority threads are used for background, ongoing tasks like checking for corruption of files on disk through recalculating checksums. Background threads basically use up idle CPU cycles.

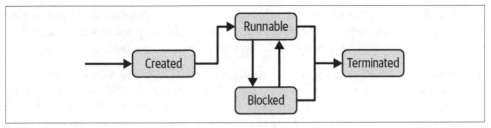

Figure 4-5. Threads states and transitions

Thread Coordination

There are many problems that require threads with different roles to coordinate their activities. Imagine a collection of threads that each accept documents from users, do some processing on the documents (e.g., generate a PDF), and then send the processed document to a shared printer pool. Each printer can only print one document at a time, so they read from a shared print queue, grabbing and printing documents in the order they arrive.

This printing problem is an illustration of the classic producer-consumer problem. Producers generate and send messages via a shared FIFO buffer to consumers. Consumers retrieve these messages, process them, and then ask for more work from the buffer. A simple illustration of this problem is shown in Figure 4-6. It's a bit like a 24-hour, 365-day buffet restaurant—the kitchen keeps producing, the waitstaff collect the food and put it in the buffet, and hungry diners help themselves. Forever.

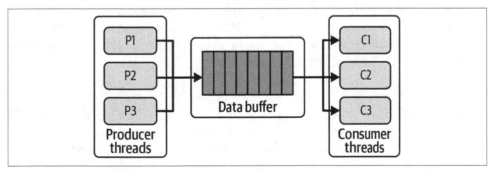

Figure 4-6. The producer-consumer problem

Like virtually all real resources, the buffer has a limited capacity. Producers generate new items, but if the buffer is full, they must wait until some item(s) have been consumed before they can add the new item to the buffer. Similarly, if the consumers are consuming faster than the producers are producing, then they must wait if there are no items in the buffer, and somehow get alerted when new items arrive.

One way for a producer to wait for space in the buffer, or a consumer to wait for an item, is to keep retrying an operation. A producer could sleep for a second, and then retry the put operation until it succeeds. A consumer could do likewise.

This solution is called *polling*, or busy waiting. It works fine, but as the second name implies, each producer and consumer are using resources (CPU, memory, maybe network?) each time they retry and fail. If this is not a concern, then cool, but in scalable systems we are always aiming to optimize resource usage, and polling can be wasteful.

A better solution is for producers and consumers to block until their desired operation, put or get respectively, can succeed. Blocked threads consume no resources and hence provide an efficient solution. To facilitate this, thread programming models provide blocking operations that enable threads to signal to other threads when an event occurs. With the producer-consumer problem, the basic scheme is as follows:

- When a producer adds an item to the buffer, it sends a signal to any blocked consumers to notify them that there is an item in the buffer.

- When a consumer retrieves an item from the buffer, it sends a signal to any blocked producers to notify them there is capacity in the buffer for new items.

In Java, there are two basic primitives, namely `wait()` and `notify()`, that can be used to implement this signaling scheme. Briefly, they work like this:

- A thread may call `wait()` within a synchronized block if some condition it requires to hold is not true. For example, a thread may attempt to retrieve a message from a buffer, but if the buffer has no messages to retrieve, it calls `wait()` and blocks until another thread adds a message, sets the condition to `true`, and calls `notify()` on the same object.

- `notify()` wakes up a thread that has called `wait()` on the object.

These Java primitives are used to implement *guarded blocks*. Guarded blocks use a condition as a guard that must hold before a thread resumes the execution. The following code snippet shows how the guard condition, *empty*, is used to block a thread that is attempting to retrieve a message from an empty buffer:

```
while (empty) {
  try {
    System.out.println("Waiting for a message");
    wait();
  } catch (InterruptedException e) {}
}
```

When another thread adds a message to the buffer, it executes `notify()` as follows:

```
// Store message.
this.message = message;
empty = false;
// Notify consumer that message is available
notify();
```

The full implementation of this example is given in the code examples in the book Git repository (*https://oreil.ly/fss-git-repo*). There are a number of variations of the `wait()` and `notify()` methods, but these go beyond the scope of what I can cover in this overview. And luckily, Java provides us with thread-safe abstractions that hide this complexity from your code.

An example that is pertinent to the producer-consumer problem is the `Blocking Queue` interface in `java.util.concurrent.BlockingQueue`. A `BlockingQueue` implementation provides a thread-safe object that can be used as the buffer in a producer-consumer scenario. There are 5 different implementations of the `Blocking Queue` interface. I'll use one of these, the `LinkedBlockingQueue`, to implement the producer-consumer. This is shown in Example 4-4.

Example 4-4. Producer-consumer with a `LinkedBlockingQueue`

```
class ProducerConsumer {
    public static void main(String[] args)
        BlockingQueue buffer = new LinkedBlockingQueue();
        Producer p = new Producer(buffer);
        Consumer c = new Consumer(buffer);
        new Thread(p).start();
        new Thread(c).start();
    }
}

class Producer implements Runnable {
    private boolean active = true;
    private final BlockingQueue buffer;
    public Producer(BlockingQueue q) { buffer = q; }
    public void run() {

        try {
            while (active) { buffer.put(produce()); }
        } catch (InterruptedException ex) { // handle exception}
    }
    Object produce() { // details omitted, sets active=false }
}

class Consumer implements Runnable {
    private boolean active = true;
    private final BlockingQueue buffer;
    public Consumer(BlockingQueue q) { buffer = q; }
    public void run() {
```

```
      try {
        while (active) { consume(buffer.take()); }
      } catch (InterruptedException ex) { // handle exception }
    }
    void consume(Object x) {  // details omitted, sets active=false }
  }
```

This solution absolves the programmer from being concerned with the implementation of coordinating access to the shared buffer, and greatly simplifies the code.

The `java.util.concurrent` package (*https://oreil.ly/XGEsn*) is a treasure trove for building multithreaded Java solutions. In the following sections, I will briefly highlight a few of these powerful and extremely useful capabilities.

Thread Pools

Many multithreaded systems need to create and manage a collection of threads that perform similar tasks. For example, in the producer-consumer problem, we can have a collection of producer threads and a collection of consumer threads, all simultaneously adding and removing items, with coordinated access to the shared buffer.

These collections are known as thread pools. Thread pools comprise several worker threads, which typically perform a similar purpose and are managed as a collection. We could create a pool of producer threads which all wait for an item to process, write the final product to the buffer, and then wait to accept another item to process. When we stop producing items, the pool can be shut down in a safe manner, so no partially processed items are lost through an unanticipated exception.

In the `java.util.concurrent` package, thread pools are supported by the `Executor Service` interface. This extends the base `Executor` interface with a set of methods to manage and terminate threads in the pool. A simple producer-consumer example using a fixed size thread pool is shown in Examples 4-5 and 4-6. The `Producer` class in Example 4-5 is a `Runnable` that sends a single message to the buffer and then terminates. The `Consumer` simply takes messages from the buffer until an empty string is received, upon which it terminates.

Example 4-5. Producer and consumer for thread pool implementation

```
class Producer implements Runnable {

  private final BlockingQueue buffer;

  public Producer(BlockingQueue q) { buffer = q; }

  @Override
  public void run() {
```

```
    try {
      sleep(1000);
      buffer.put("hello world");

    } catch (InterruptedException ex) {
      // handle exception
    }
   }
  }
 }

class Consumer implements Runnable {
  private final BlockingQueue buffer;

  public Consumer(BlockingQueue q) { buffer = q; }

  @Override
  public void run() {
      boolean active = true;
      while (active) {
          try {
              String  s = (String) buffer.take();
              System.out.println(s);
              if (s.equals("")) active = false;
          } catch (InterruptedException ex) {
              / handle exception
          }
      } /
      System.out.println("Consumer terminating");
   }
 }
```

In Example 4-6, we create a single consumer to take messages from the buffer. We then create a fixed size thread pool of size 5 to manage our producers. This causes the JVM to preallocate five threads that can be used to execute any Runnable objects that are executed by the pool.

In the for() loop, we then use the ExecutorService to run 20 producers. As there are only 5 threads available in the thread pool, only a maximum of 5 producers will be executed simultaneously. All others are placed in a wait queue which is managed by the thread pool. When a producer terminates, the next Runnable in the wait queue is executed using any available thread in the pool.

Once we have requested all the producers to be executed by the thread pool, we call the shutdown() method on the pool. This tells the ExecutorService not to accept any more tasks to run. We next call the awaitTermination() method, which blocks the calling thread until all the threads managed by the thread pool are idle and no more work is waiting in the wait queue. Once awaitTermination() returns, we know all messages have been sent to the buffer, and hence send an empty string to the buffer which will act as a termination value for the consumer.

Example 4-6. Thread pool–based producer-consumer solution

```java
public static void main(String[] args) throws InterruptedException
  {
    BlockingQueue buffer = new LinkedBlockingQueue();

    //start a single consumer
    (new Thread(new Consumer(buffer))).start();

    ExecutorService producerPool = Executors.newFixedThreadPool(5);
    for (int i = 0; i < 20; i++)
      {
        Producer producer = new Producer(buffer) ;
        System.out.println("Producer created" );
        producerPool.execute(producer);
      }

    producerPool.shutdown();
    producerPool.awaitTermination(10, TimeUnit.SECONDS);

    //send termination message to consumer
    buffer.put("");
  }
```

As with most topics in this chapter, there are many more sophisticated features in the Executor framework that can be used to create multithreaded programs. This description has just covered the basics. Thread pools are important as they enable our systems to rationalize the use of resources for threads. Every thread consumes memory; for example, the stack size for a thread is typically around 1 MB. Also, when we switch execution context to run a new thread, this consumes CPU cycles. If our systems create threads in an undisciplined manner, we will eventually run out of memory and the system will crash. Thread pools allow us to control the number of threads we create and utilize them efficiently.

I'll discuss thread pools throughout the remainder of this book, as they are a key concept for efficient and scalable management of the ever-increasing request loads that servers must satisfy.

Barrier Synchronization

I had a high school friend whose family, at dinnertime, would not allow anyone to start eating until the whole family was seated at the table. I thought this was weird, but many years later it serves as a good analogy for the concept known as barrier synchronization. Eating commenced only after all family members arrived at the table.

Multithreaded systems often need to follow such a pattern of behavior. Imagine a multithreaded image-processing system. An image arrives and a distinct segment of the image is passed to each thread to perform some transformation upon—think Instagram filters on steroids. The image is only fully processed when all threads have completed. In software systems, we use a mechanism called barrier synchronization to achieve this style of thread coordination.

The general scheme is shown in Figure 4-7. In this example, the main() thread creates four new threads and all proceed independently until they reach the point of execution defined by the barrier. As each thread arrives, it blocks. When all threads have arrived at this point, the barrier is released, and each thread can continue with its processing.

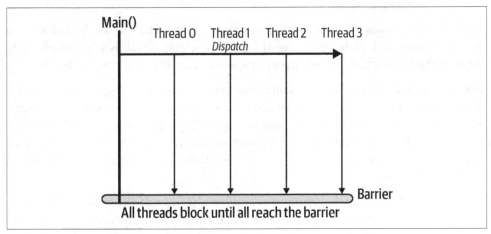

Figure 4-7. Barrier synchronization

Java provides three primitives for barrier synchronization. I'll show here how one of the three, CountDownLatch, works. The basic concepts apply to other barrier synchronization primitives.

When you create a CountDownLatch, you pass a value to its constructor that represents the number of threads that must block at the barrier before they are all allowed to continue. This is called in the thread which is managing the barrier points for the system—in Figure 4-7 this would be main():

```
CountDownLatch nextPhaseSignal = new CountDownLatch(numThreads);
```

Next, you create the worker threads that will perform some actions and then block at the barrier until they all complete. To do this, you need to pass each thread a reference to CountDownLatch:

```
for (int i = 0; i < numThreads; i++) {
        Thread worker = new Thread(new WorkerThread(nextPhaseSignal));
```

```
          worker.start();
    }
```

After launching the worker threads, the main() thread will call the .await() method to block until the latch is triggered by the worker threads:

```
    nextPhaseSignal.await();
```

Each worker thread will complete its task and, before exiting, call the .count Down() method on the latch. This decrements the latch value. When the last thread calls .countDown() and the latch value becomes zero, all threads that have called .await() on the latch transition from the *blocked* to the *runnable* state. At this stage we are assured that all workers have completed their assigned task:

```
    nextPhaseSignal.countDown();
```

Any subsequent calls to .countDown() will return immediately as the latch has been effectively triggered. Note .countDown() is nonblocking, which is a useful property for applications in which threads have more work to do after reaching the barrier.

This example illustrates using a CountDownLatch to block a single thread until a collection of threads have completed their work. You can invert this use case with a latch, however, if you initialize its value to one. Multiple threads could call .await() and block until another thread calls .countDown() to release all waiting threads. This example is analogous to a simple gate, which one thread opens to allow a collection of others to continue.

CountDownLatch is a simple barrier synchronizer. It's a single-use tool, as the initializer value cannot be reset. More sophisticated features are provided by the Cyclic Barrier and Phaser classes in Java. Armed with the knowledge of how barrier synchronization works from this section, these will be straightforward to understand.

Thread-Safe Collections

Many Java programmers, once they delve into the wonders of multithreaded programs, are surprised to discover that the collections in the java.util package are not thread safe.[2] Why, I hear you ask? The answer, luckily, is simple. It has to do with performance. Calling synchronized methods incurs overheads. Hence, to attain faster execution for single-threaded programs, the collections are not thread safe.

If you want to share an ArrayList, Map, or your favorite data structure from java.util across multiple threads, you must ensure modifications to the structure are placed in critical sections. This approach places the burden on the client of the

---

2 Except Vector and HashTable, which are legacy classes; thread safe and slow!

collection to safely make updates, and hence is error prone—a programmer might forget to make modifications in a `synchronized` block.

It's always safer to use inherently thread-safe collections in your multithreaded code. For this reason, the Java collections framework provides a factory method that creates a thread-safe version of `java.util` collections. Here's an example of creating a thread-safe list:

```
List<String> list = Collections.synchronizedList(new ArrayList<>());
```

What is really happening here is that you are creating a wrapper around the base collection class, which has `synchronized` methods. These delegate the actual work to the original class, in a thread-safe manner of course. You can use this approach for any collection in the `java.util` package, and the general form is:

```
Collections.synchronized....(new collection<>())
```

where "...." is `List`, `Map`, `Set`, and so on.

Of course, when using the synchronized wrappers, you pay the performance penalty for acquiring the monitor lock and serializing access from multiple threads. This means the whole collection is locked while a single thread makes a modification, greatly limiting concurrent performance (Amdahl's law again). For this reason, Java 5.0 included the concurrent collections package, namely `java.util.concurrent`. It contains a rich collection of classes specifically designed for efficient multithreaded access.

In fact, we've already seen one of these classes—the `LinkedBlockingQueue`. This uses a locking mechanism that enables items to be added to and removed from the queue in parallel. This finer grain locking mechanism utilizes the `java.util.concurrent.lock.Lock` class rather than the monitor lock approach. This allows multiple locks to be utilized on the same collection, hence enabling safe concurrent access.

Another extremely useful collection that provides this finer-grain locking is the `ConcurrentHashMap`. This provides the similar methods as the non–thread safe `HashMap`, but allows nonblocking reads and concurrent writes based on a `concurrencyLevel` value you can pass to the constructor (the default value is 16):

```
ConcurrentHashMap (int initialCapacity, float loadFactor,
                   int concurrencyLevel)
```

Internally, the hash table is divided into individually lockable segments, often known as shards. Locks are associated with each shard rather than the whole collection. This means updates can be made concurrently to hash table entries in different shards of the collection, increasing performance.

Retrieval operations are nonblocking for performance reasons, meaning they can overlap with multiple concurrent updates. This means retrievals only reflect the results of the most recently completed update operations at the time the retrieval is executed.

For similar reasons, iterators for a ConcurrentHashMap are what is known as weakly consistent. This means the iterator contains a copy of the hash map that reflects its state at the time the iterator is created. While the iterator is in use, new nodes may be added and existing nodes removed from the underlying hash map. However, these state changes are not reflected in the iterator.

If you need an iterator that always reflects the current hashmap state while being updated by multiple threads, then there are performance penalties to pay, and a ConcurrentHashMap is not the right approach. This is an example of favoring performance over consistency—a classic design trade-off.

Summary and Further Reading

I'll draw upon the major concepts introduced in this chapter throughout the remainder of this book. Threads are inherently components of the data processing and database platforms that we use to build scalable distributed systems. In many cases, you may not be writing explicitly multithreaded code. However, the code you write will be invoked in a multithreaded environment, which means you need to be aware of thread safety. Many platforms also expose their concurrency through configuration parameters, meaning that to tune the system's performance, you need to understand the effects of changing the various threading and thread pool settings. Basically, there's no escaping concurrency in the world of scalable distributed systems.

Finally, it is worth mentioning that while concurrent programming primitives vary across programming languages, the foundational issues don't change, and carefully designed multithreaded code to avoid race conditions and deadlocks is needed. Whether you grapple with the pthreads library (*https://oreil.ly/1pu8N*) in C/C++, or the classic CSP-inspired Go concurrency model, the problems you need to avoid are the same. The knowledge you have gained from this chapter will regardless set you on the right track, whatever language you are using.

This chapter has only brushed the surface of concurrency in general and its support in Java. The best book to continue learning more about the basic concepts of concurrency is the classic *Java Concurrency in Practice* (*JCiP*) by Brian Goetz et al. (Addison-Wesley Professional, 2006). If you understand everything in the book, you'll be writing pretty great concurrent code.

Java concurrency support has moved on considerably since Java 5. In the world of Java 12 (or whatever version is current when you read this), there are new features such as CompletableFutures, lambda expressions, and parallel streams. The functional programming style introduced in Java 8.0 makes it easy to create concurrent solutions without directly creating and managing threads. A good source of knowledge for Java 8.0 features is *Mastering Concurrency Programming with Java 8* by Javier Fernández González (Packt, 2017).

Other excellent sources include:

- Doug Lea, *Concurrent Programming in Java: Design Principles and Patterns*, 2nd ed. (Addison-Wesley Professional, 1996)
- Raoul-Gabriel Urma, Mario Fusco, and Alan Mycroft, *Modern Java in Action: Lambdas, Streams, Functional and Reactive Programming* (Manning, 2019)
- The Baeldung website (*https://oreil.ly/TmCV1*) has a comprehensive collection of articles for learning about Java concurrency and served as the basis for the dining philosophers example in this chapter.

Scalable Systems

The five chapters in Part II of this book focus on scaling request processing. The major topics covered include scaling out systems across multiple compute resources, load balancing, distributed caching, asynchronous messaging, and microservice-based architectures. I introduce the basic concepts of these architectural approaches and illustrate them with examples from widely used distributed technologies such as RabbitMQ and Google App Engine.

CHAPTER 5

Application Services

At the heart of any system lies the unique business logic that implements the application requirements. In distributed systems, this is exposed to clients through APIs and executed within a runtime environment designed to efficiently support concurrent remote calls. An API and its implementation comprise the fundamental elements of the services an application supports.

In this chapter, I'm going to focus on the pertinent issues for achieving scalability for the services tier in an application. I'll explain APIs and service design and describe the salient features of application servers that provide the execution environment for services. I'll also elaborate on topics such as horizontal scaling, load balancing, and state management that I introduced briefly in Chapter 2.

Service Design

In the simplest case, an application comprises one internet facing service that persists data to a local data store, as shown in Figure 5-1. Clients interact with the service through its published API, which is accessible across the internet.

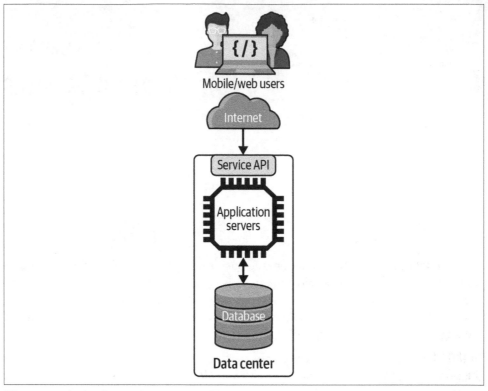

Figure 5-1. A simple service

Let's look at the API and service implementation in more detail.

Application Programming Interface (API)

An API defines a contract between the client and server. The API specifies the types of requests that are possible, the data that is needed to accompany the requests, and the results that will be obtained. APIs have many different variations, as I explained in RPC/RMI discussions in Chapter 3. While there remains some API diversity in modern applications, the predominant style relies on HTTP APIs. These are typically, although not particularly accurately, classified as RESTful.

REST is an architectural style defined by Roy Fielding in his PhD thesis.[1] A great source of knowledge on RESTful APIs and the various degrees to which web technologies can be exploited is *REST in Practice* by Jim Webber et al. (O'Reilly, 2010). Here I'll just briefly touch on the HTTP create, read, update, delete (CRUD) API pattern.

---

1 Roy T. Fielding, "Architectural Styles and the Design of Network-Based Software Architectures" (*https://oreil.ly/9dQbd*). Dissertation. University of California, Irvine, 2000.

This pattern does not fully implement the principles of REST, but it is widely adopted in internet systems today. It exploits the four code HTTP verbs, namely POST, GET, PUT, and DELETE.

A CRUD API specifies how clients perform create, read, update, and delete operations in a specific business context. For example, a user might *create* a profile (POST), *read* catalog items (GET), *update* their shopping cart (PUT), and *delete* items from their order (DELETE).

An example HTTP CRUD API for the example ski resort system (briefly introduced in Chapter 2) that uses these four core HTTP verbs is shown in Table 5-1. In this example, parameter values are passed as part of the request address and are identified by the {} notation.

Table 5-1. HTTP CRUD verbs

Verb	Uniform Resource Identifier (URI) example	Purpose
POST	*/skico.com/skiers/*	Create a new skier profile, with skier details provided in the JSON request payload. The new skier profile is returned in the JSON response.
GET	*/skico.com/skiers/{skierID}*	Get the profile information for a skier, returned in a JSON response payload.
PUT	*/skico.com/skiers/{skierID}*	Update skier profile.
DELETE	*/skico.com/skiers/{skierID}*	Delete a skier's profile as they didn't renew their pass!

Additional parameter values can be passed and returned in HTTP request and response bodies, respectively. For example, a successful request to:

```
GET /skico.com/skiers/12345
```

will return an HTTP 200 response code and the following results formatted in JSON:

```
{
    "username": "Ian123",
    "email": "i.gorton@somewhere.com"
    "city": "Seattle"
}
```

To change the skier's city, the client could issue the following PUT request to the same URI along with a request body representing the updated skier profile:

```
PUT  /skico.com/skiers/12345
{
    "username": "Ian123",
    "email": "i.gorton@somewhere.com"
    "city": "Wenatchee"
}
```

More formally, an HTTP CRUD API applies HTTP verbs on *resources* identified by URIs. In Table 5-1, for example, a URI that identifies skier 768934 would be:

```
/skico.com/skiers/768934
```

An HTTP GET request to this resource would return the complete profile information for a skier in the response payload, such as name, address, number of days visited, and so on. If a client subsequently sends an HTTP PUT request to this URI, we are expressing the intent to update the resource for skier 768934—in this example it would be the skier's profile. The PUT request would provide the complete representation for the skier's profile as returned by the GET request. Again, this would be as a payload with the request. Payloads are typically formatted as JSON, although XML and other formats are also possible. If a client sends a DELETE request to the same URI, then the skier's profile will be deleted.

Hence the combination of the HTTP verb and URI define the semantics of the API operation. Resources, represented by URIs, are conceptually like objects in object-oriented design (OOD) or entities in entity–relationship model (ER model). Resource identification and modeling hence follows similar methods to OOD and ER modeling. The focus however is on resources that need to be exposed to clients in the API. "Summary and Further Reading" on page 113 points to useful sources of information for resource design.

HTTP APIs can be specified using a notation called OpenAPI (*https://oreil.ly/Dt1P1*). At the time of writing, the latest version is 3.0. A tool called SwaggerHub (*https://oreil.ly/Xsh39*) is the de facto standard to specify APIs in OpenAPI. The specification is defined in Yet Another Markup Language (YAML), and an example is shown in the following API definition extract. It defines the GET operation on the URI /resorts. If the operation is successful, a 200 response code is returned along with a list of resorts in a format defined by a JSON schema that appears later in the specification. If for some reason the query to get a list of resorts operated by skico.com returns no entries, a 404 response code is returned along with an error message that is also defined by a JSON schema:

```
paths:
  /resorts:
    get:
      tags:
        - resorts
      summary: get a list of ski resorts in the database
      operationId: getResorts
      responses:
        '200':
          description: successful operation
          content:
            application/json:
              schema:
                $ref: '#/components/schemas/ResortsList'
        '404':
          description: Resorts not found. Unlikely unless we go broke
```

```
content:
  application/json:
    schema:
      $ref: '#/components/schemas/responseMsg'
```

API design is a complex topic in itself and delving deeply into this area is beyond the scope of this book. From a scalability perspective, there are some issues that should, however, be borne in mind:

- Each API request requires a round trip to a service, which incurs network latency. A common antipattern is known as a chatty API, in which multiple API requests are used to perform one logical operation. This commonly occurs when an API is designed following pure object-oriented design approaches. Imagine exposing `get()` and `set()` methods for individual resource properties as HTTP APIs. Accessing a resource would require multiple API requests, one for each property. This is not scalable. Use GET to retrieve the whole resource and PUT to send back an updated resource. You can also use the HTTP PATCH verb (*https:// oreil.ly/ERLY3*) to update individual properties of a resource. PATCH allows partial modification of a resource representation, in contrast to PUT that replaces the complete resource representation with new values.

- Consider using compression for HTTP APIs that pass large payloads. All modern web servers and browsers support compressed content (*https://oreil.ly/laBxS*) using the HTTP Accept-Encoding and Content-Encoding headers. Specific API requests and responses can utilize these headers by specifying the compression algorithm that is used for the content—for example, `gzip`. Compression can reduce network bandwidth and latencies by 50% or more. The trade-off cost is the compute cycles to compress and decompress the content. This is typically small compared to the savings in network transit times.

Designing Services

An application server container receives requests and routes them to the appropriate handler function to process the request. The handler is defined by the application service code and implements the business logic required to generate results for the request. As multiple simultaneous requests arrive at a service instance, each is typically allocated an individual thread context to execute the request.[2] The issue of thread handling in application servers is one I'll discuss in more detail later in this chapter.

The sophistication of the routing functionality varies widely by technology platform and language. For example, in Express.js, the container calls a specified function for

---

2 Node.js is a notable exception here as it is single threaded. However, it employs an asynchronous programming model for blocking I/O that supports handling many simultaneous requests.

requests that match an API signature—known as a route path—and HTTP method. The code example below illustrates this with a method that will be called when the client sends a GET request for a specific skier's profile, as identified by the value of :skierID:

```
app.get('/skiers/:skierID', function (req, res) {
  // process the GET request
  ProcessRequest(req.params)
})
```

In Java, the widely used Spring Framework provides an equally sophisticated method routing technique. It leverages a set of annotations that define dependencies and implement dependency injection to simplify the service code. The code snippet below shows an example of annotations usage:

```
@RestController
public class SkierController {
    @GetMapping("/skiers/{skierID}",
                produces = "application/json")
    public Profile GetSkierProfile(@PathVariable String skierID) {
        // DB query method omitted for brevity
        return GetProfileFromDB(skierID);
    }
}
```

These annotations provide the following functionality:

@RestController

Identifies the class as a controller that implements an API and automatically serializes the return object into the HttpResponse returned from the API

@GetMapping

Maps the API signature to the specific method, and defines the format of the response body

@PathVariable

Identifies the parameter as a value that originates in the path for a URI that maps to this method

Another Java technology, JEE servlets, also provides annotations, as shown in Example 5-1, but these are simplistic compared to Spring and other higher-level frameworks. The @WebServlet annotation identifies the base pattern for the URI which should cause a particular servlet to be invoked. This is /skiers in our example. The class that implements the API method must extend the HttpServlet abstract class from the javax.servlet.http package and override at least one method that implements an HTTP request handler. The four core HTTP verbs map to methods as follows:

doGet

> For HTTP GET requests

doPost

> For HTTP POST requests

doPut

> For HTTP PUT requests

doDelete

> For HTTP DELETE requests

Each method is passed two parameters, namely an HttpServletRequest and HttpServletResponse object. The servlet container creates the HttpServletRequest object, which contains members that represent the components of the incoming HTTP request. This object contains the complete URI path for the call, and it is the servlet's responsibility to explicitly parse and validate this, and extract path and query parameters if valid. Likewise, the servlet must explicitly set the properties of the response using the HttpServletResponse object.

Servlets therefore require more code from the application service programmer to implement. However, they are likely to provide a more efficient implementation as there is less generated code "plumbing" involved in request processing compared to the more powerful annotation approaches of Spring et al. This is a classic performance versus ease-of-use trade-off. You'll see lots of these in this book.

Example 5-1. Java servlet example

```java
import javax.servlet.http.*;
@WebServlet(
    name = "SkiersServlet",
    urlPatterns = "/skiers"
)
public class SkierServlet extends HttpServlet (

protected void doGet(HttpServletRequest request,
                     HttpServletResponse response) {
  // handles requests to /skiers/{skierID}
  try {
     // extract skierID from the request URI (not shown for brevity)
     String skierID  = getSkierIDFromRequest(request);
     if(skierID == null) {
        // request was poorly formatted, return error code
        response.setStatus(HttpServletResponse.SC_BAD_REQUEST);    }
     else {
        // read the skier profile from the database
        Profile profile = GetSkierProfile (skierID);
```

```
      // add skier profile as JSON to HTTP response and return 200
      response.setContentType("application/json");
      response.getWriter().write(gson.toJson(Profile));
      response.setStatus(HttpServletResponse.SC_OK);
  } catch(Exception ex) {
    response.setStatus
      (HttpServletResponse.SC_INTERNAL_SERVER_ERROR);      }

  }
} }
```

State Management

State management is a tricky, nuanced topic. The bottom line is that service implementations that need to scale should avoid storing conversational state.

What on earth does that mean? Let's start by examining the topic of state management with HTTP.

HTTP is known as *stateless* protocol. This means each request is executed independently, without any knowledge of the requests that were executed before it from the same client. Statelessness implies that every request needs to be self-contained, with sufficient information provided by the client for the web server to satisfy the request regardless of previous activity from that client.

The picture is a little more complicated that this simple description portrays, however. For example:

- The underlying socket connection between a client and server is kept open so that the overheads of connection creation are amortized across multiple requests from a client. This is the default behavior for versions HTTP/1 and above.

- HTTP supports cookies, which are known as the HTTP State Management Mechanism (*https://oreil.ly/9eGyC*). The name gives it away, really!

- HTTP/2 supports streams, compression, and encryption, all of which require state management.

So, originally HTTP was stateless, but perhaps not anymore? Armed with this confusion, I'll move on to state management in application services APIs that are built on top of HTTP.

When a user or application connects to a service, it will typically send a series of requests to retrieve and update information. *Conversational state* represents any information that is retained between requests such that a subsequent request can assume the service has retained knowledge about the previous interactions. I'll explore what this means in a simple example.

In the skier service API, a user may request their profile by submitting a GET request to the following URI:

```
GET /skico.com/skiers/768934
```

They may then use their app to modify their city attribute and send a PUT request to update the resource:

```
PUT /skico.com/skiers/
{
    "username": "Ian123",
    "email": "i.gorton@somewhere.com"
    "city": "Wenatchee"
}
```

As this URI does not identify the skier, the service must know the unique identifier of the resource to update, namely 768934. Hence, for this update operation to succeed, the service must have retained conversational state from the previous GET request.

Implementing this approach is relatively straightforward. When the service receives the initial GET request, it creates a session state object that uniquely identifies the client connection. In reality, this is often performed when a user first connects to or logs in to a service. The service can then read the skier profile from the database and utilize the session state object to store conversational state—in our example this would be skierID and likely values associated with the skier profile. When the subsequent PUT request arrives from the client, it uses the session state object to look up the skierID associated with this session and uses that to update the skier's home city.

Services that maintain conversational state are known as stateful services. Stateful services are attractive from a design perspective as they can minimize the number of times a service retrieves data (state) from the database and reduce the amount of data that is passed between clients and the services.

For services with light request loads, they make eminent sense and are promoted by many frameworks to make services easy to build and deploy. For example, JEE servlets support session management using the HttpSession object, and similar capabilities are offered by the Session object in ASP.NET.

As you scale the service implementations however, the stateful approach becomes problematic. For a single service instance, you have two problems to consider:

- If you have multiple client sessions all maintaining session state, this will utilize available service memory. The amount of memory utilized will be proportional to the number of clients the service is maintaining state for. If a sudden spike of requests arrives, how can you be certain we will not exhaust available memory and cause the service to fail?

- You also must be mindful about how long to keep session state available. A client may stop sending requests but not cleanly close their connection to allow the state to be reclaimed. All session management approaches support a default session timeout. If you set this to a short time interval, clients may see their state disappear unexpectedly. If you set the session timeout period to be too long, you may degrade service performance as it runs low on resources.

In contrast, stateless services do not assume that any conversational state from previous calls has been preserved. The service should not maintain any knowledge from earlier requests, so that each request can be processed individually. This requires the client to provide all the necessary information for the service to process the request and provide a response. This is in fact how the skier API is specified in Table 5-1, namely:

```
PUT /skico.com/skiers/768934
{
    "username": "Ian123",
    "email": "i.gorton@somewhere.com"
    "city": "Wenatchee"
}
```

A sequence diagram illustrating this stateless design is shown in Figure 5-2.

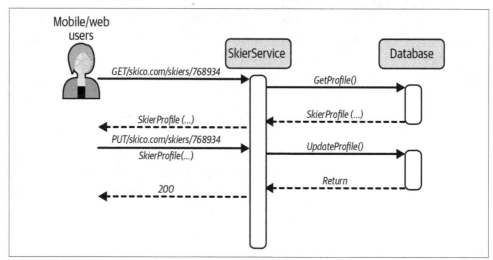

Figure 5-2. Stateless API example

Any scalable service will need stateless APIs. The reason why will become clear when I explain horizontal scaling later in this chapter. For now, the most important design implication is that for a service that needs to retain state pertaining to client sessions—the classic shopping cart example—this state must be stored externally to the service. This invariably means an external data store.

Applications Servers

Application servers are the heart of a scalable application, hosting the business services that compose an application. Their basic role is to accept requests from clients, apply application logic to the requests, and reply to the client with the request results. Clients may be external or internal, as in other services in the application that require to use the functionality of a specific service.

The technological landscape of application servers is broad and complex, depending on the language you want to use and the specific capabilities that each offers. In Java, the Java Enterprise Edition (JEE) (*https://oreil.ly/we6BN*) defines a comprehensive, feature rich, standards-based platform for application servers, with multiple different vendor and open source implementations.

In other languages, the Express.js (*https://expressjs.com*) server supports Node, Flask (*https://oreil.ly/mDZqO*) supports Python, and in Go a service can be created by incorporating the net/http package. These implementations are much more minimal and lightweight than JEE and are typically classified as web application frameworks. In Java, the Apache Tomcat server (*https://oreil.ly/6A2uP*) is a somewhat equivalent technology. Tomcat is an open source implementation of a subset of the JEE platform, namely the Java servlet, JavaServer Pages (JSP), Java Expression Language (EL), and Java WebSocket technologies.

Figure 5-3 depicts a simplified view of the anatomy of Tomcat. Tomcat implements a *servlet container*, which is an execution environment for application-defined servlets. Servlets are dynamically loaded into this container, which provides life cycle management and a multithreaded runtime environment.

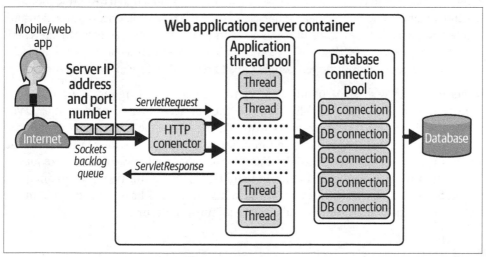

Figure 5-3. Anatomy of a web application server

Requests arrive at the IP address of the server, which is listening for traffic on specific ports. For example, by default Tomcat listens on port 8080 for HTTP requests and 8443 for HTTPS requests. Incoming requests are processed by one or more listener threads. These create a TCP/IP socket connection between the client and server. If network requests arrive at a frequency that cannot be processed by the TCP listener, pending requests are queued up in the *Sockets Backlog*. The size of the backlog is operating system dependent. In most Linux versions the default is 100.

Once a connection is established, the TCP requests are marshalled by, in this example, an *HTTP Connector* which generates the HTTP request (`HttpServletRequest` object as in Figure 5-2) that the servlet can process. The HTTP request is then dispatched to an application container thread to process.

Application container threads are managed in a thread pool, essentially a Java `Executor`, which by default in Tomcat is a minimum size of 25 threads and a maximum of 200. If there are no available threads to handle a request, the container maintains them in a queue of runnable tasks and dispatches these as soon as a thread becomes available. This queue by default is size `Integer.MAX_VALUE`—that is, essentially unbounded.[3] By default, if a thread remains idle for 60 seconds, it is killed to free up resources in the Java virtual machine.

For each request, the method that corresponds with the HTTP request is invoked in a thread. The servlet method processes the HTTP request headers, executes the business logic, and constructs a response that is marshalled by the container back into a TCP/IP packet and sent over the network to the client.

In processing the business logic, servlets often need to query an external database. This requires each thread executing the servlet methods to obtain a database connection and execute database queries. In many databases, especially relational ones, connections are limited resources as they consume memory and system resources in both the client and database server. For this reason, a fixed-size database connection pool is typically utilized. The pool hands out open connections to requesting threads on demand.

When a servlet wishes to submit a query to the database, it requests a connection from the pool. If one is available, access to the connection is granted to the servlet until it indicates it has completed its work. At that stage the connection is returned to the pool and made available for another servlet to utilize. As the container thread pool is typically larger than the database connection pool, a servlet may request a connection when none are available. To handle this, the connection pool maintains a request queue and hands out open connections on a FIFO basis, and threads in the queue are blocked until there is availability or a timeout occurs.

---

3 See Apache Tomcat 9 Configuration Reference (*https://oreil.ly/QYgQ0*) for default Tomcat Executor configuration settings.

An application server framework such as Tomcat is hence highly configurable for different workloads. For example, the size of the thread and database connection pools can be specified in configuration files that are read at startup.

The complete Tomcat container environment runs within a single JVM, and hence processing capacity is limited by the number of vCPUs available and the amount of memory allocated as heap size. Each allocated thread consumes memory, and the various queues in the request-processing pipeline consume resources while requests are waiting. This means that request response time will be governed by both the request-processing time in the servlet business logic as well as the time spent waiting in queues for threads and connections to become available.

In a heavily loaded server with many threads allocated, context switching may start to degrade performance, and available memory may become limited. If performance degrades, queues grow as requests wait for resources. This consumes more memory. If more requests are received than can be queued up and processed by the server, then new TCP/IP connections will be refused, and clients will see errors. Eventually, an overloaded server may run out of resources and start throwing exceptions and crash.

Consequently, time spent tuning configuration parameters to efficiently handle anticipated loads is rarely wasted. Systems tend to degrade in performance well before they reach 100% utilization (*https://oreil.ly/iq25y*). Once any resource—CPU utilization, memory usage, network, disk accesses, etc.—gets close to full utilization, systems exhibit less predictable performance. This is because more time is spent on time-wasting tasks such as thread context switching and memory garbage collecting. This inevitably affects latencies and throughput. Thus, having a utilization target is essential. Exactly what these thresholds should be is extremely application dependent.

Monitoring tools available with web application frameworks enable engineers to gather a range of important metrics, including latencies, active requests, queue sizes, and so on. These are invaluable for carrying out data-driven experiments that lead to performance optimization.

Java-based application frameworks such as Tomcat support the Java Management Extensions (JMX) framework (*https://oreil.ly/P06Wc*), which is a standard part of the Java Standard Edition platform. JMX enables frameworks to expose monitoring information based on the capabilities of MBeans, which represent a resource of interest (e.g., thread pool, database connections usage). This enables an ecosystem of tools to offer capabilities for monitoring JMX-supported platforms. These range from JConsole (*https://oreil.ly/xCxjh*), which is available in the Java Development Kit (JDK) by default, to powerful open source technologies such as JavaMelody (*https://oreil.ly/RAWfY*) and many expensive commercial offerings.

Horizontal Scaling

A core principle of scaling a system is being able to easily add new processing capacity to handle increased load. For most systems, a simple and effective approach is deploying multiple instances of stateless server resources and using a load balancer to distribute the requests across these instances. This is known as horizontal scaling and is illustrated in Figure 5-4. Stateless service replicas and a load balancer are both necessary for horizontal scaling.

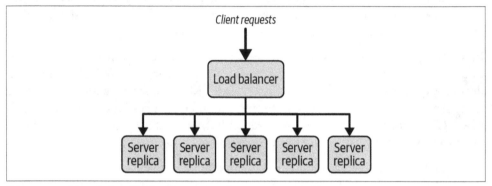

Figure 5-4. Simple load balancing example

Service replicas are deployed on their own (virtual) hardware. If we have two replicas, we double our processing capacity. If we have ten replicas, we have potentially 10x capacity. This enables our system to handle increased loads. The aim of horizontal scaling is to create a system-processing capacity that is the sum of the total resources available.

The servers need to be stateless, so that any request can be sent to any service replica to handle. This decision is made by the load balancer, which can use various policies to distribute requests. If the load balancer can keep each service replica equally busy, then we are effectively using the processing capacity provided by the service replicas.

If our services are stateful, the load balancer needs to always route requests from the same server to the same service replica. As client sessions have indeterminate durations, this can lead to some replicas being much more heavily loaded than others. This creates an imbalance and is not effective in using the available capacity evenly across replicas. I'll return to this issue in more detail in the next section on load balancing.

 Technologies like Spring Session and plugins to Tomcat's clustering platform allow session state to be externalized in general purpose distributed caches like Redis and memcached. This effectively makes our services stateless. Load balancers can distribute requests across all replicated services without concern for state management. I'll cover the topic of distributed caches in Chapter 6.

Horizontal scaling also increases availability. With one service instance, if it fails, the service is unavailable. This is known as a *single point of failure (SPoF)*—a bad thing, and something to avoid in any scalable distributed system. Multiple replicas increase availability. If one replica fails, requests can be directed to any replica—remember, they are stateless. The system will have reduced capacity until the failed server is replaced, but it will still be available. The ability to scale is crucial, but if a system is unavailable, then the most scalable system ever built is still somewhat ineffective!

Load Balancing

Load balancing aims to effectively utilize the capacity of a collection of services to optimize the response time for each request. This is achieved by distributing requests across the available services to ideally utilize the collective service capacity. The objective is to avoid overloading some services while underutilizing others.

Clients send requests to the IP address of the load balancer, which redirects requests to target services, and relays the results back to the client. This means clients never contact the target services directly, which is also beneficial for security as the services can live behind a security perimeter and not be exposed to the internet.

Load balancers may act at the *network level* or the *application level*. These are often called *layer 4* and *layer 7* load balancers, respectively. The names refer to network transport layer at layer 4 in the Open Systems Interconnection (OSI) reference model (*https://oreil.ly/6ctRe*), and the application layer at layer 7. The OSI model defines network functions in seven abstract layers. Each layer defines standards for how data is packaged and transported.

Network-level load balancers distribute requests at the network connection level, operating on individual TCP or UDP packets. Routing decisions are made on the basis of client IP addresses. Once a target service is chosen, the load balancer uses a technique called network address translation (NAT). This changes the destination IP address in the client request packet from that of the load balancer to that of the chosen target. When a response is received from the target, the load balancer changes the source address recorded in the packet header from the target's IP address to its own. Network load balancers are relatively simple as they operate on the individual packet level. This means they are extremely fast, as they provide few features beyond choosing a target service and performing NAT functionality.

In contrast, application-level load balancers reassemble the complete HTTP request and base their routing decisions on the values of the HTTP headers and on the actual contents of the message. For example, a load balancer can be configured to send all POST requests to a subset of available services, or distribute requests based on a query string in the URI. Application load balancers are sophisticated reverse proxies. The richer capabilities they offer means they are slightly slower than network load balancers, but the powerful features they offer can be utilized to more than make up for the overheads incurred.

To give you some idea of the raw performance difference between network- and application-layer load balancers, Figure 5-7 compares the two in a simple application scenario. The load balancing technology under test is the AWS Application and Network Elastic Load Balancers (ELBs) (*https://oreil.ly/imwKF*). Each load balancer routes requests to one of 4 replicas. These execute the business logic and return results to the clients via the load balancer. Client load varies from a lightly loaded 32 concurrent clients to a moderate 256 concurrent clients. Each client sends a sequence of requests with no delay between receiving the results from one request and sending the next request to the server.

You can see from Figure 5-5 that the network load balancer delivers on average around 20% higher performance for the 32, 64, and 128 client tests. This validates the expected higher performance from the less sophisticated network load balancer. For 256 clients, the performance of the two load balancers is essentially the same. This is because the capacity of the 4 replicas is exceeded and the system has a bottleneck. At this stage the load balancers make no difference to the system performance. You need to add more replicas to the load balancing group to increase system capacity, and hence throughput.

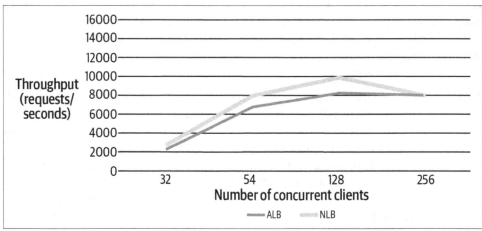

Figure 5-5. Comparing load balancer performance[4]

In general, a load balancer has the following features that will be explained in the following sections:

---

[4] Experimental results by Ruijie Xiao, from Northeastern University's MS program in computer science in Seattle.

- Load distribution policies
- Health monitoring
- Elasticity
- Session affinity

Load Distribution Policies

Load distribution policies dictate how the load balancer chooses a target service to process a request. Any load balancer worth its salt will offer several load distribution policies—HAProxy offers 10 (*https://oreil.ly/AYawR*). The following are four of the most commonly supported across all load balancers:

Round robin
> The load balancer distributes requests to available servers in a round-robin fashion.

Least connections
> The load balancer distributes new requests to the server with the least open connections.

HTTP header field
> The load balancer directs requests based on the contents of a specific HTTP header field. For example, all requests with the header field X-Client-Location:US,Seattle could be routed to a specific set of servers.

HTTP operation
> The load balancer directs requests based on the HTTP verb in the request.

Load balancers will also allow services to be allocated weights. For example, standard service instances in the load balancing pool may have 4 vCPUs and each is allocated a weight of 1. If a service replica running on 8 vCPUs is added, it can be assigned a weight of 2 so the load balancer will send twice as many requests its way.

Health Monitoring

A load balancer will periodically send pings and attempt connections to test the health of each service in the load balancing pool. These tests are called health checks. If a service becomes unresponsive or fails connection attempts, it will be removed from the load balancing pool and no requests will be sent to that host. If the connection to the service has experienced a transient failure, the load balancer will reincorporate the service once it becomes available and healthy. If, however, it has failed, the service will be removed from the load balancer target pool.

Elasticity

Spikes in request loads can cause the service capacity available to a load balancer to become saturated, leading to longer response times and eventually request and connection failures. *Elasticity* is the capability of an application to dynamically provision new service capacity to handle an increase in requests. As load increases, new replicas are started and the load balancer directs requests to these. As load decreases, the load balancer stops services that are no longer needed.

Elasticity requires a load balancer to be tightly integrated with application monitoring, so that scaling policies can be defined to determine when to scale up and down. Policies may specify, for example, that capacity for a service should be increased when the average service CPU utilization across all instances is over 70%, and decreased when average CPU utilization is below 40%. Scaling policies can typically be defined using any metrics that are available through the monitoring system.

An example of elastic load balancing is the AWS Auto Scaling groups. An Auto Scaling group is a collection of service instances available to a load balancer that is defined with a minimum and maximum size. The load balancer will ensure the group always has the minimum numbers of services available, and the group will never exceed the maximum number. This scheme is illustrated in Figure 5-6.

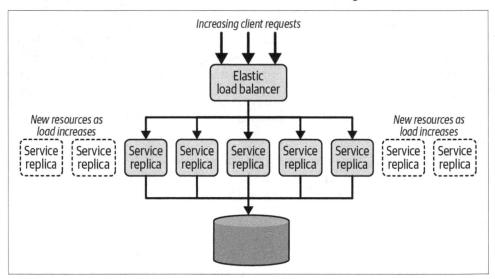

Figure 5-6. Elastic load balancing

Typically, there are two ways to control the number of replicas in a group. The first is based on a schedule, when the request load increases and decreases are predictable. For example, you may have an online entertainment guide and publish the weekend events for a set of major cities at 6 p.m. on Thursday. This generates a higher load until Sunday at noon. An Auto Scaling group could easily be configured to provision new services at 6 p.m. Thursday and reduce the group size to the minimum at noon Sunday.

If increased load spikes are not predictable, elasticity can be controlled dynamically by defined scaling policies based on application metrics such as average CPU and memory usage and number of messages in a queue. If the upper threshold of the policy is exceeded, the load balancer will start one or more new service instances until performance drops below the metric threshold. Instances need time to start—often a minute or more—and hence a *warm-up* period can be defined until the new instance is considered to be contributing to the group's capacity. When the observed metric value drops below the lower threshold defined in the scaling policy, *scale in* or *scale down* commences and instances will be automatically stopped and removed from the pool.

Elasticity is a key feature that allows services to scale dynamically as demand grows. For highly scalable systems with fluctuating workloads, it is pretty much a mandatory capability for providing the necessary capacity at minimum costs.

Session Affinity

Session affinity, or sticky sessions, are a load balancer feature for stateful services. With sticky sessions, the load balancer sends all requests from the same client to the same service instance. This enables the service to maintain in-memory state about each specific client session.

There are various ways to implement sticky sessions. For example, HAProxy provides a comprehensive set of capabilities (*https://oreil.ly/Nt7EH*) to maintain client requests on the same service in the face of service additions, removals, and failures. AWS Elastic Load Balancing (ELB) generates an HTTP cookie that identifies the service replica a client's session is associated with. This cookie is returned to the client, which must send it in subsequent requests to ensure session affinity is maintained.

Sticky sessions can be problematic for highly scalable systems. They lead to a load imbalance problem, in which, over time, clients are not evenly distributed across services. This is illustrated in Figure 5-7, where two clients are connected to one service while another service remains idle.

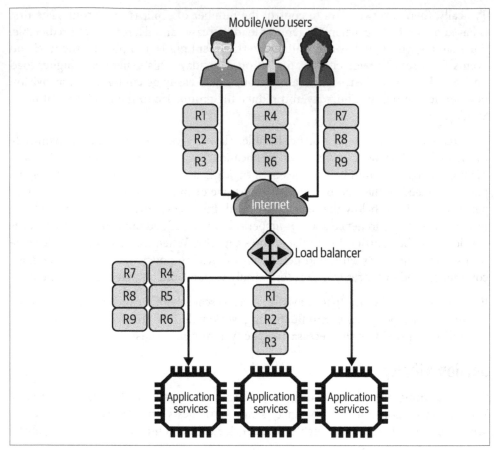

Figure 5-7. Load imbalance with sticky sessions

Load imbalance occurs because client sessions last for varying amounts of time. Even if sessions are evenly distributed initially, some will terminate quickly while others will persist. In a lightly loaded system, this tends to not be an issue. However, in a system with millions of sessions being created and destroyed constantly, load imbalance is inevitable. This will lead to some service replicas being underutilized, while others are overwhelmed and may potentially fail due to resource exhaustion. To help alleviate load imbalance, load balancers usually provide policies such as sending new sessions to instances with the least connections or fastest response times. These help direct new sessions away from heavily loaded services.

Stateful services have other downsides. When a service inevitably fails, how do the clients connected to that server recover the state that was being managed? If a service instance becomes slow due to high load, how do clients respond? In general, stateful servers create problems that in large scale systems can be difficult to design around and manage.

Stateless services have none of these downsides. If one fails, clients get an exception and retry, with their request routed to another live service replica. If a service is slow due to a transient network outage, the load balancer takes it out of the service group until it passes health checks or fails. All application state is either externalized or provided by the client in each request, so service failures can be handled easily by the load balancer.

Stateless services enhance scalability, simplify failure scenarios, and ease the burden of service management. For scalable applications, these advantages far outweigh the disadvantages, and hence their adoption in most major, large-scale internet sites such as Netflix (*https://oreil.ly/3F1Is*).

Finally, bear in mind that scaling one collection of services through load balancing may well overwhelm downstream services or databases that the load balanced services depend on. Just like with highways, adding eight traffic lanes for 50 miles will just cause bigger traffic chaos if the highway ends at a set of traffic lights with a one-lane road on the other side. We've all been there, I'm sure. I'll address these issues in Chapter 9.

Summary and Further Reading

Services are the heart of a scalable software system. They define the contract as an API that specifies their capabilities to clients. Services execute in an application server container environment that hosts the service code and routes incoming API requests to the appropriate processing logic. Application servers are highly programming language dependent, but in general provide a multithreaded programming model that allows services to process many requests simultaneously. If the threads in the container thread pool are all utilized, the application server queues up requests until a thread becomes available.

As request loads grow on a service, we can scale it out horizontally using a load balancer to distribute requests across multiple instances. This architecture also provides high availability as the multiple-service configuration means the application can tolerate failures of individual instances. The service instances are managed as a pool by the load balancer, which utilizes a load distribution policy to choose a target service replica for each request. Stateless services scale easily and simplify failure scenarios by allowing the load balancer to simply resend requests to responsive targets. Although most load balancers will support stateful services using a feature called sticky sessions, stateful services make load balancing and handling failures more complex. Hence, they are not recommended for highly scalable services.

API design is a topic of great complexity and debate. An excellent overview of basic API design and resource modeling is available on the Thoughtworks blog (*https://oreil.ly/qCl1B*).

The Java Enterprise Edition (JEE) is an established and widely deployed server-side technology. It has a wide range of abstractions for building rich and powerful services. The Oracle tutorial (*https://oreil.ly/IGW1N*) is an excellent starting point for appreciating this platform.

Much of the knowledge and information about load balancers is buried in the documentation provided by the technology suppliers. You choose your load balancer and then dive into the manuals. For an excellent, broad perspective on the complete field of load balancing, *Server Load Balancing* by Tony Bourke (O'Reilly, 2001) is a good resource.

CHAPTER 6
Distributed Caching

Caches exist in many places in an application. The CPUs that run your applications have fast, multilevel hardware caches to reduce relatively slow main memory accesses. Database engines can make use of main memory to cache the contents of the data store so that in many cases queries do not have to touch relatively slow disks.

Distributed caching is an essential ingredient of a scalable system. Caching makes the results of expensive queries and computations available for reuse by subsequent requests at low cost. By not having to reconstruct the cached results for every request, the capacity of the system is increased, and it can scale to handle greater workloads.

I'll cover two flavors of caching in this chapter. Application caching requires business logic that incorporates the caching and access of precomputed results using distributed caches. Web caching exploits mechanisms built into the HTTP protocol to enable caching of results within the infrastructure provided by the internet. When used effectively, both will protect your services and databases from heavy read traffic loads.

Application Caching

Application caching is designed to improve request responsiveness by storing the results of queries and computations in memory so they can be subsequently served by later requests. For example, think of an online newspaper site where readers can leave comments. Once posted, articles change infrequently, if ever. New comments tend to get posted soon after an article is published, but the frequency drops quickly with the age of the article. Hence an article can be cached on first access and reused by all subsequent requests until the article is updated, new comments are posted, or no one wants to read it anymore.

In general, caching relieves databases of heavy read traffic, as many queries can be served directly from the cache. It also reduces computation costs for objects that are expensive to construct, for example, those needing queries that span several different databases. The net effect is to reduce the computational load on our services and databases and create headroom, or capacity for more requests.

Caching requires additional resources, and hence cost, to store cached results. However, well-designed caching schemes are low cost compared to upgrading database and service nodes to cope with higher request loads. As an indication of the value of caches, approximately 3% of infrastructure at Twitter (*https://oreil.ly/OdvXp*) is dedicated to application-level caches. At Twitter scale, operating hundreds of clusters, that is a lot of infrastructure!

Application-level caching exploits dedicated distributed cache engines. The two predominant technologies in this area are memcached (*https://memcached.org*) and Redis (*https://redis.io*). Both are essentially distributed in-memory hash tables designed for arbitrary data (strings, objects) representing the results of database queries or downstream service API calls. Common use cases for caches are storing user session data, dynamic web pages, and results of database queries. The cache appears to application services as a single store, and objects are allocated to individual cache servers using a hash function on the object key.

The basic scheme is shown in Figure 6-1. The service first checks the cache to see if the data it requires is available. If so, it returns the cached contents as the results—this is known as a *cache hit*. If the data is not in the cache—a *cache miss*—the service retrieves the requested data from the database and writes the query results to the cache so it is available for subsequent client requests without querying the database.

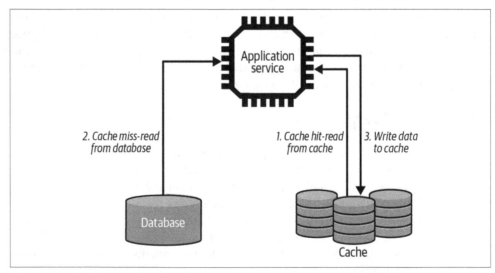

Figure 6-1. Application-level caching

For example, at a busy winter resort, skiers and snowboarders can use their mobile app to get an estimate of the lift wait times across the resort. This enables them to plan and avoid congested areas where they will have to wait to ride a lift for 15 minutes or more!

Every time a skier loads a lift, a message is sent to the company's service that collects data about skier traffic patterns. Using this data, the system can estimate lift wait times from the number of skiers who ride a lift and the rate they are arriving. This is an expensive calculation, taking maybe a second or more at busy times, as it requires aggregating potentially tens of thousands of lift ride records and performing the wait time calculation. For this reason, once the results are calculated, they are deemed valid for five minutes. Only after this time has elapsed is a new calculation performed and results produced.

The following code example shows how a stateless `LiftWaitService` might work. When a request arrives, the service first checks the cache to see if the latest wait times are available. If they are, the results are immediately returned to the client. If the results are not in the cache, the service calls a downstream service which performs the lift wait calculations and returns them as a `List`. These results are then stored in the cache and then returned to the client:

```
public class LiftWaitService {
    public List getLiftWaits(String resort) {
      List liftWaitTimes = cache.get("liftwaittimes:" + resort);
        if (liftWaitTimes == null) {
          liftWaitTimes = skiCo.getLiftWaitTimes(resort);
          // add result to cache, expire in 300 seconds
          cache.put("liftwaittimes:" + resort, liftWaitTimes, 300);
      }
    return liftWaitTimes;
      }
    }
```

Cache access requires a key with which to associate the results. In this example, the key is constructed with the string "`liftwaittimes:`" concatenated with the resort identifier that is passed by the client to the service. This key is then hashed by the cache to identify the server where the cached value resides.

When a new value is written to the cache, a value of 300 seconds is passed as a parameter to the `put` operation. This is known as a *time to live* (TTL) value. It tells the cache that after 300 seconds this key-value pair should be evicted from the cache as the value is no longer current (also known as stale).

While the cache value is valid, all requests will utilize it. This means there is no need to perform the expensive lift wait time calculation for every call. A cache hit on a fast network will take maybe a millisecond—much faster than the lift wait times calculation. When the cache value is evicted after 300 seconds, the next request will result in a cache miss. This will result in the calculation of the new values to be stored in the cache. Therefore, if we get N requests in a 5-minute period, N-1 requests are served from the cache. Imagine if N is 10,000? This is a lot of expensive calculations saved, and CPU cycles that your database can use to process other queries.

Using an expiry time like the TTL is a common way to invalidate cache contents. It ensures a service doesn't deliver stale, out-of-date results to a client. It also enables the system to have some control over cache contents, which are typically limited. If cached items are not flushed periodically, the cache will fill up. In this case, a cache will adopt a policy such as *least recently used* or *least accessed* to choose cache entries to evict and create space for more current, timely results.

Application caching can provide significant throughput boosts, reduced latencies, and increased client application responsiveness. The key to achieving these desirable qualities is to satisfy as many requests as possible from the cache. The general design principle is to maximize the cache hit rate and minimize the cache miss rate. When a cache miss occurs, the request must be satisfied through querying databases or downstream services. The results of the request can then be written to the cache and hence be available for further accesses.

There's no hard-and-fast rule on what the cache hit rate should be, as it depends on the cost of constructing the cache contents and the update rate of cached items. Ideal cache designs have many more reads than updates. This is because when an item must be updated, the application needs to invalidate cache entries that are now stale because of the update. This means the next request will result in a cache miss.[1]

When items are updated regularly, the cost of cache misses can negate the benefits of the cache. Service designers therefore need to carefully consider query and update patterns an application experiences, and construct caching mechanisms that yield the most benefit. It is also crucial to monitor the cache usage once a service is in production to ensure the hit and miss rates are in line with design expectations. Caches will provide both management utilities and APIs to enable monitoring of the cache usage characteristics. For example, memcached makes a large number of statistics available, including the hit and miss counts as shown in the snippet of output below:

```
STAT get_hits 98567
STAT get_misses 11001
STAT evictions 0
```

Application-level caching is also known as the *cache-aside* pattern (*https://oreil.ly/ 3Ip0A*). The name references the fact that the application code effectively bypasses the

---

1 Some application use cases may make it possible for a new cache entry to be created at the same time an update is made. This can be useful if some keys are "hot" and will have a great likelihood of being accessed again before the next update. This is known as an "eager" cache update.

data storage systems if the required results are available in the cache. This contrasts with other caching patterns in which the application always reads from and writes to the cache. These are known as *read-through*, *write-through*, and *write-behind* caches, defined as follows:

Read-through

The application satisfies all requests by accessing the cache. If the data required is not available in the cache, a loader is invoked to access the data systems and load the results in the cache for the application to utilize.

Write-through

The application always writes updates to the cache. When the cache is updated, a writer is invoked to write the new cache values to the database. When the database is updated, the application can complete the request.

Write-behind

Like write-through, except the application does not wait for the value to be written to the database from the cache. This increases request responsiveness at the expense of possible lost updates if the cache server crashes before a database update is completed. This is also known as a write-back cache, and internally is the strategy used by most database engines.

The beauty of these caching approaches is that they simplify application logic. Applications always utilize the cache for reads and writes, and the cache provides the "magic" to ensure the cache interacts appropriately with the backend storage systems. This contrasts with the cache-aside pattern, in which application logic must be cognizant of cache misses.

Read-through, write-through, and write-behind strategies require a cache technology that can be augmented with an application-specific handler to perform database reads and writes when the application accesses the cache. For example, NCache (*https:// oreil.ly/v6Xio*) supports *provider interfaces* that the application implements. These are invoked automatically on cache misses for read-through caches and on writes for write-through caches. Other such caches are essentially dedicated database caches, and hence require cache access to be identical to the underlying database model. An example of this is Amazon's DynamoDB Accelerator (DAX) (*https://oreil.ly/lfltM*). DAX sits between the application code and DynamoDB, and transparently acts as a high-speed, in-memory cache to reduce database access times.

One significant advantage of the cache-aside strategy is that it is resilient to cache failure. In circumstances when the cache is unavailable, all requests are essentially handled as a cache miss. Performance will suffer, but services will still be able to satisfy requests. In addition, scaling cache-aside platforms such as Redis and memcached is straightforward due to their simple, distributed hash table model. For these reasons, the cache-aside pattern is the primary approach seen in massively scalable systems.

Web Caching

One of the reasons that websites are so highly responsive is that the internet is littered with web caches. Web caches store a copy of a given resource—for example, a web page or an image, for a defined time period. The caches intercept client requests and if they have a requested resource cached locally, they return the copy rather than forwarding the request to the target service. Hence, many requests can be satisfied without placing a burden on the service. Also, as the caches are physically closer to the client, the requests will have lower latencies.

Figure 6-2 gives an overview of the web caching architecture. Multiple levels of caches exist, starting with the client's web browser cache and local organization-based caches. ISPs will also implement general web proxy caches, and reverse proxy caches can be deployed within the application services execution domain. Web browser caches are also known as private caches (for a single user). Organizational and ISP proxy caches are shared caches that support requests from multiple users.

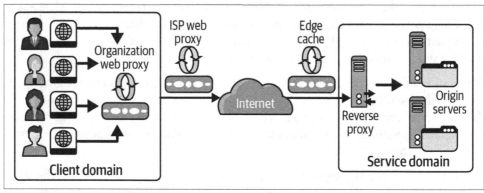

Figure 6-2. Web caches in the internet

Edge caches, also known as content delivery networks (CDNs), live at various strategic geographical locations globally, so that they cache frequently accessed data close to clients. For example, a video streaming provider may configure an edge cache in Sydney, Australia to serve video content to Australasian users rather than streaming content across the Pacific Ocean from US-based origin servers. Edge caches are deployed globally by CDN providers. Akamai, the original CDN provider, has over 2,000 locations and delivers up to 30% of internet traffic globally (*https://oreil.ly/ s73lC*). For media-rich sites with global users, edge caches are essential.

Caches typically store the results of GET requests only, and the cache key is the URI of the associated GET. When a client sends a GET request, it may be intercepted by one or more caches along the request path. Any cache with a fresh copy of the requested resource may respond to the request. If no cached content is found, the request is served by the service endpoint, which is also called the origin server in web technology parlance.

Services can control what results are cached and for how long they are stored by using HTTP caching directives. Services set these directives in various HTTP response headers, as shown in this simple example:

```
Response:
HTTP/1.1 200 OK Content-Length: 9842
Content-Type: application/json
Cache-Control: public
Date: Fri, 26 Mar 2019 09:33:49 GMT
Expires: Fri, 26 Mar 2019 09:38:49 GMT
```

I will describe these directives in the following subsections.

Cache-Control

The Cache-Control HTTP header can be used by client requests and service responses to specify how the caching should be utilized for the resources of interest. Possible values are:

no-store
    Specifies that a resource from a request response should not be cached. This is typically used for sensitive data that needs to be retrieved from the origin servers each request.

no-cache
    Specifies that a cached resource must be revalidated with an origin server before use. I discuss revalidation in the section "Etag" on page 122.

private
    Specifies a resource can be cached only by a user-specific device such as a web browser.

public
    Specifies a resource can be cached by any proxy server.

max-age
    Defines the length of time in seconds a cached copy of a resource should be retained. After expiration, a cache must refresh the resource by sending a request to the origin server.

Expires and Last-Modified

The Expires and Last-Modified HTTP headers interact with the max-age directive to control how long cached data is retained.

Caches have limited storage resources and hence must periodically evict items from memory to create space. To influence cache eviction, services can specify how long resources in the cache should remain valid, or *fresh*. When a request arrives for a fresh resource, the cache serves the locally stored results without contacting the origin server. Once any specified retention period for a cached resource expires, it becomes stale and becomes a candidate for eviction.

Freshness is calculated using a combination of header values. The `"Cache-Control: max-age=N"` header is the primary directive, and this value specifies the freshness period in seconds.

If `max-age` is not specified, the `Expires` header is checked next. If this header exists, then it is used to calculate the freshness period. The `Expires` header specifies an explicit date and time after which the resource should be considered stale. For example:

```
Expires: Wed, 26 Oct 2022 09:39:00 GMT
```

As a last resort, the `Last-Modified` header can be used to calculate resource retention periods. This header is set by the origin server to specify when a resource was last updated, and uses the same format as the `Expires` header. A cache server can use `Last-Modified` to determine the freshness lifetime of a resource based on a heuristic calculation that the cache supports. The calculation uses the `Date` header, which specifies the time a response message was sent from an origin server. A resource retention period subsequently becomes equal to the value of the `Date` header minus the value of the `Last-Modified` header divided by 10.

Etag

HTTP provides another directive that can be used to control cache item freshness. This is known as an `Etag`. An `Etag` is an opaque value that can be used by a web cache to check if a cached resource is still valid. I'll explain this using an example in the following.

Going back to our winter resort example, the resort produces a weather report at 6 a.m. every day during the winter season. If the weather changes during the day, the resort updates the report. Sometimes this happens two or three times each day, and sometimes not at all if the weather is stable. When a request arrives for the weather report, the service responds with a maximum age to define cache freshness, and also an `Etag` that represents the version of the weather report that was last issued. This is shown in the following HTTP example, which tells a cache to treat the weather report resource as fresh for at least 3,600 seconds, or 60 minutes. The `Etag` value, namely `"blackstone-weather-03/26/19-v1"`, is simply generated using a label that the service defines for this particular resource. In this example, the `Etag` represents the first version of the report for the Blackstone Resort on March 26th, 2019. Other common strategies are to generate the `Etag` using a hash algorithm such as MD5:

```
Request:
GET /skico.com/weather/Blackstone

Response:
HTTP/1.1 200 OK Content-Length: ...
Content-Type: application/json
Date: Fri, 26 Mar 2019 09:33:49 GMT
Cache-Control: public, max-age=3600
ETag: "blackstone-weather-03/26/19-v1"
<!-- Content omitted -->
```

For the next hour, the web cache simply serves this cached weather report to all clients who issue a GET request. This means the origin servers are freed from processing these requests—the outcome that we want from effective caching. After an hour though, the resource becomes stale. Now, when a request arrives for a stale resource, the cache forwards it to the origin server with a `If-None-Match` directive along with the `Etag` to inquire if the resource, in our case the weather report, is still valid. This is known as *revalidation*.

There are two possible responses to this request:

- If the `Etag` in the request matches the value associated with the resource in the service, the cached value is still valid. The origin server can therefore return a 304 (Not Modified) response, as shown in the following example. No response body is needed as the cached value is still current, thus saving bandwidth, especially for large resources. The response may also include new cache directives to update the freshness of the cached resource.

- The origin server may ignore the revalidation request and respond with a 200 OK response code, a response body and `Etag` representing the latest version of the weather report:

```
Request:
GET /upic.com/weather/Blackstone
If-None-Match: "blackstone-weather-03/26/19-v1"
Response:
HTTP/1.1 304 Not Modified
Cache-Control: public, max-age=3600
```

In the service implementation, a mechanism is needed to support revalidation. In our weather report example, one strategy is as follows:

Generate a new daily report
The weather report is constructed and stored in a database, with the `Etag` as an attribute.

GET *requests*

When any GET request arrives, the service returns the weather report and the Etag. This will also populate web caches along the network response path.

Conditional GET *requests*

For conditional requests with the If-None-Match: directive, look up the Etag value in the database and return 304 if the value has not changed. If the stored Etag has changed, return 200 along with the latest weather report and a new Etag value.

Update the weather report

A new version of the weather report is stored in the database and the Etag value is modified to represent this new version of the response.

When used effectively, web caching can significantly reduce latencies and save network bandwidth. This is especially true for large items such as images and documents. Further, as web caches handle requests rather than application services, this reduces the request load on origin servers, creating additional capacity.

Proxy caches such as Squid (*https://oreil.ly/wZGrG*) and Varnish (*https://oreil.ly/NvvwX*) are extensively deployed on the internet. Web caching is most effective when deployed for static data (images, videos, and audio streams) as well as infrequently changing data such as weather reports. The powerful facilities provided by HTTP caching in conjunction with proxy and edge caches are therefore invaluable tools for building scalable applications.

Summary and Further Reading

Caching is an essential component of any scalable distribution. Caching stores information that is requested by many clients in memory and serves this information as the results to client requests. While the information is still valid, it can be served potentially millions of times without the cost of re-creation.

Application caching using a distributed cache is the most common approach to caching in scalable systems. This approach requires the application logic to check for cached values when a client request arrives and return these if available. If the cache hit rate is high, with most requests being satisfied with cached results, the load on backend services and databases can be considerably reduced.

The internet also has a built in, multilevel caching infrastructure. Applications can exploit this through the use of cache directives that are part of HTTP headers. These directives enable a service to specify what information can be cached, for how long it should be cached, and employ a protocol for checking to see if a stale cache entry is still valid. Used wisely, HTTP caching can significantly reduce request loads on downstream services and databases.

Caching is a well established area of software and systems, and the literature tends to be scattered across many generic and product-specific sources. A great source of "all things caching" is Gerardus Blokdyk's *Memcached*, 3rd ed. (5StarCooks, 2021). While the title gives away the product-focused content, the knowledge contained can be translated easily to cache designs with other competing technologies.

A great source of information on HTTP/2 in general is *Learning HTTP/2: A Practical Guide for Beginners* by Stephen Ludin and Javier Garza (O'Reilly, 2017). And while dated, *Web Caching* by Duane Wessels (O'Reilly, 2001) contains enough generic wisdom to remain a very useful reference.

CDNs are a complex, vendor-specific topic in themselves. They come into their own for media-rich websites with a geographically dispersed group of users that require fast content delivery. For a highly readable overview of CDNs, Ogi Djuraskovic's site (*https://oreil.ly/I4K5L*) is worth checking out.

CHAPTER 7

Asynchronous Messaging

Inevitably for a distributed systems book, I've spent a fair bit of time in the preceding chapters discussing communications issues. Communication is fundamental to distributed systems, and it is a major issue that architects need to incorporate into their system designs.

So far, these discussions have assumed a synchronous messaging style. A client sends a response and waits for a server to respond. This is how most distributed communications are designed to occur, as the client requires an instantaneous response to proceed.

Not all systems have this requirement. For example, when I return some goods I've purchased online, I take them to my local UPS or FedEx store. They scan my QR code, and I give them the package to process. I do not then wait in the store for confirmation that the product has been successfully received by the vendor and my payment returned. That would be dull and unproductive. I trust the shipping service to deliver my unwanted goods to the vendor and expect to get a message a few days later when it has been processed.

We can design our distributed systems to emulate this behavior. Using an asynchronous communications style, clients, known as producers, send their requests to an intermediary messaging service. This acts as a delivery mechanism to relay the request to the intended destination, known as the consumer, for processing. Producers "fire and forget" the requests they send. Once a request is delivered to the messaging service, the producer moves on to the next step in their logic, confident that the requests it sends will eventually get processed. This improves system responsiveness, in that producers do not have to wait until the request processing is completed.

In this chapter I'll describe the basic communication mechanisms that an asynchronous messaging system supports. I'll also discuss the inherent trade-offs between throughput and data safety—basically, making sure your systems don't lose messages. I'll also cover three key messaging patterns that are commonly deployed in highly scalable distributed systems.

To make these concepts concrete, I'll describe RabbitMQ (*https://oreil.ly/j9eHD*), a widely deployed open source messaging system. After introducing the basics of the technology, I'll focus on the core set of features you need to be aware of in order to design a high-throughput messaging system.

Introduction to Messaging

Asynchronous messaging platforms are a mature area of technology, with multiple products in the space.[1] The venerable IBM MQ Series appeared in 1993 and is still a mainstay of enterprise systems. The Java Messaging Service (JMS), an API-level specification, is supported by multiple JEE vendor implementations. RabbitMQ, which I'll use as an illustration later in this chapter, is arguably the most widely deployed open source messaging system. In the messaging world, you will never be short of choice.

While the specific features and APIs vary across all these competing products, the foundational concepts are pretty much identical. I'll cover these in the following subsections, and then describe how they are implemented in RabbitMQ in the next section. Once you appreciate how one messaging platform works, it is relatively straightforward to understand the similarities and differences inherent in the competition.

Messaging Primitives

Conceptually, a messaging system comprises the following:

Message queues
    Queues that store a sequence of messages

Producers
    Send messages to queues

Consumers
    Retrieve messages from queues

Message broker
    Manages one or more queues

This scheme is illustrated in Figure 7-1.

---

1 A helpful overview of the messaging technologies landscape can be found at *https://oreil.ly/KMvTp*.

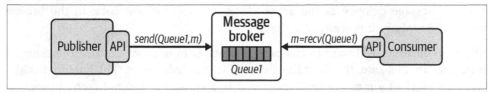

Figure 7-1. A simple messaging system

A message broker is a service that manages one or more queues. When messages are sent from producers to a queue, the broker adds messages to the queue in the order they arrive—basically a FIFO approach. The broker is responsible for efficiently managing message receipt and retention until one or more consumers retrieve the messages, which are then removed from the queue. Message brokers that manage many queues and many requests can effectively utilize many vCPUs and memory to provide low latency accesses.

Producers send messages to a named queue on a broker. Many producers can send messages to the same queue. A producer will wait until an acknowledgment message is received from the broker before the send operation is considered complete.

Many consumers can take messages from the same queue. Each message is retrieved by exactly one consumer. There are two modes of behavior for consumers to retrieve messages, known as *pull* or *push*. While the exact mechanisms are product-specific, the basic semantics are common across technologies:

- In pull mode, also known as polling, consumers send a request to the broker, which responds with the next message available for processing. If there are no messages available, the consumer must poll the queue until messages arrive.

- In push mode, a consumer informs the broker that it wishes to receive messages from a queue. The consumer provides a callback function that should be invoked when a message is available. The consumer then blocks (or does other work) and the message broker delivers messages to the callback function for processing when they are available.

Generally, utilizing the push mode when available is much more efficient and recommended. It avoids the broker being potentially swamped by requests from multiple consumers and makes it possible to implement message delivery more efficiently in the broker.

Consumers will also acknowledge message receipt. Upon consumer acknowledgment, the broker is free to mark a message as delivered and remove it from the queue. Acknowledgment may be done automatically or manually.

If automatic acknowledgment is used, messages are acknowledged as soon as they are delivered to the consumer, and before they are processed. This provides the lowest latency message delivery as the acknowledgment can be sent back to the broker before the message is processed.

Often a consumer will want to ensure a message is fully processed before acknowledgment. In this case, it will utilize manual acknowledgments. This guards against the possibility of a message being delivered to a consumer but not being processed due to a consumer crash. It does, of course, increase message acknowledgment latency. Regardless of the acknowledgment mode selected, unacknowledged messages effectively remain on the queue and will be delivered at some later time to another consumer for processing.

Message Persistence

Message brokers can manage multiple queues on the same hardware. By default, message queues are typically memory based, in order to provide the fastest possible service to producers and consumers. Managing queues in memory has minimal overheads, as long as memory is plentiful. It does, however, risk message loss if the server were to crash.

To guard against message loss—a practice known as data safety—queues can be configured to be persistent. When a message is placed on a queue by a producer, the operation does not complete until the message is written to disk. This scheme is depicted in Figure 7-2. Now, if a message broker should fail, on reboot it can recover the queue contents to the state they existed in before the failure, and no messages will be lost. Many applications can't afford to lose messages, and hence persistent queues are necessary to provide data safety and fault tolerance.

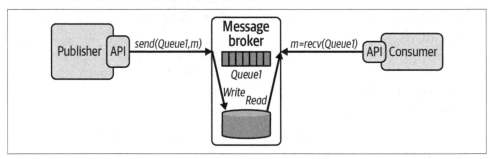

Figure 7-2. Persisting messages to disk

Persistent queues have an inherent increase in the response time for send operations, with the trade-off being enhanced data safety. Brokers will usually maintain the queue contents in memory as well as on disk so messages can be delivered to consumers with minimal overhead during normal operations.

Publish–Subscribe

Message queues deliver each message to exactly one consumer. For many use cases, this is exactly what you want—my online purchase return needs to be consumed just once by the originating vendor—so that I get my money back.

Let's extend this use case. Assume the online retailer wants to do an analysis of all purchase returns so it can detect vendors who have a high rate of returns and take some remedial action. To implement this, you could simply deliver all purchase return messages to the respective vendor *and* the new analysis service. This creates a one-to-many messaging requirement, which is known as a publish–subscribe architecture pattern. In publish–subscribe systems, message queues are known as *topics*. A topic is basically a message queue that delivers each published message to one of more subscribers, as illustrated in Figure 7-3.

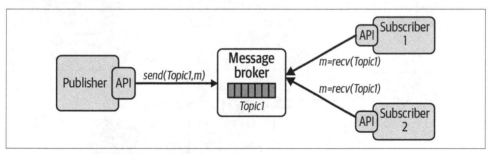

Figure 7-3. A publish–subscribe broker architecture

With publish–subscribe, you can create highly flexible and dynamic systems. Publishers are decoupled from subscribers, and the number of subscribers can vary dynamically. This makes the architecture highly extensible as new subscribers can be added without any changes to the existing system. It also makes it possible to perform message processing by a number of consumers in parallel, thus enhancing performance.

Publish–subscribe places an additional performance burden on the message broker. The broker is obliged to deliver each message to all active subscribers. As subscribers will inevitably process and acknowledge messages at different times, the broker needs to keep messages available until all subscribers have consumed each message. Utilizing a push model for message consumption provides the most efficient solution for publish–subscribe architectures.

Publish–subscribe messaging is a key component for building distributed, event-driven architectures. In event-driven architectures, multiple services can publish events related to some state changes using message broker topics. Services can register interest in various event types by subscribing to a topic. Each event published on the topic is then delivered to all interested consumer services. I'll return to event-driven architectures when microservices are covered in Chapter 9.[2]

Message Replication

In an asynchronous system, the message broker is potentially a single point of failure. A system or network failure can cause the broker to be unavailable, making it impossible for the systems to operate normally. This is rarely a desirable situation.

For this reason, most message brokers enable logical queues and topics to be physically replicated across multiple brokers, each running on their own node. If one broker fails, then producers and consumers can continue to process messages using one of the replicas. This architecture is illustrated in Figure 7-4. Messages published to the leader are mirrored to the follower, and messages consumed from the leader are removed from the follower.

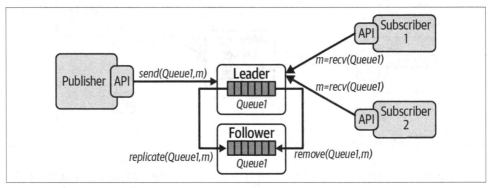

Figure 7-4. Message queue replication

The most common approach to message queue replication is known as a leader-follower architecture. One broker is designated as the leader, and producers and consumers send and receive messages respectively from this leader. In the background, the leader replicates (or mirrors) all messages it receives to the follower, and removes messages that are successfully delivered. This is shown in Figure 7-4 with the *replicate* and *remove* operations. How precisely this scheme behaves and the effects it has on broker performance is inherently implementation, and hence product dependent.

With leader-follower message replication, the follower is known as a hot standby, basically a replica of the leader that is available if the leader fails. In such a failure scenario, producers and consumers can continue to operate by switching over to accessing the follower. This is also called *failover*. Failover is implemented in the

---

2 Chapter 14 of *Fundamentals of Software Architecture* by Mark Richards and Neal Ford is an excellent source of knowledge for event-driven architectures.

client libraries for the message broker, and hence occurs transparently to producers and consumers.

Implementing a broker that performs queue replication is a complicated affair. There are numerous subtle failure cases that the broker needs to handle when duplicating messages. I'll start to raise these issues and describe some solutions in Chapters 10 and 11 when discussions turn to scalable data management.

 Some advice: don't contemplate *rolling your own* replication scheme, or any other complex distributed algorithm for that matter. The software world is littered with failed attempts to build application-specific distributed systems infrastructure, just because the solutions available "don't do it quite right for our needs" or "cost too much." Trust me—your solution will not work as well as existing solutions and development will cost more than you could ever anticipate. You will probably end up throwing your code away. These algorithms are really hard to implement correctly at scale.

Example: RabbitMQ

RabbitMQ is one of the most widely utilized message brokers in distributed systems. You'll encounter deployments in all application domains, from finance to telecommunications to building environment control systems. It was first released around 2009 and has developed into a full-featured, open source distributed message broker platform with support for building clients in most mainstream languages.

The RabbitMQ broker is built in Erlang, and primarily provides support for the Advanced Message Queuing Protocol (AMQP) open standard.[3] AMQP emerged from the finance industry as a cooperative protocol definition effort. It is a binary protocol, providing interoperability between different products that implement the protocol. Out of the box, RabbitMQ supports AMQP v0-9-1, with v1.0 support via a plugin.

Messages, Exchanges, and Queues

In RabbitMQ, producers and consumers use a client API to send and receive messages from the broker. The broker provides the store-and-forward functionality for messages, which are processed in a FIFO manner using queues. The broker implements a messaging model based on a concept called exchanges, which provide a flexible mechanism for creating messaging topologies.

An exchange is an abstraction that receives messages from producers and delivers them to queues in the broker. Producers only ever write messages to an exchange.

---

3 Other protocols such as STOMP and MQTT are supported via plugins.

Messages contain a message payload and various attributes known as message metadata. One element of this metadata is the *routing key*, which is a value used by the exchange to deliver messages to the intended queues.

Exchanges can be configured to deliver a message to one or more queues. The message delivery algorithm depends on the exchange type and rules called bindings, which establish a relationship between an exchange and a queue using the routing key. The three most commonly used exchange types are shown in Table 7-1.

Table 7-1. Exchange types

Exchange type	Message routing behavior
Direct	Delivers a message to a queue based on matching the value of a routing key which is published with each message
Topic	Delivers a message to one or more queues based on matching the routing key and a pattern used to bind a queue to the exchange
Fanout	Delivers a message to all queues that are bound to the exchange, and the routing key is ignored

Direct exchanges are typically used to deliver each message to one destination queue based on matching the routing key.[4] Topic exchanges are a more flexible mechanism based on pattern matching that can be used to implement sophisticated publish–subscribe messaging topologies. Fanout exchanges provide a simple one-to-many broadcast mechanism, in which every message is sent to all attached queues.

Figure 7-5 depicts how a direct exchange operates. Queues are bound to the exchange by consumers with three values, namely "France," "Spain," and "Portugal." When a message arrives from a publisher, the exchange uses the attached routing key to deliver the message to one of the three attached queues.

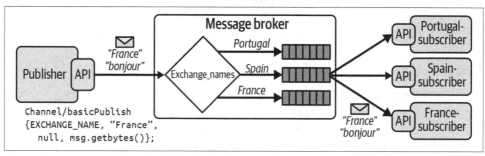

Figure 7-5. An example of a RabbitMQ direct exchange

---

4 Consumers can call queueBind() multiple times to specify that their destination should receive messages for more than one routing key value. This approach can be used to create one-to-many message distribution. Topic exchanges are more powerful for one-to-many messaging.

The following code shows an excerpt of how a direct exchange is configured and utilized in Java. RabbitMQ clients, namely producer and consumer processes, use a *channel* abstraction to establish communications with the broker (more on channels in the next section). The producer creates the exchange in the broker and publishes a message to the exchange with the routing key set to "France." A consumer creates an anonymous queue in the broker, binds the queue to the exchange created by the publisher, and specifies that messages published with the routing key "France" should be delivered to this queue.

Producer:

```
channel.exchangeDeclare(EXCHANGE_NAME, "direct");
channel.basicPublish(EXCHANGE_NAME, "France", null, message.getBytes());
```

Consumer:

```
String queueName = channel.queueDeclare().getQueue();
channel.queueBind(queueName, EXCHANGE_NAME, "France");
```

Distribution and Concurrency

To get the most from RabbitMQ in terms of performance and scalability, you must understand how the platform works under the covers. The issues of concern relate to how clients and the broker communicate, and how threads are managed.

Each RabbitMQ client connects to a broker using a RabbitMQ connection. This is basically an abstraction on top of TCP/IP, and can be secured using user credentials or TLS. Creating connections is a heavyweight operation, requiring multiple round trips between the client and server, and hence a single long-lived connection per client is the common usage pattern.

To send or receive messages, clients use the connection to create a RabbitMQ channel. Channels are a logical connection between a client and the broker, and only exist in the context of a RabbitMQ connection, as shown in the following code snippet:

```
ConnectionFactory connFactory = new ConnectionFactory();
Connection rmqConn = connFactory.createConnection();
Channel channel = rmqConn.createChannel();
```

Multiple channels can be created in the same client to establish multiple logical broker connections. All communications over these channels are multiplexed over the same RabbitMQ (TCP) connection, as shown in Figure 7-6. Creating a channel requires a network round trip to the broker. Hence for performance reasons, channels should ideally be long-lived, with channel churn, namely constantly creating and destroying channels, avoided.

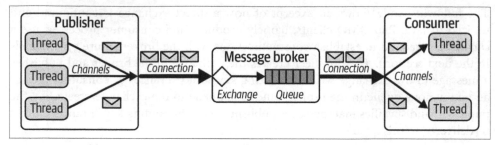

Figure 7-6. RabbitMQ connections and channels

To increase the throughput of RabbitMQ clients, a common strategy is to implement multithreaded producers and consumers. Channels, however, are not thread safe, meaning every thread requires exclusive access to a channel. This is not a concern if your client has long-lived, stateful threads and can create a channel per thread, as shown in Figure 7-6. You start a thread, create a channel, and publish or consume away. This is a channel-per-thread model.

In application servers such as Tomcat or Spring however, the solution is not so simple. The life cycle and invocation of threads is controlled by the server platform, not your code. The solution is to create a global channel pool upon server initialization. This precreated collection of channels can be used on demand by server threads without the overheads of channel creation and deletion per request. Each time a request arrives for processing, a server thread takes the following steps:

- Retrieves a channel from the pool
- Sends the message to the broker
- Returns the channel to pool for subsequent reuse

While there is no native RabbitMQ capability to do this, in Java you can utilize the Apache Commons Pool library (*https://oreil.ly/zcxvE*) to implement a channel pool. The complete code for this implementation is included in the accompanying code repository for this book. The following code snippet shows how a server thread uses the `borrowObject()` and `returnObject()` methods of the Apache `GenericObjectPool` class (*https://oreil.ly/lVPId*). You can tune the minimum and maximum size of this object pool using setter methods to provide the throughput your application desires:

```
private boolean sendMessageToQueue(JsonObject message) {
  try {
    Channel channel = pool.borrowObject();
      channel.basicPublish(// arguments omitted for brevity)
      pool.returnObject(channel);
      return true;
  } catch (Exception e) {
```

```
        logger.info("Failed to send message to RabbitMQ");
        return false;
    }
}
```

On the consumer side, clients create channels that can be used to receive messages. Consumers can explicitly retrieve messages on demand from a queue using the `basicGet()` API, as shown in the following example:

```
boolean autoAck = true;
GetResponse response = channel.basicGet(queueName, autoAck);
if (response == null) {
    // No message available. Decide what to do …
} else {
    // process message
}
```

This approach uses the *pull* model (polling). Polling is inefficient as it involves busy-waiting, obliging the consumer to continually ask for messages even if none are available. In high-performance systems, this is not the approach to use.

The alternative and preferable method is the *push* model. The consumer specifies a callback function that is invoked for each message the RabbitMQ broker sends, or pushes, to the consumer. Consumers issue a call to the `basicConsume()` API. When a message is available for the consumer from the queue, the RabbitMQ client library on the consumer invokes the callback in another thread associated with the channel. The following code example shows how to receive messages using an object of type `DefaultConsumer` that is passed to `basicConsume()` to establish a connection:

```
boolean autoAck = true;
channel.basicConsume(queueName, autoAck, "tag",
    new DefaultConsumer(channel) {
        @Override
        public void handleDelivery(String consumerTag,
                                   Envelope envelope,
                                   AMQP.BasicProperties properties,
                                   byte[] body)
            throws IOException
        {
            // process the message
        }
    });
```

Reception of messages on a single channel is single threaded. This makes it necessary to create multiple threads and allocate a channel-per-thread or channel pool in order to obtain high message consumption rates. The following Java code extract shows how this can be done. Each thread creates and configures its own channel and specifies the callback function—`threadCallback()`—that should be called by the RabbitMQ client when a new message is delivered:

```
Runnable runnable = () -> {
    try {
        final Channel channel = connection.createChannel();
        channel.queueDeclare(QUEUE_NAME, true, false, false, null);
        // max one message per receiver

        final DeliverCallback threadCallback = (consumerTag, delivery)
          -> {
            String message =
                new String(delivery.getBody(), StandardCharsets.UTF_8);
            // process the message
        };
        channel.basicConsume(QUEUE_NAME,
                             false, threadCallback, consumerTag -> {});
        //
    } catch (IOException e) {
        logger.info(e.getMessage());
    }
```

Another important aspect of RabbitMQ to appreciate in order to obtain high performance and scalability is the thread model used by the message broker. In the broker, each queue is managed by a single thread. This means you can increase throughput on a multicore node if you have at least as many queues as cores on the underlying node. Conversely, if you have many more highly utilized queues than cores on your broker node, you are likely to see some performance degradation.

Like most message brokers, RabbitMQ performs best when consumption rates keep up with production rates. When queues grow long, in the order of tens of thousands of messages, the thread managing a queue will experience more overheads. By default, the broker will utilize 40% of the available memory of the node it is running on. When this limit is reached, the broker will start to throttle producers, slowing down the rate at which the broker accepts messages, until the memory usage drops below the 40% threshold. The memory threshold is configurable and again, this is a setting that can be tuned to your workload to optimize message throughput.[5]

Data Safety and Performance Trade-offs

All messaging systems present a dilemma around a performance versus reliability trade-off. In this particular case, the core issue is the reliability of message delivery, commonly known as data safety. You want your messages to transit between producer and consumer with minimum latency, and of course you don't want to lose any messages along the way. Ever. If only it were that simple. These are distributed systems, remember.

---

5 A complete description of how the RabbitMQ server memory can be configured is available at the RabbitMQ Memory Alarms page (*https://oreil.ly/Ayp2I*).

When a message transits from producer to consumer, there are multiple failure scenarios you have to understand and cater for in your design. These are:

- A producer sends a message to a broker and message is not successfully accepted by the broker.
- A message is in a queue and the broker crashes.
- A message is successfully delivered to the consumer but the consumer fails before fully processing the message.

If your application can tolerate message loss, then you can choose options that maximize performance. It probably doesn't matter if occasionally you lose a message from an instant messaging application. In this case your system can ignore message safety issues and run full throttle. This isn't the case for, say, a purchasing system. If purchase orders are lost, the business loses money and customers. You need to put safeguards in place to ensure data safety.

RabbitMQ, like basically all message brokers, has features that you can utilize to guarantee end-to-end message delivery. These are:

Publisher-confirms
A publisher can specify that it wishes to receive acknowledgments from the broker that a message has been successfully received. This is not default publisher behavior and must be set as a channel attribute by calling the `confirmSelect()` method. Publishers can wait for acknowledgments synchronously, or asynchronously by registering a callback function.

Persistent messages and message queues
If a message broker fails, all messages stored in memory for each queue are lost. To survive a broker crash, queues need to be configured as persistent (durable). This means messages are written to disk as soon as they arrive from publishers. When a broker is restarted after a crash, it recovers all persistent queues and messages. In RabbitMQ, both queues and individual messages need to be configured as persistent to provide a high level of data safety.

Consumer manual acknowledgments
A broker needs to know when it can consider a message successfully delivered to a consumer so it can remove the message from the queue. In RabbitMQ, this occurs either immediately after a message is written to a TCP socket, or when the broker receives an explicit client acknowledgment. These two modes are known as automatic and manual acknowledgments, respectively. Automatic acknowledgments risk data safety as a connection or a consumer may fail before the consumer processes the message. For data safety, it is therefore important to utilize manual acknowledgments to make sure a message has been both received and processed before it is evicted from the queue.

In a nutshell, you need publisher acknowledgments, persistent queues and messages, and manual consumer acknowledgments for complete data safety. Your system will almost certainly take a performance hit, but you won't lose messages.

Availability and Performance Trade-Offs

Another classic messaging system trade-off is between availability and performance. A single broker is a single point of failure, and hence the system will be unavailable if the broker crashes or experiences a transient network failure. The solution, as is typical for increasing availability, is broker and queue replication.

RabbitMQ provides two ways to support high availability, known as mirrored queues and quorum queues. While the details in implementation differ, the basics are the same, namely:

- Two or more RabbitMQ brokers need to be deployed and configured as a cluster.
- Each queue has a leader version, and one or more followers.
- Publishers send messages to the leader, and the leader takes responsibility for replicating each message to the followers.
- Consumers also connect to the leader, and when messages are successfully acknowledged at the leader, they are also removed from followers.
- As all publisher and consumer activity is processed by the leader, both quorum and mirrored queues enhance availability but do not support load balancing. Message throughput is limited by the performance possible for the leader replica.

There are numerous differences in the exact features (*https://oreil.ly/UNy9z*) supported by quorum and mirrored queues. The key difference, however, revolves around how messages are replicated and how a new leader is selected in case of leader failure. Quorum in this context essentially means a majority. If there are five queue replicas, then at least three replicas—the leader and two followers—need to persist a newly published message. Quorum queues implement an algorithm known as RAFT to manage replication and elect a new leader when a leader becomes available. I'll discuss RAFT in some detail in Chapter 12.

Quorum queues must be persistent and are therefore designed to be utilized in use cases when data safety and availability take priority over performance. They have other advantages over the mirrored queue implementation in terms of failure handling. For these reasons, the mirrored queue implementation will be deprecated in future versions.

Messaging Patterns

With a long history of usage in enterprise systems, a comprehensive catalog of design patterns (*https://oreil.ly/DuhYA*) exists for applications that utilize messaging. While many of these are concerned with best design practices for ease of construction and modification of systems and message security, a number apply directly to scalability in distributed systems. I'll explain three of the most commonly utilized patterns in the next sections.

Competing Consumers

A common requirement for messaging systems is to consume messages from a queue as quickly as possible. With the competing consumers pattern (*https://oreil.ly/WHatQ*), this is achieved by running multiple consumer threads and/or processes that concurrently processes messages. This enables an application to scale out message processing by horizontally scaling the consumers as needed. The general design is shown in Figure 7-7.

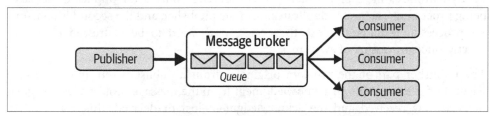

Figure 7-7. The competing consumers pattern

Using this pattern, messages can be distributed across consumers dynamically using either the push or a pull model. Using the push approach, the broker is responsible for choosing a consumer to deliver a message to. A common method, which, for example, is implemented in RabbitMQ and ActiveMQ, is a simple round-robin distribution algorithm. This ensures an even distribution of messages to consumers.

With the pull approach, consumers simply consume messages as quickly as they can process them. Assuming a multithreaded consumer, if one consumer is running on an 8-core node and another on a 2-core node, we'd expect the former would process approximately four times the amount of messages of the latter. Hence, load balancing occurs naturally with the pull approach.

There are three key advantages to this pattern, namely:

Availability
    If one consumer fails, the system remains available, and its share of messages is simply distributed to the other competing consumers.

Failure handling
> If a consumer fails, unacknowledged messages are delivered to another queue consumer.

Dynamic load balancing
> New consumers can be started under periods of high load and stopped when load is reduced, without the need to change any queue or consumer configurations.

Support for competing consumers will be found in any production-quality messaging platform. It is a powerful way to scale out message processing from a single queue.

Exactly-Once Processing

As I discussed in Chapter 3, transient network failures and delayed responses can cause a client to resend a message. This can potentially lead to duplicate messages being received by a server. To alleviate this issue, we need to put in place measures to ensure idempotent processing.

In asynchronous messaging systems, there are two sources for duplicate messages being processed. The first is duplicates from the publisher, and the second is consumers processing a message more than once. Both need to be addressed to ensure exactly-once processing of every message.

The publisher part of the problem originates from a publisher retrying a message when it does not receive an acknowledgment from the message broker. If the original message was received and the acknowledgment lost or delayed, this may lead to duplicates on the queue. Fortunately, some message brokers provide support for this duplicate detection, and thus ensure duplicates do not get published to a queue. For example, the ActiveMQ Artemis release can remove duplicates (*https://oreil.ly/ WZnGm*) that are sent from the publisher to the broker. The approach is based on the solution I described in Chapter 3, using client-generated, unique *idempotency key* values for each message. Publishers simply need to set a specific message property to a unique value, as shown in the following code:

```
ClientMessage msg = session.createMessage(true);
UUID idKey = UUID.randomUUID();  // use as idempotence key
msg.setStringProperty(HDR_DUPLICATE_DETECTION_ID, idKey.toString() );
```

The broker utilizes a cache to store idempotency key values and detect duplicates. This effectively eliminates duplicate messages from the queue, solving the first part of your problem.

On the consumer side, duplicates occur when the broker delivers a message to a consumer, which processes it and then fails to send an acknowledgment (consumer crashes or the network loses the acknowledgment). The broker therefore redelivers the message, potentially to a different consumer if the application utilizes the competing consumer pattern.

It's the obligation of consumers to guard against duplicate processing. Again, the mechanisms I described in Chapter 3, namely maintaining a cache or database of idempotency keys for messages that have been processed. Most brokers will set a message header that indicates if a message is a redelivery. This can be used in the consumer implementation of idempotence. It doesn't guarantee a consumer has seen the message already. It just tells you that the broker delivered it and the message remains unacknowledged.

Poison Messages

Sometimes messages delivered to consumers can't be processed. There are numerous possible reasons for this. Probably most common are errors in producers that send messages that cannot be handled by consumers. This could be for reasons such as a malformed JSON payload or some unanticipated state change, for example, a *StudentID* field in a message for a student who has just dropped out from the institution and is no longer active in the database. Regardless of the reason, these *poison messages* have one of two effects:

- They cause the consumer to crash. This is probably most common in systems under development and test. Sometimes, though, these issues sneak into production, when failing consumers are sure to cause some serious operational headaches.

- They cause the consumer to reject the message as it is not able to successfully process the payload.

In either case, assuming consumer acknowledgments are required, the message remains on the queue in an unacknowledged state. After some broker-specific mechanism, typically a timeout or a negative acknowledgment, the poison message will be delivered to another consumer for processing, with predictable, undesirable results.

If poison messages are not somehow detected, they can be delivered indefinitely. This at best takes up processing capacity and hence reduces system throughput. At worst it can bring a system to its knees by crashing consumers every time a poison message is received.

The solution to poison message handling is to limit the number of times a message can be redelivered. When the redelivery limit is reached, the message is automatically moved to a queue where problematic requests are collected. This queue is traditionally and rather macabrely known as the *dead-letter queue*.

As you no doubt expect by now, the exact mechanism for implementing poison message handling varies across messaging platforms. For example, Amazon Simple Queue Service (SQS) defines a policy that specifies the dead-letter queue that is associated with an application-defined queue. The policy also states after how many redeliveries a message should be automatically moved from the application queue to the dead-letter queue. This value is known as the maxReceiveCount.

In SQS, each message has a ReceiveCount attribute, which is incremented when a message is not successfully processed by a consumer. When the ReceiveCount exceeds the defined maxReceiveCount value for a queue, SQS moves the message to the dead-letter queue. Sensible values for redelivery vary with application characteristics, but a range of three to five is common.

The final part of poison message handling is diagnosing the cause for messages being redirected to the dead-letter queue. First, you need to set some form of monitoring alert that sends a notification to engineers that a message has failed processing. At that stage, diagnosis will comprise examining logs for exceptions that caused processing to fail and analyzing the message contents to identify producer or consumer issues.

Summary and Further Reading

Asynchronous messaging is an integral component of scalable system architectures. Messaging is particularly attractive in systems that experience peaks and troughs in request. During peak times, producers can add requests to queues and respond rapidly to clients, without having to wait for the requests to be processed.

Messaging decouples producers from consumers, making it possible to scale them independently. Architectures can take advantage of this by elastically scaling producers and consumers to match traffic patterns and balance message throughput requirements with costs. Message queues can be distributed across multiple brokers to scale message throughput. Queues can also be replicated to enhance availability.

Messaging is not without its dangers. Duplicates can be placed on queues, and messages can be lost if queues are maintained in memory. Deliveries to consumers can be lost, and a message can be consumed more than once if acknowledgments are lost. These data safety issues require attention to detail in design so that tolerance for duplicate messages and message loss is matched to the system requirements.

If you are interested in acquiring a broad and deep knowledge of messaging architectures and systems, the classic book *Enterprise Integration Patterns* by Gregor Hohpe and Bobby Woolf (Addison-Wesley Professional, 2003) should be your first stop. Other excellent sources of knowledge tend to be messaging platform specific, and as there are a lot of competing platforms, there's a lot of books to choose from. My favorite RabbitMQ books for general messaging wisdom and RabbitMQ-specific information are *RabbitMQ Essentials*, 2nd ed., by David Dossot and Lovisa Johansson (Packt, 2014) and *RabbitMQ in Depth* by Gavin M. Roy (Manning, 2017).

On a final note, the theme of asynchronous communications and the attendant advantages and problems will permeate the remainder of this book. Messaging is a key component of microservice-based architectures (Chapter 9) and is foundational to how distributed databases function. And you'll certainly recognize the topics of this chapter when I cover streaming systems and event-driven processing in Part IV.

CHAPTER 8

Serverless Processing Systems

Scalable systems experience widely varying patterns of usage. For some applications, load may be high during business hours and low or nonexistent during nonbusiness hours. Other applications, for example, an online concert ticket sales system, might have low background traffic 99% of the time. But when tickets for a major series of shows are released, the demand can spike by 10,000 times the average load for a number of hours before dropping back down to normal levels.

Elastic load balancing, as described in Chapter 5, is one approach for handling these spikes. Another is serverless computing, which I'll examine in this chapter.

The Attractions of Serverless

The transition of major organizational IT systems from on-premises to public cloud platforms deployments seems inexorable. Organizations from startups to government agencies to multinationals see clouds as digital transformation platforms and a foundational technology to improve business continuity.

Two of the great attractions of cloud platforms are their pay-as-you-go billing and ability to rapidly scale up (and down) virtual resources to meet fluctuating workloads and data volumes. This ability to scale, of course, doesn't come for free. Your applications need to be architected to leverage the scalable services (*https://oreil.ly/lbMBp*) provided by cloud platforms. And of course, as I discussed in Chapter 1, cost and scale are indelibly connected. The more resources a system utilizes for extended periods, the larger your cloud bills will be at the end of the month.

Monthly cloud bills can be big. Really big. Even worse, unexpectedly big! Cases of "sticker shock" for significant cloud overspend are rife—in one survey, 69% of respondents regularly overspent on their cloud budget by more than 25% (*https://oreil.ly/har0N*). In one well-known case, $500K was spent on an Azure task before it was noticed (*https://oreil.ly/flEER*). Reasons attributed to overspending are many, including lack of deployment of autoscaling solutions, poor long-term capacity planning, and inadequate exploitation of cloud architectures leading to bloated system footprints.

On a cloud platform, architects are confronted with a myriad of architectural decisions. These decisions are both broad, in terms of the overall architectural patterns or styles the systems adopts—for example, microservices, N-tier, event driven—and narrow, specific to individual components and the cloud services that the system is built upon.

In this sense, architecturally significant decisions pervade all aspects of the system design and deployment on the cloud. And the collective consequences of these decisions are highly apparent when you receive your monthly cloud spending bill.

Traditionally, cloud applications have been deployed on an infrastructure as a service (IaaS) platform utilizing virtual machines (VMs). In this case, you pay for the resources you deploy regardless of how highly utilized they are. If load increases, elastic applications can spin up new virtual machines to increase capacity, typically using the cloud-provided load balancing service. Your costs are essentially proportional to the type of VMs you choose, the duration they are deployed for, and the amount of data the application stores and transmits.

Major cloud providers offer an alternative to explicitly provisioning virtual processing resources. Known as *serverless* platforms, they do not require any compute resources to be statically provisioned. Using technologies such as AWS Lambda or Google App Engine (GAE), the application code is loaded and executed on demand, when requests arrive. If there are no active requests, there are essentially no resources in use and no charges to meet.

Serverless platforms also manage autoscaling (up and down) for you. As simultaneous requests arrive, additional processing capacity is created to handle requests and, ideally, provide consistently low response times. When request loads drop, additional processing capacity is decommissioned, and no charges are incurred.

Every serverless platform varies in the details of its implementation. For example, a limited number of mainstream programming languages and application server frameworks are typically supported. Platforms provide multiple configuration settings that can be used to balance performance, scalability and costs. In general, costs are proportional to the following factors:

- The type of processing instance chosen to execute a request
- The number of requests and processing duration for each request

- How long each application server instance remains resident on the serverless infrastructure

However, the exact parameters used vary considerably across vendors. Every platform is proprietary and different in subtle ways. The devil lurks, as usual, in the details. So, let's explore some of those devilish details specifically for the GAE and AWS Lambda platforms.

Google App Engine

Google App Engine (GAE) was the first offering from Google as part of what is now known as the Google Cloud Platform (GCP). It has been in general release since 2011 and enables developers to upload and execute HTTP-based application services on Google's managed cloud infrastructure.

The Basics

GAE supports developing applications in Go, Java, Python, Node.js, PHP, .NET, and Ruby. To build an application on GAE, developers can utilize common HTTP-based application frameworks that are built with the GAE runtime libraries provided by Google. For example, in Python, applications can utilize Flask, Django, and web2py, and in Java the primary supported platform is servlets built on the Jetty JEE web container.

Application execution is managed dynamically by GAE, which launches compute resources to match request demand levels. Applications generally access a managed persistent storage platform such as Google's Firestore (*https://oreil.ly/XWhwm*) or Google Cloud SQL (*https://oreil.ly/7boAD*), or interact with a messaging service like Google's Cloud Pub/Sub (*https://oreil.ly/T5Zn7*).

GAE comes in two flavors, known as the standard environment and the flexible environment. The basic difference is that the standard environment is more closely managed by GAE, with development restrictions in terms of language versions supported. This tight management makes it possible to scale services rapidly in response to increased loads. In contrast, the flexible environment is essentially a tailored version of Google Compute Engine (GCE), which runs applications in Docker containers (*https://www.docker.com*) on VMs. As its name suggests, it gives more options in terms of development capabilities that can be used, but is not as suitable for rapid scaling.

In the rest of this chapter, I'll focus on the highly scalable standard environment.

GAE Standard Environment

In the standard environment, developers upload their application code to a GAE project that is associated with a base project URL. This code must define HTTP endpoints that can be invoked by clients making requests to the URL. When a request is received, GAE will route it to a processing instance to execute the application code. These are known as resident instances for the application and are the major component of the cost incurred for utilizing GAE.

Each project configuration can specify a collection of parameters that control when GAE loads a new instance or invokes a resident instance. The two simplest settings control the minimum and maximum instances that GAE will have resident at any instant. The minimum can be zero, which is perfect for applications that have long periods of inactivity, as this incurs no costs.

When a request arrives and there are no resident instances, GAE dynamically loads an application instance and invokes the processing for the endpoint. Multiple simultaneous requests can be sent to the same instance, up to some configured limit (more on this when I discuss autoscaling later in this chapter). GAE will then load additional instances on demand until the specified maximum instance value is reached. By setting the maximum, an application can put a lid on costs, albeit with the potential for increased latencies if load continues to grow.

As mentioned previously, standard environment applications can be built in Go, Java, Python, Node.js, PHP, and Ruby. As GAE itself is responsible for loading the runtime environment for an application, it restricts the supported versions (*https://oreil.ly/HEoR0*) to a small number per programming language. The language used also affects the time to load a new instance on GAE. For example, a lightweight runtime environment such as Go will start on a new instance in less than a second. In comparison, a more bulky JVM is on the order of 1–3 seconds on average. This load time is also influenced by the number of external libraries that the application incorporates.

Hence, while there is variability across languages, loading new instances is relatively fast. Much faster than booting a virtual machine, anyway. This makes the standard environment extremely well suited for applications that experience rapid spikes in load. GAE is able to quickly add new resident instances as request volumes increase. Requests are dynamically routed to instances based on load, and hence assume a purely stateless application model to support effective load distribution. Subsequently, instances are released with little delay once the load drops, again reducing costs.

GAE's standard environment is an extremely powerful platform for scalable applications, and one I'll explore in more detail in the case study later in this chapter.

Autoscaling

Autoscaling is an option that you specify in an `app.yaml` file that is passed to GAE when you upload your server code. An autoscaled application is managed by GAE according to a collection of default parameter values, which you can override in your `app.yaml`. The basic scheme is shown in Figure 8-1.

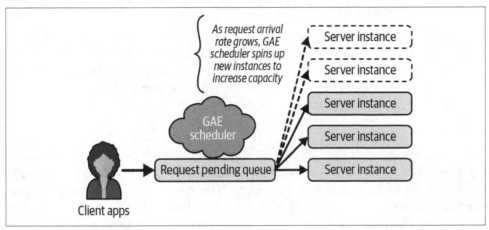

Figure 8-1. GAE autoscaling

GAE basically manages the number of deployed processing instances for an application based on incoming traffic load. If there are no incoming requests, then GAE will not schedule any instances. When a request arrives, GAE deploys an instance to process the request.

Deploying an instance can take anywhere between a few hundred ms to a few seconds depending on the programming language you are using (*https://oreil.ly/VLKTO*). This means latency can be high for initial requests if there are no resident instances. To mitigate this instance loading latency effects, you can specify a minimum number of instances to keep available for processing requests. This, of course, costs money.

As the request load grows, the GAE scheduler will dynamically load more instances to handle requests. Three parameters control precisely how scaling operates, namely:

Target CPU utilization
> Sets the CPU utilization threshold above which more instances will be started to handle traffic. The range is 0.5 (50%) to 0.95 (95%). The default is 0.6 (60%).

Maximum concurrent requests
> Sets the maximum number of concurrent requests an instance can accept before the scheduler spawns a new instance. The default value is 10, and the maximum is 80. The documentation (*https://oreil.ly/QcuzZ*) doesn't state the minimum allowed value, but presumably 1 would define a single-threaded service.

Target throughput utilization

> This is used in conjunction with the value specified for maximum concurrent requests to specify when a new instance is started. The range is 0.5 (50%) to 0.95 (95%). The default is 0.6 (60%). It works like this: when the number of concurrent requests for an instance reaches a value equal to maximum concurrent requests value multiplied by the target throughput utilization, the scheduler tries to start a new instance.

Got that? As is hopefully apparent, these three settings interact with each other, making configuration somewhat complex. By default, an instance will handle 10 × 0.6 = 6 concurrent requests before a new instance is created. And if these 6 (or fewer) requests cause the CPU utilization for an instance to go over 60%, the scheduler will also try to create a new instance.

But wait, there's more!

You can also specify values to control when GAE adds new instances based on the time requests spend in the request pending queue (see Figure 8-1) waiting to be dispatched to an instance for processing. The max-pending-latency parameter specifies the maximum amount of time that GAE should allow a request to wait in the pending queue before starting additional instances to handle requests and reduce latency. The default value is 30 ms. The lower the value, the quicker an application will scale. And the more it will probably cost you.[1]

These auto-scaling parameter settings give us the ability to fine-tune a service's behavior to balance performance and cost. How modifying these parameters will affect an application's behavior is, of course, dependent on the precise functionality of the service. The fact that there are subtle interplays between these parameters makes this tuning exercise somewhat complicated, however. I'll return to this topic in the case study section later in this chapter, and explain a simple, platform-agnostic approach you can take to service tuning.

AWS Lambda

AWS Lambda is Amazon's serverless platform. The underlying design principles and major features echo that of GAE and other serverless platforms. Developers upload code which is deployed as services known as Lambda functions. When invoked, Lambda supplies a language-specific execution environment to run the function code.

---

1 There's also an optional min-pending-latency parameter, with a default value of zero. If you are brave, how the minimum and maximum values work together is explained in this documentation (*https://oreil.ly/ GKbDR*).

A simple example of a Python Lambda function is shown in the following code. This function simply extracts a message from the input event and returns it unaltered as part of an HTTP 200 response. In general, you implement a function that takes an event and a context parameter. The event is a JSON-formatted document encapsulating data for a Lambda function to process. For example, if the Lambda function handles HTTP requests, the event will contain HTTP headers and the request body. The context contains metadata about the function and runtime environment, such as the function version number and available memory in the execution environment:

```
import json

def lambda_handler(event, context):
    event_body = json.loads(event['body'])
    response = {
        'statusCode': 200,
        'body': json.dumps({ event_body['message'] })
    }

    return response
```

Lambda functions can be invoked by external clients over HTTP. They can also be tightly integrated with other AWS services. For example, this enables Lambda functions to be dynamically triggered when new data is written to the AWS S3 storage service or a monitoring event is sent to the AWS CloudWatch service. If your application is deeply embedded in the AWS ecosystem, Lambda functions can be of great utility in designing and deploying your architecture.

Given the core similarities between serverless platforms, in this section I'll just focus on the differentiating features of Lambda from a scalability and cost perspective.

Lambda Function Life Cycle

Lambda functions can be built in a number of languages and support common service containers such as Spring for Java and Flask for Python. For each supported language, namely Node.js, Python, Ruby, Java, Go, and .NET-based code, Lambda supports a number of runtime versions. The runtime environment version is specified at deployment time along with the code, which is uploaded to Lambda in a compressed format.[2]

Lambda functions must be designed to be stateless so that the Lambda runtime environment can scale the service on demand. When a request first arrives for the API defined by the Lambda function, Lambda downloads the code for the function,

---

2 As of 2021, Lambda also supports services that are built using Docker containers. This gives the developer the scope to choose language runtime when creating the container image.

initializes a runtime environment and any instance specific initialization (e.g., creating a database connection), and finally invokes the function code handler.

This initial invocation is known as a cold start, and the time taken is dependent on the language environment selected, the size of the function code, and time taken to initialize the function. Like in GAE, lightweight languages such as Node.js and Go will typically take a few hundred milliseconds to initialize, whereas Java or .NET are heavier weight and can take a second or more.

Once an API execution is completed, Lambda can use the deployed function runtime environment for subsequent requests. This means cold start costs are not incurred. However, if a burst of requests arrive simultaneously, multiple runtime instances will be initialized, one for each request (*https://oreil.ly/0XixC*). Unlike GAE, Lambda does not send multiple concurrent requests to the same runtime instance. This means all these simultaneous requests will incur additional response times due to cold start costs.

If a new request does not arrive and a resident runtime instance is not immediately reutilized, Lambda *freezes* the execution environment. If subsequent requests arrive, the environment is *thawed* and reused. If more requests do not arrive for the function, after a platform-controlled number of minutes Lambda will deactivate a frozen instance so it does not continue to consume platform resources.[3]

Cold start costs can be mitigated by using *provisioned concurrency*. This tells Lambda to keep a minimum number of runtime instances resident and ready to process requests with no cold start overheads. The "no free lunch" principle applies of course, and charges increase based on the number of provisioned instances. You can also make a Lambda function a target of an AWS Application Load Balancer (ALB), in a similar fashion to that discussed in Chapter 5. For example, a load balancer policy that increases the provisioned concurrency for a function at a specified time, in anticipation of an increase in traffic, can be defined.

Execution Considerations

When you define a Lambda function, you specify the amount of memory that should be allocated to its runtime environment. Unlike GAE, you do not specify the number of vCPUs to utilize. Rather, the computation power is allocated in proportion to the memory specified, which is between 128 MB and 10 GB.

Lambda functions are charged for each millisecond of execution. The cost per millisecond grows with the amount of memory allocated to the runtime environment. For example, at the time of writing the costs per millisecond for a 2 GB instance are twice that of a 1 GB instance (*https://oreil.ly/dRuvn*). Lambda does not specify precisely

---

[3] This experiment (*https://oreil.ly/ziptj*) describes how long idle functions are kept resident.

how much more compute capacity this additional memory buys your function, however. Still, the larger the amount of memory allocated, then the faster your Lambda functions will likely execute.[4]

This situation creates a subtle trade-off between performance and costs. Let's examine a simple example based on the costs for 1 GB and 2 GB instances mentioned above, and assume that 1 millisecond of execution on a 1 GB instance incurs 1 mythical cost unit, and a millisecond on a 2 GB instance incurs 2 mythical cost units.

With 1 GB of memory, I'll assume this function executes in 40 milliseconds, thus incurring 40 cost units. With 2 GB of memory allocated, and commensurately more CPU allocation, the same function takes 10 milliseconds, meaning you part with 20 cost units from your AWS wallet. Hence your bills will be reduced by 50% and you will get 4x faster execution by allocating more memory to the function. Tuning can surely pay dividends.

This is obviously very dependent on the actual processing your Lambda function performs. Still, if your service is executed several billion times a month, this kind of somewhat nonintuitive tuning exercise may result in significant cost savings and greater scalability.

Finding this sweet spot that provides faster response times at similar or lower costs is a performance tuning experiment that can pay high dividends at scale. Lambda makes this a relatively straightforward experiment to perform as there is only one parameter (memory allocation) to vary. The case study later in this chapter will explain an approach that can be used for platforms such as GAE, which have multiple interdependent parameters that control scalability and costs.

Scalability

As the number of concurrent requests for a function increases, Lambda will deploy more runtime instances to scale the processing. If the request load continues to grow, Lambda reuses available instances and creates new instances as needed. Eventually, when the request load falls, Lambda scales down by stopping unused instances. That's the simple version, anyway. In reality, it is a tad more complicated.

All Lambda functions have a built-in concurrency limit for request bursts. Interestingly, this default burst limit varies depending on the AWS region where the function is deployed. For example, in US West (Oregon), a function can scale up to 3,000 instances to handle a burst of requests, whereas in Europe (Frankfurt) the limit is 1,000 instances.[5]

---

4 Per the AWS Lambda documentation (*https://oreil.ly/9mydQ*), "At 1,769 MB, a function has the equivalent of one vCPU (one vCPU-second of credits per second)."

5 Established customers can negotiate with AWS to increase these limits.

Regardless of the region, once the burst limit is reached, a function can scale at a rate of 500 instances per minute. This continues until the demand is satisfied and requests start to drop off. If the request load exceeds the capacity that can be processed by 500 additional instances per minute, Lambda throttles the function and returns an HTTP 429 to clients, who must retry the request.

This behavior is depicted in Figure 8-2. During the request burst, the number of instances grows rapidly up to the region-defined burst limit. After that, only 500 new instances can be deployed per minute. During this time, requests that cannot be satisfied by the available instances are throttled. As the request load drops, instances are removed from the platform until a steady state of traffic resumes.

Precisely how many concurrent client requests a function can handle depends on the processing time for the function. For example, assume we have 3,000 deployed instances, and each request takes on average 100 milliseconds to process. This means that each instance can process 10 requests per second, giving a maximum throughput of $(3,000 \times 10) = 30,000$ requests per second.

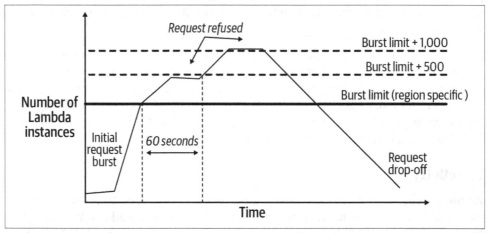

Figure 8-2. Scaling an AWS Lambda function

To complete the picture, you need to be aware that the burst concurrency limit actually applies to all functions in the region associated with a single AWS account. So, if you deploy three different Lambda functions in the same region under one account, their *collective number* of deployed instances is controlled by the burst limit that determines the scaling behavior. This means if one function is suddenly and unexpectedly heavily loaded, it can consume the burst limit and negatively impact the availability of other functions that wish to scale at the same time.

To address this potential conflict, you can fine-tune the concurrency levels associated with each individual Lambda function deployed under the same AWS account in the same region.[6] This is known as *reserved concurrency*. Each individual function can be associated with a value that is less than the burst limit.[7] This value defines the maximum number of instances of that function that can be executed concurrently.

Reserved concurrency has two implications:

- The Lambda function with reserved concurrency always has execution capacity available exclusively for its own invocations. It cannot be unexpectedly starved by concurrent invocations of other functions in the region.

- The reserved capacity caps the maximum number of resident instances for that function. Requests that cannot be processed when the number of instances is at the reserved value fail with an HTTP 429 error.

As should be apparent from this discussion, AWS Lambda provides a powerful and flexible serverless environment. With care, the runtime environment can be configured to scale effectively to handle high-volume, bursty request loads. It has become an integral part of the AWS toolbox for many organizations' internal and customer-facing applications.[8]

Case Study: Balancing Throughput and Costs

Getting the required performance and scalability at lowest cost from a serverless platform almost always requires tweaking of the runtime parameter settings. When your application is potentially processing many millions of requests per day, even a 10% cost reduction can result in significant monetary savings. Certainly, enough to make your boss and clients happy.

All serverless platforms vary in the parameter settings you can tune. Some are relatively straightforward, such as AWS Lambda in which choosing the amount of memory for a function is the dominant tuning parameter. The other extreme is perhaps Azure Functions, which has multiple parameter settings and deployment limits that differ based on which of three hosting plans are selected.[9]

GAE sits between these two, with a handful of parameters that govern autoscaling behavior. I'll use this as an example of how to approach application tuning.

---

6 Alternatively, if the Lambda usage is across different applications, it could be separated into different accounts. AWS account design and usage is, however, outside the scope of this book.

7 Actually, this maximum reserved concurrency for a function is the (Burst Limit –100). AWS reserves 100 concurrent instances for all functions that are not associated with explicit concurrency limits. This ensures that all functions have access to some spare capacity to execute.

8 See *https://oreil.ly/nVnNe* for an interesting set of curated case studies from Lambda users.

9 Scaling Azure functions is covered in the documentation (*https://oreil.ly/Uz7lX*).

Choosing Parameter Values

There are three main parameters that govern how GAE autoscales an application, as I explained earlier in this chapter. Table 8-1 lists these parameters along with possible values ranges.

Table 8-1. GAE autoscaling parameters

Parameter name	Minimum	Maximum	Default
target_throughput_utilization	0.5	0.95	0.6
target_cpu_utilization	0.5	0.95	0.6
max_concurrent_requests	1	80	10

Given these ranges, the question for a software architect is, simply, how do you choose the parameter values that provide the required performance and scalability at lowest cost? Probably the hardest part is figuring out where to start.

Even with three parameters, there is a large combination of possible settings that, potentially, interact with each other. How do you know that you have parameter settings that are serving both your users and your budgets as close to optimal as possible? There's some good general advice available (*https://oreil.ly/W2pJl*), but you are still left with the problem of choosing parameter values for your application.

For just the three parameters listed in Table 8-1, there are approximately 170K different configurations. You can't test all of them. If you put your engineering hat on, and just consider values in increments of 0.05 for throughput and CPU utilization, and increments of 10 for maximum concurrent requests, you still end up with around 648 possible configurations. That is totally impractical to explore, especially as we really don't know a priori how sensitive our service behavior is going to be to any parameter value setting. So, what can you do?

One way to approach tuning a system is to undertake a parameter study (*https://oreil.ly/l6his*). Also known as a parametric study, the approach comprises three basic steps:

- Nominate the parameters for evaluation.
- Define the parameter ranges and discrete values within those ranges.
- Analyze and compare the results of each parameter variation.

To illustrate this approach, I'll lead you through an example based on the three parameters in Table 8-1. The aim is to find the parameter settings that give ideally the highest throughput at the lowest cost. The application under test was a GAE Go service that performs reads and writes to a Google Firestore database. The application logic was straightforward, basically performing three steps:

- Input parameter validation
- Database access
- Formatting and returning results

The ratio of write to read requests was 80% to 20%, thus defining a write-heavy workload. I also used a load tester that generated an uninterrupted stream of requests from 512 concurrent client threads at peak load, with short warm-up and cooldown phases of 128 client threads.

GAE Autoscaling Parameter Study Design

For a well-defined parameter study, you need to:

- Choose the parameter ranges of interest.
- Within the defined ranges for each parameter, choose one or two intermediate values.

For the example Go application with simple business logic and database access, intuition seems to point to the default GAE CPU utilization and concurrent request settings to be on the low side. Therefore, I chose these two parameters to vary, with the following values:

```
target_cpu_utilization: {0.6, 0.7. 0.8}
max_concurrent_requests: {10, 35, 60, 80}
```

This defines 12 different application configurations, as shown by the entries in Table 8-2.

Table 8-2. Parameter study selected values

cpu_utilization				
0.6	10	35	60	80
0.7	10	35	60	80
0.8	10	35	60	80

The next step is to run load tests on each of the 12 configurations. This was straightforward and took a few hours over two days. Your load-testing tool will capture various test statistics. In this example, you are most interested in overall average throughput obtained and the cost of executing each test. The latter should be straightforward to obtain from the serverless monitoring tools available.

Now, I'll move on to the really interesting part—the results.

Results

Table 8-3 shows the mean throughput for each test configuration. The highest throughput of 6,178 requests per second is provided by the {CPU80, max10} configuration. This value is 1.7% higher than that provided by the default settings {CPU60, max10}, and around 9% higher than the lowest throughput of 5,605 requests per second. So the results show a roughly 10% variation from lowest to highest throughput. Same code. Same request load. Different configuration parameters.

Table 8-3. Mean throughput for each test configuration

Throughput	max10	max35	max60	max80
CPU60	6,006	6,067	5,860	5,636
CPU70	6,064	6,121	5,993	5,793
CPU80	6,178	5,988	5,989	5,605

Now I'll factor in cost. In Table 8-4, I've normalized the cost for each test run by the cost of the default GAE configuration {CPU60, max10}. So, for example, the cost of the {CPU70, max10} configuration was 18% higher than the default, and the cost of the {CPU80, max80} configuration was 45% lower than the default.

Table 8-4. Mean cost for each test configuration normalized to default configuration cost

Normalized instance hours	max10	max35	max60	max80
CPU60	100%	72%	63%	63%
CPU70	118%	82%	63%	55%
CPU80	100%	72%	82%	55%

There are several rather interesting observations we can make from these results:

- The default settings {CPU60, max10} give neither the highest performance nor lowest cost. This configuration makes Google happy, but maybe not your client.
- We obtain 3% higher performance with the {CPU80, max10} configuration at the same cost of the default configuration.
- We obtain marginally (approximately 2%) higher performance with 18% lower costs from the {CPU70, max35} configuration as compared to the default configuration settings.
- We obtain 96% of the default configuration performance at 55% of the costs with the {CPU70, max80} test configuration. That is a pretty decent cost saving for slightly lower throughput.

Armed with this information, you can choose the configuration settings that best balance your costs and performance needs. With multiple, dependent configuration parameters, you are unlikely to find the "best" setting through intuition and expertise. There are too many intertwined factors at play for that to happen. Parameter studies let you quickly and rigorously explore a range of parameter settings. With two or three parameters and three or four values for each, you can explore the parameter space quickly and cheaply. This enables you to see the effects of the combinations of values and make educated decisions on how to deploy your application.

Summary and Further Reading

Serverless platforms are a powerful tool for building scalable applications. They eliminate many of the deployment complexities associated with managing and updating clusters of explicitly allocated virtual machines. Deployment is as simple as developing the service's code, and uploading it to the platform along with a configuration file. The serverless platform you are using takes care of the rest.

In theory, anyway.

In practice, of course, there are important dials and knobs that you can use to tune the way the underlying serverless platforms manage your functions. These are all platform-specific, but many relate to performance and scalability, and ultimately the amount of money you pay. The case study in this chapter illustrated this relationship and provided you with an approach you can utilize to find that elusive sweet spot that provides the required performance at lower costs than the default platform parameter settings provide.

Exploiting the benefits of serverless computing requires you to buy into a cloud service provider. There are many to choose from, but all come with the attendant vendor lock-in and downstream pain and suffering if you ever decide to migrate to a new platform.

There are open source serverless platforms such as Apache OpenWhisk (*https://oreil.ly/YaXC3*) that can be deployed to on-premises hardware or cloud-provisioned virtual resources. There are also solutions such as the Serverless Framework (*https://oreil.ly/1EpoR*) that are provider-independent. These make it possible to deploy applications written in Serverless to a number of mainstream cloud providers, including all the usual suspects. This delivers code portability but does not insulate the system from the complexities of different provider deployment environments. Inevitably, achieving the required performance, scalability, and security on a new platform is not going to be a walk in the park.

A great source of information on serverless computing is Jason Katzer's *Learning Serverless* (O'Reilly, 2020). I'd also recommend two extremely interesting articles that discuss the current state of the art and future possibilities for serverless computing. These are:

- D. Taibi et al., "Serverless Computing: Where Are We Now, and Where Are We Heading?" *IEEE Software*. 38, no. 1 (Jan.–Feb. 2021): 25–31, doi: 10.1109/MS.2020.3028708.
- J. Schleier-Smith et al., "What Serverless Computing Is and Should Become: The Next Phase of Cloud Computing," *Communications of the ACM* 64, no. 5 (May 2021): 76–84.

Finally, serverless platforms are a common technology for implementing *microservices architectures*. Microservices are an architectural pattern for decomposing an application into multiple independently deployable and scalable parts. This design approach is highly amenable to a serverless-based implementation, and conveniently, is the topic we cover in the next chapter.

CHAPTER 9

Microservices

You don't often see strong links between a mainstream software architectural style and an Italian-inspired, globally popular cuisine. This is, however, the case with microservices and pizza. The roots of microservices can be traced back to around 2008 when the approach was pioneered at scale by the internet giants we all know. At Amazon, the "two-pizza rule" (*https://oreil.ly/F2xjL*) emerged as a governing principle of team size for a single system component, which subsequently became known as a microservice. What is the two-pizza rule? Very simply, every internal team should be small enough that it can be fed with two pizzas.

It is a misconception, however, that microservices are in some sense smaller than a service. The defining characteristic of a microservice (*https://oreil.ly/7e0Cj*) is their scope, organized around a business capability. Put very simply, microservices are an approach to designing and deploying fine-grained, highly cohesive, and loosely coupled services that are composed to fulfill the system's requirements. These fine-grained services, or microservices, are independently deployed and must communicate and coordinate when necessary to handle individual system requests. Hence, by their very nature, microservices architectures are distributed systems, and must deal with the various scalability, performance, and availability issues I have described in previous chapters.

Microservices are a popular, modern architectural style with plenty of engineering advantages in the right context. For example, small, agile teams with single microservice responsibilities can iterate and evolve features quickly, and deploy updated versions independently. Each microservice is a black box to the rest of the system and can choose an architecture and technology stack internally that best suits the team's and application's needs. Major new system functionalities can be built as microservices and composed into the application architecture with minimal impact on the rest of the system.

In this chapter, I'll briefly describe microservices and explain their key characteristics. I'll touch on the major engineering and architectural principles behind a microservices approach and provide pointers to excellent sources of general design knowledge. The main focus of the chapter, given the topic of this book, is the inherently distributed nature of microservices and how they behave at scale. I will describe some problems that emerge as coupled microservices are placed under load and solutions that you need to design into your architecture to build scalable, resilient applications.

The Movement to Microservices

In many ways, microservice-based architectures have benefited from a confluence of software engineering and technology innovation that has emerged over the last decade. Small, agile teams, continuous development and integration practices, and deployment technologies have collectively provided fertile ground for the fine-grained architectural approach embodied by microservices. Microservice-based architectures are a catalyst for exploiting these advances to deploy flexible, extensible, and scalable systems. Let's examine their origins and some features.

Monolithic Applications

Since the dawn of IT systems, the monolithic architectural style has dominated enterprise applications. Essentially, this style decomposes an application into multiple logical modules or services, which are built and deployed as a single application. These services offer endpoints that can be called by external clients. Endpoints provide security and input validation and then delegate the requests to shared business logic, which in turn will access a persistent store through a data access objects (DAO) layer. This design is depicted in Figure 9-1 for an example university management system that has capabilities to handle student course assignments and timetables, room scheduling, fee payments, and faculty and advisor interactions

This architecture encourages the creation of reusable business logic and DAOs that can be shared across service implementations. DAOs are mapped to database entities, and all service implementations share a single database.

Popular platforms such as IBM WebSphere and Microsoft .NET enable all the services to be built and deployed as a single executable package. This is where the term *monolith*—the complete application—originates. APIs, business logic, data access, and so forth are all wrapped up in a single deployment artifact.

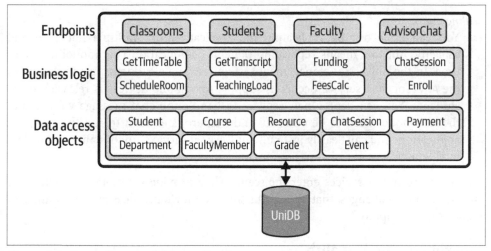

Figure 9-1. Example monolithic application

Monolithic applications, unsurprisingly given the longevity of the approach, have many advantages. The architectural approach is well understood and provides a solid foundation for new applications. It enjoys extensive automation in development frameworks in many languages. Testing is straightforward, as is deployment as there is just a single application package to manage. System and error monitoring is also simplified as the application runs on one (probably quite powerful) server.

Scaling up is the simplest way to improve responsiveness and capacity for monolithic applications. Scaling out is also possible. Two or more copies of the monolith can be provisioned, and a load balancer utilized to distribute requests. This works for both stateful and stateless services, as long as the load balancer supports session affinity for stateful designs.

Monoliths can start to become problematic as system features and request volumes grow. This problem has two fundamental elements:

Code base complexity
> As the size of the application and engineering team grows, adding new features, testing, and refactoring become progressively more difficult. Technical debt inevitably builds, and without significant investments in engineering, the code becomes more and more fragile. Engineering becomes harder without continual and concerted refactoring efforts to maintain architectural integrity and code quality. Development cadence increases for rolling out new features.

Scaling out

You can scale out by replicating the application on multiple nodes to add capacity. But this means replicating the *entire* application (the monolith) every time. In the university management system, assume a sudden spike in the use of the `AdvisorChat` service occurs as support for mobile devices is released to the students. You can deploy new replicas to handle the chat message volume, but the new nodes need to be powerful and numerous enough to run the complete application. You can't easily just pull out the chat service functionality and scale it independently.

This is where microservices enter the scene. They provide solutions to engineering and scale out challenges that monoliths almost inevitably face as the volume of requests grows rapidly.

Breaking Up the Monolith

A microservice architecture decomposes the application functionality into multiple independent services that communicate and coordinate when necessary. Figure 9-2 shows how the university management system from Figure 9-1 might be designed using microservices. Each microservice is totally self-contained, encapsulating its own data storage where needed, and offers an API for communications.

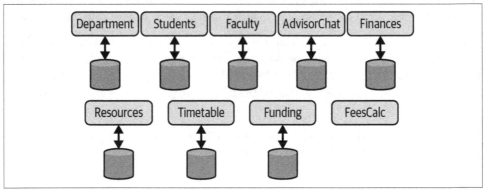

Figure 9-2. A microservice architecture example

Microservices offer the following advantages as systems grow in code size and request load:

Code base

Following the two-pizza rule, an individual service should not be more complex than a small team size can build, evolve, and manage. As a microservice is a black box, the team has full autonomy to choose their own development stack and data management platform.[1] Given the narrower, highly cohesive scope of functionality that a well-designed microservice supports, this should result in lower code complexity and higher development cadence for new features. In addition, revisions of the microservice can be independently deployed as needed. If the API the microservice supports is stable, the change is transparent to dependent services.

Scale out

Individual microservices can be scaled out to meet request volume and latency requirements. For example, to satisfy the ever-demanding and chatting students, the AdvisorChat microservice can be replicated as needed behind its own load balancer to provide low response times. This is depicted in Figure 9-3. Other services that experience light loads can simply run on a single node or be replicated at low cost to eliminate single points of failure and enhance availability.

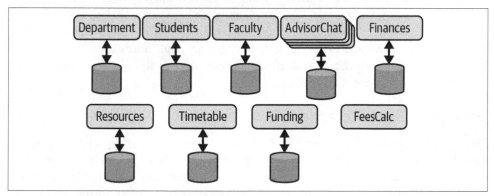

Figure 9-3. Independently scaling a microservice

One of the key design decisions when moving to a microservices architecture is how to decompose the system functionality into individual services. Domain-driven design (DDD) (*https://oreil.ly/cS9GJ*) provides a suitable method for identifying microservices, as the necessarily self-contained nature of microservices maps well to the notion of bounded contexts in DDD. These topics are beyond the scope of this chapter but are essential knowledge for architects of microservice-based applications.

There is always a balancing act though. Microservices are by their very nature distributed. Often, the purity of the domain model needs to be analyzed and adjusted to meet the reality of the costs of distributed communications and the complexity of system management and monitoring. You need to factor in request loads and the

---

1 Standardization of the development stack across microservices does, of course, have advantages, as Susan Fowler explains in *Production-Ready Microservices* (O'Reilly, 2016).

interactions needed to serve these requests, so that excessive latencies aren't incurred by multiple interactions between microservices.

For example, `Faculty` and `Funding` are excellent candidates for microservices. However, if satisfying requests such as "get funding by faculty" or "find funding opportunities for faculty" incur excessive communications, performance and reliability could be impacted. Merging microservices may be a sensible option in such circumstances. Another common approach is to duplicate data across coupled microservices. This enables a service to access the data it needs locally, simplifying the design and reducing data access response times.

Duplicate data is, of course, a trade-off. It takes additional storage capacity and development effort to ensure all duplicated data converges to a consistent state. Duplicate data updates can be initiated immediately when data changes to attempt to minimize the time interval that the duplicates are inconsistent. Alternatively, if the business context allows, periodic duplication (e.g., hourly or daily) can operate, perhaps executed by a scheduled task that is invoked when request loads are low. As the demands on performance and scalability on an application grow, the cost and complexity of duplicate data is typically small compared to the problems that a major refactoring of the system would present.

Deploying Microservices

To support frequent updates and benefit from the agility afforded by small teams, you need to be able to deploy new microservice versions easily and quickly. This is where we start to infringe on the world of continuous deployment and DevOps, which is way beyond the scope of this book (see "Summary and Further Reading" on page 180 for reading recommendations). Still, deployment options impinge on the ease of scalability for a microservice. I'll just describe one common approach for deploying microservices in this section.

Serverless processing platforms, as I described in Chapter 8, are an attractive microservices deployment approach. A microservice can be built to expose its API on the serverless platform of your choice. The serverless option has three advantages:

Deployment is simple
> Just upload the new executable package for your microservice to the endpoint you have configured for your function.

Pay by usage
> If your service has periods of low-volume requests, your costs are low, even zero.

Ease of scaling
> The platform you choose handles scaling of your function. You control precisely how this works through configuration parameters, but the serverless option takes the heavy lifting out of scalability.

When you deploy all your microservices on a serverless platform, you expose multiple endpoints that clients need to invoke. This introduces complexity as clients need to be able to discover the location (host IP address and port) of each microservice. What if you decide to refactor your microservices by perhaps combining two in or order to eliminate network calls? Or move an API implementation from one microservice to another? Or even change the endpoint (IP address and port) of an API?

Exposing backend changes directly to clients is never a good idea. The Gang of Four book taught us this many years ago with the façade pattern in object-oriented systems.[2] In microservices, you can exploit an analogous approach using the API gateway pattern (*https://oreil.ly/7aJ7h*). An API gateway essentially acts as a single entry point for all client requests, as shown in Figure 9-4. It insulates clients from the underlying architecture of the microservices that implement the application functionality. Now, if you refactor your underlying APIs or even choose to deploy on a radically different platform such as a private cloud, clients are oblivious to changes.

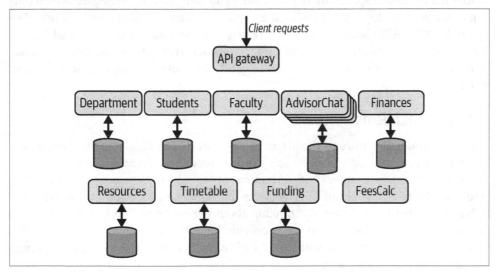

Figure 9-4. The API gateway pattern

There are multiple API gateway implementations you can exploit in your systems. These range from powerful open source solutions such as the NGINX Plus (*https://oreil.ly/8JXlJ*) and Kong (*https://oreil.ly/2fcNb*) API gateways to cloud vendor–specific managed offerings. The general range of functions, listed as follows, is similar:

- Proxy incoming client API requests with low millisecond latencies to backend microservices that implement the API. Mapping between client-facing APIs,

---

2 Erich Gamma et al., *Design Patterns: Elements of Reusable Object-Oriented Software* (Addison Wesley Professional, 1994).

handled by the API gateway, and backend microservice APIs is performed through admin tools or configuration files. Capabilities and performance vary across products, sometimes quite significantly, especially under high request loads.[3]

- Provide authentication and authorization for requests.

- Define rules for throttling each API. Setting the maximum number of requests a microservice can handle per second can be used to ensure backend processing is not overwhelmed.

- Support a cache for API results so that requests can be handled without invoking backend services.

- Integrate with monitoring tools to support analysis of API usage, latencies, and error metrics.

Under heavy request spikes, there is, of course, the danger of the API gateway becoming a bottleneck. How this is handled by your API gateway is product-specific. For example, AWS API Gateway has a 10K requests per second limit, with an additional burst quota of up to 5K requests/second.[4] The Kong API gateway is stateless, hence it is possible to deploy multiple instances and distribute the requests using a load balancer.

Principles of Microservices

There's considerably more to the art and science of designing, deploying, and evolving microservices-based architectures. I've just scratched the surface in the discussions so far in this chapter. Before I move on to address some of the scalability and availability challenges of microservices that must be addressed due to their distributed nature, it's worth briefly thinking about the core principles of microservices as defined by Sam Newman in his excellent *Building Microservices* book (O'Reilly, 2015). I've listed them here with some additional commentary alluding to performance and scalability aspects.

Microservices should be:

Modeled around a business domain
  The notion of bounded contexts provides a starting point for the scope of a microservice. Business domain boundaries may need rethinking in the context

---

3 An excellent NGINX study (*https://oreil.ly/sBNNM*) benchmarks the performance of API gateways. It is performed by one of the vendors, so a hint of caution in interpreting results is required. Studies like this are valuable in assessing potential solutions.

4 This limit can be increased (*https://oreil.ly/GzaL7*).

---

of coupling between microservices and the performance overheads it may introduce.

Highly observable

Monitoring of each service is essential to ensure they are behaving as expected, processing requests with low latencies, and error conditions are logged. In distributed systems, observability is an essential characteristic for effective operations.

Hide implementation details

Microservices are black boxes. Their API is a contract which they are guaranteed to support, but how this is carried out is not exposed externally. This gives freedom for each team to choose development stacks that can be optimized to the requirements of the microservice.

Decentralize all the things

One thing to decentralize is the processing of client requests that require multiple calls to downstream microservices. These are often called workflows. There are two basic approaches to achieving this, namely orchestration and choreography. "Workflows" on page 171 describes these topics.

Isolate failure

The failure of one microservice should not propagate to others and bring down the application. The system should continue to operate, although probably with some degraded service quality. Much of the rest of this chapter addresses this principle specifically.

Deploy independently

Every microservice should be independently deployable, to enable teams to roll out enhancements and modifications without any dependency on the progress of other teams.

Culture of automation

Development and DevOps tooling and practices are absolutely essential to gain the benefits of microservices. Automation makes it faster and more robust to make changes to the deployed system frequently. This frequency may be, for example, hourly or daily, depending on the system and the pace of development.

Workflows

Orchestration and choreography are commonly used for implementing use cases that require access to more than one microservice (e.g., in Figure 9-4). A faculty member may wish to get a list of the classes they are teaching in a semester and the resources available for audio-visual within each classroom they have been allocated to. Implementing this use case requires access to the *Faculty*, *Timetable*, and *Resources* microservices.

There are two basic approaches to implement this workflow:

Peer-to-peer choreography
> The required microservices communicate directly to satisfy the request. This shares the responsibility and knowledge of processing the workflow across each autonomous microservice. Communications may be synchronous or utilize an asynchronous, typically publish–subscribe approach.

Centralized orchestration
> The logic to implement the workflow is embedded in a single component, often a dedicated microservice. This communicates with the domain services and sends the results back to the user.

There are trade-offs with both approaches. For example, orchestration makes it simpler to monitor the progress of a request as the logic is in one place. It may, however, create bottlenecks if the request load is high, and you must be careful to ensure the orchestrator doesn't become a single point of failure.

A good discussion of these trade-offs can be found on page 256 of *The Fundamentals of Software Architecture* book (*https://oreil.ly/82uJo*) I recommended in Chapter 1. An excellent example of these trade-offs and solutions at scale is Netflix's Conductor (*https://oreil.ly/D2Px6*) orchestration engine.

Resilience in Microservices

One of the frequently unstated truisms of distributed systems is that, for the vast amount of the time, systems operate without catastrophic errors. Networks are fast and reliable, machines and disks rarely crash, the foundational platforms you use for hosting microservices and messaging and databases are incredibly robust. This is especially true when systems are handling low request volumes, and have plenty of CPU, memory, and network bandwidth to keep their users extremely happy. Of course, your system still has to be prepared for intermittent failures that will occur, usually at the most inconvenient of times!

Things start to get really fun when request frequencies and volumes increase. Threads contend for processing time, memory becomes scarce, network connections become saturated, and latencies increase. This is when individual microservices start behaving unpredictably. Then, all bets are off.

To ensure your systems don't fail suddenly as loads increase, there are a number of necessary precautions you need to take. I'll explain the nature of the problems that you need to be aware of, and the solutions available, in the following subsections.

Cascading Failures

Figure 9-5 depicts a simple microservices architecture. A request arrives at microservice A. To process this request, it calls microservice B, which in turn calls microservice C. Once microservice C responds, B can return the results to A, which in turn can respond to the client. The numbers in the figure represent this sequence for an individual request.

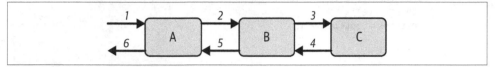

Figure 9-5. Microservices with dependencies

Now I'll assume that the request load on microservice A grows. This means A will exert more load on B, which will in turn exert more load on C. For some reason, such as lack of processing capacity or database contention, this causes the response times from microservice C to increase, which creates back pressure on B and causes it to respond more slowly to A.

If the increased load is sustained for a period of time, threads in the microservices A and B are blocked waiting for requests to be handled by downstream processing. Let's assume microservice C becomes overloaded—perhaps the request pattern causes database deadlocks on frequently updated keys, or the network connection to C's database becomes unstable. In an overloaded state, response times increase and B's threads become blocked waiting for results. Remember from Chapter 2, application servers have fixed-size thread pools. Once all threads in B are occupied making calls to C, if requests continue to arrive at high volumes, they will be queued until a thread is available. Response times from B to A start to grow, and in an instant all of A's threads will be blocked waiting for B to respond.

At this stage, things will likely start to break. TCP requests will time out and throw an error to the caller. New connections will be refused as the dependent service is overloaded. Microservices may fail if memory is exhausted, or the increased load uncovers subtle bugs that weren't revealed during testing. These errors ripple, or cascade back through the call chain. In the example in Figure 9-5, the slow responses from C can cause requests to A and B to fail.

The insidious nature of cascading failures is that they are triggered by slow response times of dependent services. If a downstream service simply fails or is unavailable due to a system crash or transient network failure, the caller gets an error immediately and can respond accordingly. This is not the case with services that gradually slow down. Requests return results, just with longer response times. If the overwhelmed component continues to be bombarded with requests, it has no time to recover and response times continue to grow.

This situation is often exacerbated by clients that, upon request failure, immediately retry the operation, as illustrated in the following code snippet:

```
int retries = RETRY_COUNT;
while (retries > 0) {
   try {
       callDependentService();
       return true;
     } catch (RemoteCallException ex) {
        logError(e);
        retries = retries - 1;
   }
   return false;
```

Immediate retries simply maintain the load on the overwhelmed microservice, with very predictable results, namely another exception. Overload situations don't disappear in a few milliseconds. In fact, they are likely to persist for many seconds or even minutes. Retries just keep the pressure on.

The retry example can be improved by techniques such as exponential backoff (*https://oreil.ly/CzCdE*), namely inserting a growing delay between retries. This potentially can help relieve the downstream overload, but the delay becomes part of the latency experienced by the caller, which often doesn't help matters.

Cascading failures are common in distributed systems. Whether caused by overwhelmed services, or error conditions such as bugs or network problems, there are explicit steps you need to take to guard against them.

Fail fast pattern

The core problem with slow services is that they utilize system resources for requests for extended periods. A requesting thread is stalled until it receives a response. For example, let's assume we have an API that normally responds within 50 ms. This means each thread can process around 20 requests per second. If one request is stalled for 3 seconds due to an outlier response time, then that's $(3 \times 20) - 1 = 59$ requests that could have been processed.

Even with the best designed APIs for a microservice, there will be outlier responses. Real workloads exhibit a long-tail response time profile, as illustrated in Figure 9-6. A small number of requests takes significantly longer—sometimes 20 or a 100 times more—than the average response time. This can be for a number of reasons. Garbage collection in the server, database contention, excessive context switching, system page faults, and dropped network requests are all common causes for this long tail.

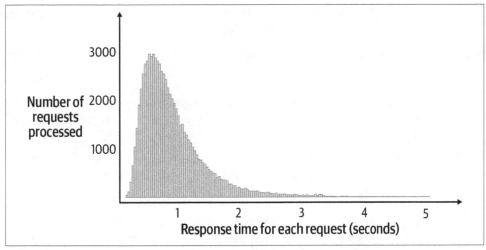

Figure 9-6. Typical long-tail response time

As you can observe from this graph, the vast majority of requests have low response times, which is great. However, a significant number are over one second and a small number much, much slower—over 4 seconds, in fact.

We can quantify the percentage of slow requests using percentiles. Percentiles give a far richer and more accurate view of response times from a microservice than averages. For example, if we measure response times and calculate percentiles under expected loads, we may get the following:

P50: 200 milliseconds
P95: 1,200 milliseconds
P99: 3,000 milliseconds

This means that 50% of requests are served in less than 200 milliseconds, 95% are served within 1,200 milliseconds, and 99% percent within 3,000 milliseconds. These numbers in general look pretty good. But let's assume our API handles 200 million requests per day (approximately 2,314 requests per second). This means 1%, or 2 million requests, take greater than 3 seconds, which is 15 times slower than the 50th percentile (the median). And some requests will be significantly longer than 3 seconds given the long-tail response time pattern we see in Figure 9-6.

Long response times are never good things, technically or for client engagement. In fact, many studies have shown how longer response times have negative effects on system usage. For example, the BBC reported (*https://oreil.ly/A6atg*) that it sees 10% less users for every additional second a page takes to load. Fast, stable response times are great for business, and one way to achieve this is to reduce the long tail. This also has the effect of decreasing the overall average response time for a service, as the average is skewed heavily by a small number of slow responses.

A common way to eliminate long response times is to fail fast. There are two main ways (*https://oreil.ly/qwUcg*) to achieve this:

- When a request takes longer than some predefined time limit, instead of waiting for it to complete, the client returns an error to its caller. This releases the thread and other resources associated with the request.
- Enable throttling on a server. If the request load exceeds some threshold, immediately fail the request with an HTTP 503 error. This indicates to the client that the service is unavailable.

Exactly how these strategies are put into action is extremely technology-specific. For example, a client making an HTTP request can configure the TCP read timeout (*https://oreil.ly/CGEg2*). This specifies how long a client should wait for to receive a response from the server. In our example in Figure 9-6, we could configure the read timeout to the P99 value, namely 3 seconds or a little higher. Then, if a client hasn't received any response within the read timeout period, an exception is raised. In Java, it's a `java.net.SocketTimeoutException`.

Throttling, or rate limiting, is a feature available in many load balancers and API gateway technologies. When some defined limits are reached, the load balancer will simply reject requests, protecting the resources it controls from overload. This enables the service to process requests with consistent low response times. It's also possible to implement some lightweight monitoring logic inside your microservice to implement throttling. You might keep a count of in-flight requests, and if the count exceeds a defined maximum, new requests are rejected. A slightly more sophisticated approach could track a metric like the average response time, or P99s, using a sliding window algorithm. If the metric of interest is increasing, or exceeds some defined threshold, again requests can be immediately rejected.

There's one more thing to consider when failing requests. A principle of microservices is fault isolation. This means the failure of part of the system doesn't make the whole application unavailable. Requests can continue to be processed, but with some degraded capabilities.

A key thing to consider is whether it is necessary to propagate the error back to the original caller. Or can some canned, default response be sent that masks the fact that the request was not correctly processed? For example, when you sign into a streaming video service, the first page will show your watchlist so you can return to your favorite shows as quickly as possible. If, however, the request to retrieve your watchlist fails, or takes too long, a default collection of popular "shows you might like" can be returned. The application is still available.

This approach works really well for transient, ephemeral failures. By the time the request is issued again by the users, the problem will probably be resolved. And there's a good chance the user won't even have noticed. Some transient errors, however, don't resolve in a second or two. That's when you need a more robust approach.

Circuit breaker pattern

If a microservice starts to throw errors due to an overload situation, or a flaky network, it makes little sense to keep trying to send requests to the API. Rather than failing fast, which still incurs a timeout delay, it is better to back off immediately from sending further requests and allow some time for the error situation to resolve. This can be achieved using the circuit breaker pattern, which protects remote endpoints from being overwhelmed when some error conditions occur.

Just like in electrical systems, clients can use a circuit breaker to protect a server from overload. The circuit breaker is configured to monitor some condition, such as error response rates from an endpoint, or the number of requests sent per second. If the configured threshold is reached—for example, 25% of requests are throwing errors—the circuit breaker is triggered. This moves the circuit breaker into an OPEN state, in which all calls return with an error immediately, and no attempt is made to call the unstable or unavailable endpoint.

The circuit breaker then rejects all calls until some suitably configured timeout period expires. At that stage, the circuit breaker moves to the HALF_OPEN state. Now, the circuit breaker allows client calls to be issued to the protected endpoint. If the requests still fail, the timeout period is reset and the circuit breaker stays open. However, if the request succeeds, the circuit breaker transitions to the CLOSED state and requests start to flow to the target endpoint. This scheme is illustrated in Figure 9-7.

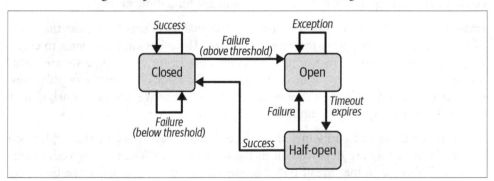

Figure 9-7. Circuit breaker pattern

Circuit breakers are essential to reduce the resources utilized for operations that are almost certain to fail. The client fails fast, and the OPEN circuit breaker relieves load on an overwhelmed server by ensuring requests do not reach it. For overloaded services, this creates an opportunity to stabilize. When the service (hopefully) recovers, the circuit breaker resets automatically and normal operations resume.

There are numerous libraries available for incorporating circuit breakers into your applications. One popular library for Python, CircuitBreaker (*https://oreil.ly/mZJiw*), is illustrated in the following code example. You simply decorate the external call you want to protect with @circuit, and specify the value of the parameters you wish to set to customize the circuit breaker behavior. In this example, we trigger the circuit breaker after 20 successive failures are detected, and the circuit breaker stays open for 5 seconds until it transitions to the half open state:

```
from circuitbreaker import circuit

@circuit(failure_threshold=20,expected_exception=RequestException,
        recovery_timeout=5)
def api_call():
```

Circuit breakers are highly effective for fault isolation. They protect clients from faulty operations of dependent services and allow services to recover. In read-heavy scenarios, requests can often return default or cached results when the circuit breaker is open. This effectively hides the fault from clients and doesn't degrade service throughput and response times. Ensure you tie circuit breaker triggers into your monitoring and logging infrastructure so that the cause of faults can be diagnosed.

Bulkhead Pattern

The term bulkhead is inspired by large shipbuilding practices. Internally the ship is divided into several physical partitions, ensuring if a leak occurs in one part of the boat's hull, only a single partition is flooded and the boat, rather importantly, continues to float. Basically, bulkheads are a damage limitation strategy.

Imagine a microservice with two endpoints. One enables clients to request the status of their current orders placed through the service. The other enables clients to create new orders for products. In normal operations, the majority of requests are status requests, entailing a fast cache or database read. Occasionally, when a popular new product is released, a flood of new order requests can arrive simultaneously. These are much more heavyweight, requiring database inserts and writes to queues.

Requests for these two endpoints share a common thread pool in the application server platform they are deployed on in the microservice. When a new order surge arrives, all threads in the thread pool become occupied by new order creations and status requests are essentially starved from gaining resources. This leads to unacceptable response times and potentially client calls seeing exceptions if a fail fast approach is used.

Bulkheads help us solve this problem. We can reserve a number of threads in a microservice to handle specific requests. In our example, we could specify that the new order request has a maximum of 150 threads of the shared thread pool available for its exclusive use. This ensures that when a new order request burst occurs, we can still handle status requests with acceptable response times because there is additional capacity in the thread pool.

The Java Resilience4j library (*https://oreil.ly/UeMAA*) provides an implementation of the bulkhead pattern using the functional programming features of Java 8 onward. The bulkhead pattern segregates remote resource calls in their own thread pools so that a single overloaded or failing service does not consume all threads available in the application server.

The following example code shows how to create a bulkhead that allows a maximum of 150 concurrent requests. If 150 threads are in use for the service that you wish to restrict with the bulkhead, requests will wait a maximum of 1 second before the default BulkheadFullException exception is thrown:

```
// configure the bulkhead
BulkheadConfig config = BulkheadConfig.custom()
            .maxConcurrentCalls(150)
            .maxWaitDuration(Duration.ofSeconds(1))
            .build();
BulkheadRegistry registry = BulkheadRegistry.of(config);
// create the bulkhead
Bulkhead newOrderBulkhead = registry.bulkhead("newOrder");
```

Next, you specify that the OrderService.newOrder() method should be decorated with the bulkhead. This ensures that a maximum of 150 invocations of this method can occur concurrently:

```
// decorate the OrderService.newOrder method with the bulkhead
Supplier<OrderOutcome> orderSupplier = () ->
    OrderService.newOrder(OrderInfo);
// decorate NewOrder with the bulkhead configuration
Supplier<OrderOutcome> bukheadOrderSupplier =
    bulkhead.decorateSupplier(bulkhead, orderSupplier);
```

Spring-boot simplifies the creation of a bulkhead using its dependency injection capabilities. You can specify the configuration of the bulkhead in the applica tion.yml file, shown as follows:

```
server:
  tomcat:
    threads:
      max: 200
resilience4j.bulkhead:
  instances:
    OrderService:
      maxConcurrentCalls: 150
      maxWaitDuration: 1000ms
```

In the code, you simply use the `@Bulkhead` decorator to specify the method that should be subject to the bulkhead behavior. In the following example, a fallback method is also specified. This will be invoked when the bulkhead capacity is reached, and requests wait for more than 1 second:

```
@Bulkhead(name = "OrderService", fallbackMethod = "newOrderBusy")
    public OrderOutcome newOrder(OrderInfo inf){// details omitted}
```

In the Wild: Scaling Microservices

Amazon and Netflix were among the early pioneers, around 2009, of microservice-based architectures at scale. Since then, much has been learned, and of course the scale of the systems built on microservices has grown incredibly. To deal with modern systems scale, Uber has evolved its microservice architecture to be based around collections of related services, known as domains, as described in this excellent technical blog post (*https://oreil.ly/XXW1J*).

Sam Newton's book chapter "Microservices at Scale" (*https://oreil.ly/sBR7Z*) includes a case study that illustrates the importance of the fail fast, circuit breaker, and bulkhead patterns. It is a forensic description of how cascading failures occur when slow service responses are encountered.

Finally, it should be emphasized that sometimes microservices are not always the right approach. A case study (*https://oreil.ly/rKMc1*) describing how the benefits of microservices added unnecessary complexity at Istio is well worth a read.

Summary and Further Reading

Embracing microservices requires you to adopt new design and development practices to create a collection of fine-grained, cohesive components to satisfy your application requirements. In addition, you also need to confront the new opportunities and complexities of distributed systems. If you adopt microservices, you simply have no choice.

This chapter has given a brief overview of the motivations for microservices and the advantages they can afford. In the context of this book, the ability to independently scale individual microservices to match increasing demand is often invaluable.

Microservices are frequently coupled, needing to communicate to satisfy a single request. This makes them susceptible to cascading failures. These occur when a microservice starts to return requests with increasing response times—caused, for example, by an overload in requests or transient network errors. Slow response times cause back pressure in the calling services, and eventually a failure in one can cause all dependent services to crash.

Patterns for avoiding cascading failures include failing fast using timeouts and circuit breakers. These essentially give the stressed microservice time to recover and stop cascading failures from occurring. The bulkhead pattern is similar in intent. It can be used to ensure requests to one API in a microservice don't utilize all available resources during a request burst. By setting a maximum limit on the number of threads in the application server a particular API can demand, processing capacity for other APIs can be guaranteed.

Microservices are a major topic in software architecture. For a complete and comprehensive coverage of the topic, there is no better source than Sam Newman's *Building Microservices*, 2nd Edition (O'Reilly, 2021). This will take you on an in-depth journey following the design, development, and deployment of microservices-based systems.

Microservices require extensive automation of the development process. The 2011 classic *Continuous Delivery: Reliable Software Releases through Build, Test, and Deployment Automation* by Jez Humble and David Farley (Addison-Wesley Professional) is an ideal place to start for a comprehensive introduction to the topic. Another excellent source of information is *DevOps: A Software Architect's Perspective* by Len Bass, Ingo Weber, and Liming Zhu (Addison-Wesley Professional, 2015). The world of DevOps is a fast-moving and technologically rich domain, and your favorite search engine is the best place to find information on the various build, configuration, test, deployment, and monitoring platforms that comprise modern DevOps pipelines.

Next, Part III of this book focuses on the topic of the storage layer. I'll be describing the core principles and algorithms that determine how we can distribute data stores to achieve scalability, availability, and consistency. The theory will be complemented by examining how a number of widely used databases operate in distributed systems, and the various approaches and architectural trade-offs they take.

Scalable Distributed Databases

Part III takes us into the complex realm of scaling the data tier. This is where distributed systems theory is most prominent. As systems introduce data replicas to facilitate scalability, other system qualities such as availability and especially consistency must be addressed—these qualities are indelibly entwined in distributed data systems. I'll motivate the need for the algorithms that make distributed databases function and sketch out some of the algorithms that are utilized. I'll then illustrate how these algorithms are manifested in major distributed databases including MongoDB, Google Cloud Spanner, and Amazon DynamoDB.

CHAPTER 10

Scalable Database Fundamentals

In the early 2000s, the world of databases was a comparatively calm and straightforward place. There were a few exceptions, but the vast majority of applications were built on relational database technologies. Systems leveraged one of a handful of relational databases from the major vendors, and these still dominate the top ten spots in database market share ranking today (*https://oreil.ly/sa8qD*).

If you could jump into a time machine and look at a similar ranking from 2001, you'd probably find 7 of the current top 10—all relational databases—in similar places to the ones they occupy in 2022. But if you examine the top 20 in 2022, at least 10 of the current database engines listed did not exist 20 years ago, and most of these are not relational. The market has expanded and diversified.

This chapter is the first of four in Part III that focuses on the data—or persistent storage—tier. I'll cover the ever-changing and evolving scalable database landscape, including distributed nonrelational and relational approaches, and the fundamental approaches that underpin these technologies.

In this chapter, I'll explain how traditional relational databases have evolved to adopt distributed architectures to address scalability. I'll then introduce some of the main characteristics of the new generation of databases that have emerged to natively support distribution. Finally, I'll describe the architectures utilized for distributing data across multiple database nodes and the trade-offs inherent with these approaches regardless of the data models they support.

Distributed Databases

The data systems we build today dwarf those of 20 years ago, when relational databases ruled the earth. This growth in data set size and complexity has been driven by internet-scale applications. These create and manage vast quantities of heterogeneous data for literally tens of millions of users. This includes, for example, user profiles, user preferences, behavioral data, images and videos, sales data, advertising, sensor readings, monitoring data, and much more. Many data sets are simply far too big to fit on a single machine.

This has necessitated the evolution of database engines to manage massive collections of distributed data. New generations of relational and nonrelational database platforms have emerged, with a wide range of competing capabilities aimed at satisfying different use cases and scalability requirements. Simultaneously, the development of low-cost, powerful hardware has made it possible to cost-effectively distribute data across literally hundreds or even thousands of nodes and disks. This enhances both scalability and, by replicating data, availability.

Another major driver of database engine innovation has been the changing nature of the application requirements that populate the internet today. The inherent strengths of relational databases, namely transactions and consistency, come at a performance cost that is not always justified in sites like Twitter and Facebook. These don't have requirements for every user to always see the same version of, for example, my tweets or timeline updates. Who cares if the latest photo of my delicious dinner is seen immediately by some of my followers and friends, while others have to wait a few seconds to admire the artful dish I'm consuming?

With tens of thousands to millions of users, it is possible to relax the various data constraints that relational databases support and attain enhanced performance and scalability. This enables the creation of new, nonrelational data models and natively distributed database engines, designed to support the variety of use cases for today's applications. There are trade-offs, of course. These manifest themselves in the range of features a database supports and the complexity of its programming model.

Scaling Relational Databases

Databases that support the relational model and SQL query language represent some of the most mature, stable, and powerful software platforms that exist today. You'll find relational databases lurking behind systems in every type of application domain you can imagine. They are incredibly complex and amazingly successful technologies.

Relational database technology was designed and matured when data sets were relatively small by today's standards, and the database could run on a single machine. As data sets have grown, approaches to scale databases have emerged. I'll briefly cover these with some examples in the following subsections.

Scaling Up

Relational databases were designed to run on a single machine, which enables shared memory and disks to be exploited to store data and process queries. This makes it possible for database engines to be customized to run on machines with multiple CPUs, disks, and large shared memories. Database engines can exploit these resources to execute many thousands of queries in parallel to provide extremely high throughput.

Figure 10-1 depicts the scale-up scenario. The database is migrated to new, more powerful (virtual) hardware. While there is database administration magic to perform the migration and tune the database configuration to effectively exploit the new resources, the application code should require no changes.

There are three main downsides to this approach:

Cost
 Hardware costs tend to grow exponentially as the computational resources offered grow.

Availability
 You still have a single database node, albeit a powerful one. If it becomes unavailable, your system is down. A multitude of high availability (HA) solutions exist that offer mechanisms to detect unavailability and failover to a backup copy of the database. Many HA solutions are database vendor dependent.

Growth
 If your database continues to grow, another migration to more powerful hardware is inevitable.

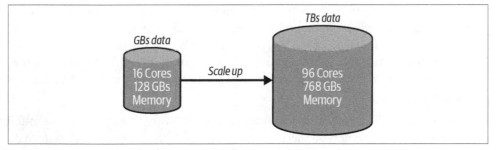

Figure 10-1. Example of a relational database scale-up scenario

Scaling up is indeed attractive in many applications. Still, in high-volume applications, there are two common scenarios in which scaling up becomes problematic. First, the database grows to exceed the processing capability of a single node. Second, low latency database accesses are required to service clients spread around the globe. Traversing intercontinental networks just doesn't cut it.

In both cases, distributing a database is necessary.

Scaling Out: Read Replicas

A common first step to increasing a database's processing capacity is to scale out using read replicas. You configure one or more nodes as read replicas of the main database. The main database node is known as the primary, and read replicas are known as secondaries. The secondaries maintain a copy of the main database. Writes are only possible to the primary, and all changes are then asynchronously replicated to secondaries. Secondaries may be physically located in different data centers or different continents to support global clients.

This architecture is shown in Figure 10-2.

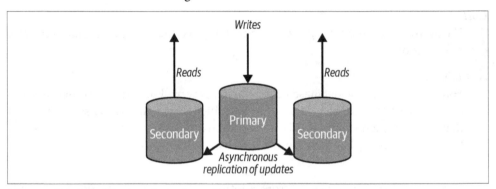

Figure 10-2. Distribution through read replication

This approach enhances scalability by directing all reads to the read replicas.[1] It is hence highly effective for applications that must support read-heavy workloads. Reads can be scaled by adding more secondaries, reducing the load on the primary. This enables it to more efficiently handle writes. In addition, if the primary becomes unavailable due to a transient failure, read requests directed to secondaries are not interrupted.

As there is a delay between when data is written to the primary and then successfully replicated to the secondaries, there is a chance that clients may read stale data from secondaries. Application must therefore be aware of this possibility. In normal operations, the time between updating the primary and the secondaries should be small, for example, a few milliseconds. The smaller this time window, then the less chance there is of a stale read.

Read replication and primary/secondary–based database architectures are topics I'll return to in much more detail in this and the following chapters.

---

1 The primary can typically be configured to handle reads as well as writes. This is all highly application-dependent.

Scale Out: Partitioning Data

Splitting up, or partitioning data in a relational database, is a technique for distributing the database over multiple independent disk partitions and database engines. Precisely how partitioning is supported is highly product-specific. In general, there are two strategies: horizontal partitioning and vertical partitioning.

Horizontal partitioning splits a logical table into multiple physical partitions. Individual rows are allocated to a partition based on some partitioning strategy. Common partitioning strategies are to allocate rows to partitions based on some value in the row, or to use a hash function on the primary key. As shown in Figure 10-3, you can allocate a row to a partition based on the value of the *region* field in each row.

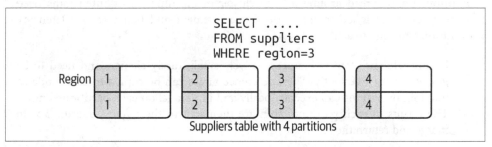

Figure 10-3. Horizontal database partitioning

Vertical partitioning, also known as row splitting, partitions a table by the columns in a row. Like normalization, vertical partitioning splits a row into one or more parts, but for the reasons of physical rather than conceptual optimization. A common strategy is to partition a row between static, read-only data and dynamic data. Figure 10-4 shows a simple vertical partitioning for an inventory system that employs this scheme.

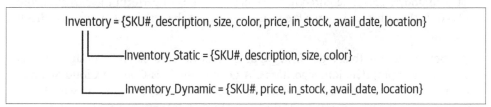

Figure 10-4. Vertical database partitioning

Relational database engines will have various levels of support for data partitioning. Some facilitate partitioning tables on disk. Others support partitioning data across nodes to scale horizontally in a distributed system.

Regardless, the very nature of relational schemas, with data split across multiple tables, makes it problematic to devise a general partitioning strategy for distribution. Horizontal partitions of data ideally distribute tables across multiple nodes. However, if a single request needs to access data from multiple nodes, or join data from distributed partitioned tables, a high level of network traffic and request coordination is required. This may not give the performance benefits you expect. These issues are briefly covered in the following sidebar.

Distributed Joins

SQL joins are complex to implement in distributed relational databases. The longevity of SQL engines means they are highly optimized for joins on a single database, as Franck Pachot describes in his excellent *The myth of NoSQL (vs. RDBMS) "joins don't scale"* blog post (*https://oreil.ly/ZHszB*). However, when relational tables are partitioned and spread around a large cluster of machines, distributed joins need to be carefully designed to minimize data movement and hence reduce latencies. Common strategies to achieve this are:

- Define reference tables that are relatively small, rarely change, and need to be joined against frequently. These reference tables can be copied to each node so that join operations can execute locally and in parallel on each partitioned node. The results of each partition's join are then sent to the request coordinator to merge and return the result set.

- Use partition keys or secondary indexes in joins. Again, this allows joins to execute locally and in parallel on each partition using the indexed fields.

- Ensure one side of the join has a highly selective filter that reduces the set of rows to a small collection. This can then be sent to each partitioned node and the join proceeds as in a reference table join. This approach minimizes data movement.

Joins that involve large collections of data on each side of the join, don't join on partition keys, and create large result sets require data shuffling and movement between nodes. This is required to move data to nodes to perform the partition, and subsequently gather and merge the results. These are the joins that are most difficult to scale.

The bottom line is that high throughput queries need to carefully design schema and choose appropriate join algorithms. A great example is Google's Cloud Spanner distributed relational database. Spanner has multiple join algorithms and will choose algorithms automatically. But as the documentation states (*https://oreil.ly/uCdhx*):

> Join operations can be expensive. This is because JOINs can significantly increase the number of rows your query needs to scan, which results in slower queries. Google advises you to test with different join algorithms. Choosing the right join algorithm can improve latency, memory consumption, or both. For queries that are critical for your workload, you are advised to specify the most performant join method and join order in your SQL statements for more consistent performance.

Example: Oracle RAC

Despite the inherent problems of partitioning relational models and the complexities of SQL queries at scale, vendors have worked in the last two decades to scale out relational databases. One notable example is Oracle's Real Applications Cluster (RAC) database (*https://oreil.ly/i0p6D*).

Oracle's RAC database was released in 2001 to provide a distributed version of the Oracle database engine for high-volume, highly available systems. Essentially, Oracle makes it possible to deploy a cluster of up to 100 Oracle database engines that all access the same physical database.

To avoid the data partitioning problem, Oracle RAC is an example of a *shared-everything* database. The clustered database engines access a single, shared data store of the data files, logs, and configuration files that comprise an Oracle database. To the database client, the clustered deployment is transparent and appears as a single database engine.

The physical storage needs to be accessible to all nodes using a network-accessible storage solution known as Storage Area Network (SAN). SANs provide high-speed network access to the Oracle database. SANs also must provide hardware-level disk mirroring to create multiple copies of application and system data in order to survive disk failure. Under high load, the SAN can potentially become a bottleneck. High-end SANs are extremely specialized storage devices that are expensive beasts to acquire.

Two proprietary software components are required for Oracle RAC deployments, namely:

Clusterware
> Supports communications and coordination between the clustered database engines. It manages, for example, cluster node membership, node failover, and high availability.

Cache Fusion
> Enables the individual caches in each clustered database node to be effectively shared so that accesses to the persistent store are minimized.

An overview of a RAC system is shown in Figure 10-5.

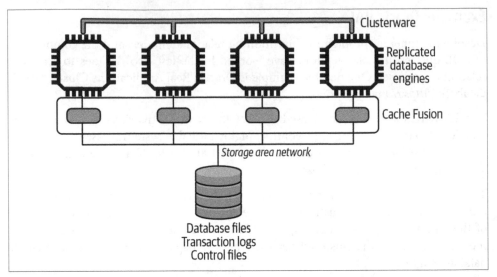

Figure 10-5. Oracle RAC overview

Oracle RAC illustrates one architectural approach, namely shared everything, to scaling a relational database. It adds processing capacity and high availability to an Oracle deployment while requiring (in theory anyway) no application code changes. The database requires multiple proprietary Oracle software components and expensive redundant storage and interconnect hardware. Add Oracle license costs, and you don't have a low-cost solution by any means.

Many Oracle customers have adopted this technology in the last 20 years. It's mature and proven, but through the lens of today's technology landscape, is based on an architecture that offers limited on-demand scalability at high costs. The alternative, namely a shared-nothing architecture that exploits the widely available low-cost commodity compute nodes and storage is the approach I'll focus on going forward.

The Movement to NoSQL

I'm not brave enough to try and construct a coherent narrative describing the forces that brought about the creation of a new generation of NoSQL database technologies.[2] My personal inclination is that this innovation was driven by a confluence of reasons that started to gather momentum in the early 2000s. In no particular order, some of these reasons were:

---

2 NoSQL probably stands for Not Only SQL, but this is somewhat vacuous. It's best to regard NoSQL as a simple label rather than an acronym.

- The development of powerful, low-cost, commodity hardware, including multi-core CPUs, faster, larger disks, and increased network speeds.

- The emergence of applications that dealt with unstructured data types and rapidly evolving business and data models. No longer was the "one size fits all" approach of relational adherents applicable to these new use cases.

- Increased need for scalability and availability for internet-facing applications.

- New opportunities to gather raw data and utilize this for new business insights and analytics.

Combined with the complexities of scaling relational databases for massive data sets that I've described in this chapter, the time was rife for a new database paradigm. Much of the database and distributed systems theory that was needed for such innovation was known, and this created fertile ground for the emergence of a whole collection of new database platforms.

The NoSQL database ecosystem that blossomed to address the evolving business and technological landscape of the early 2000s is by no means a homogeneous place. Several different approaches emerged and were implemented to some extent in various (mostly open source) databases. In general, however, the core characteristics of the NoSQL movement are:

- Simplified data models that can be easily evolved
- Proprietary query languages with limited or no support for joins
- Native support for horizontal scaling on low-cost, commodity hardware

I'll look at each of these characteristics in turn in the following subsections. But before that, consider this: how do NoSQL databases survive without the capability to execute JOIN-like queries? The answer lies in how you model data with NoSQL.

NoSQL JOIN

For illustration, and at the time of writing, CouchBase, Oracle NoSQL, and MongoDB support some form of joins, often with limitations. Oracle NoSQL joins are limited to hierarchically related tables only. MongoDB's $lookup operation allows only one of the collections to be partitioned. Cassandra, DynamoDB, Riak, and Redis have no support for join operations. Graph databases like Neo4j and OrientDB use graph traversal algorithms and operations and hence have no need for joins.

Data model normalization, as encouraged by relational databases, provides a proven technique for modeling the *problem domain*. It creates models with a single entry for every data item, which can be referenced when needed. Updates just need to modify the canonical data reference, and the update is then available to all queries that reference the data. Due to the power of SQL and joins, you don't have to think too hard about all the weird and wonderful ways the data will be accessed, both immediately and in the future. Your normalized model should (in theory) support any reasonable query for the application domain, and SQL is there to make it possible.

With NoSQL, the emphasis changes from problem domain modeling to modeling the *solution domain*. Solution domain modeling requires you to think about the common data access patterns the application must support, and to devise a data model that supports these accesses. For reading data, this means your data model must *prejoin* the data you need to service a request. Essentially, you produce what relational modelers deem a denormalized data model. You are trading off flexibility for efficiency.

Another way of thinking about solution domain modeling is to create a table per use case. As an example, skiers and snowboarders love to use their apps to list how many days they have visited their favorite mountains each season, how many lifts they rode, and what the weather was like. Using normalization, you'd probably produce something like the following as a logical data model and create tables that implement the model:

```
SnowSportPerson = {ssp_id, ssp_name, address, dob, ……….}
Resort = {resort_id, resort_name, location, …..}
Visit = {ssp_id, resort_id, date, numLifts, vertical, …..}
Weather = {resort_id, date, maxtemp, mintemp, wind, …}
```

Using SQL, it's straightforward JOIN wizardry to generate a list of visits for a specific person that looks like the following:

Summary Ian Gorton *Number of days:* 2

Date	Resort	Number of lifts	Total vertical feet	Max/min temperature (F)	Wind speed (mph)
Dec 2nd 2021	49 Degrees North	17	27,200	27/19	11
Dec 9th	Silver Mt.	14	22,007	32/16	3

In NoSQL data modeling, you create a data model that has the results the query needs all together in a table. As shown in the following, a VisitDay has all the data items needed to generate each line in the list above. You just have to sum the number of VisitDay objects in the results set to calculate the number of days for a single person.[3]

---

3 Most NoSQL databases support embedded or nested data objects. This makes it possible to create a single database object for a person's resort visits and update this object every time a new visit occurs. This simplifies reads as a query just retrieves one object that contains all the visit data needed. Depending on the database, updates may not be as efficient as inserts. This is a very database-specific issue.

```
VisitDay = {date, resort_name, ssp_id, ssp_name, numLifts, vertical, maxtemp,
mintemp, wind}
```

The *SnowSportPerson*, *Resort*, and *Weather* tables would remain unchanged from your original model. This means we have duplicated data across your logical tables. In this example, most of the data in these tables is write-once and never changes (e.g., weather conditions for a particular day), so duplication just uses more disk space—not a major problem in modern systems.

Imagine, though, if a resort name changes. It does actually happen occasionally. This update would have to retrieve all *VisitDay* entries for that resort and update the resort name in every entry. In a very large database, this update might take a few tens of seconds or more, but as it's a data maintenance operation, it can be run one dark night so that the new name appears magically to users the next day.

So there you have it. If you design your data model to efficiently process requests based on major use cases, complex operations like joins are unnecessary. Add to this that it becomes easier to partition and distribute data and the benefits start to stack up at scale. The trade-offs are that, typically, reads are faster and writes are slower. You also have to think carefully about how to implement updates to duplicate data and maintain data integrity.

Normalization

The design of relational databases encourages normalization. Normalization structures the business domain data to eliminate data redundancy and support data integrity. Normalization is a complex topic that is beyond the scope of this book. In a nutshell, the result of normalization is a data model that adheres to the rules described by one of six—yes, six—major normal forms.[4] Each normal form defines rules for how the domain data should be organized into a collection of tables and columns.

In reality, many databases I have seen over many years are designed to the rules defined by third normal form (3NF). I've heard rumors of fourth normal form databases, but suspect any higher normal forms have never left the environs of academia.

Essentially, 3NF data models are designed to simplify data management. Domain data is split among multiple relations such that every data item has a single entry that can be referenced by a unique identifier when required. Data in 3NF data models can be mechanically translated into a relational schema and instantiated by a relational database engine. Applications can then use the SQL query language to INSERT, UPDATE, SELECT, and DELETE data from the database.

---

4 Chris Date, *Database Design and Relational Theory: Normal Forms and All That Jazz*, 2nd ed. (Apress, 2012).

It's not uncommon, however, for relational data models to be demoralized to enhance query performance and application scalability. This insight is one of the key tenets that underpins the simpler data models that are supported by NoSQL databases.

NoSQL Data Models

As illustrated in Figure 10-6, there are four main NoSQL data models, all of which are somewhat simpler than the relational model.

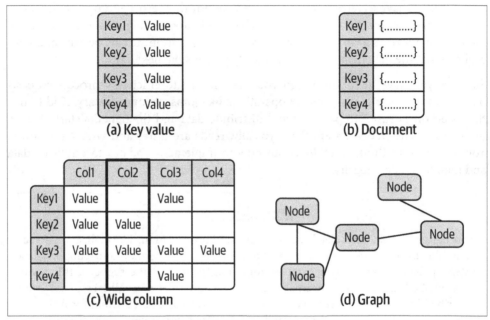

Figure 10-6. NoSQL data models

Fundamentally there are subtle overlaps between these models. But ignoring these subtleties, the four are:

Key-value

> Key-value (KV) databases are basically a hash map. Every object in the database has a unique key that is used to retrieve data associated with that key. To the database, the data associated with the key is typically opaque to the database engine. It can be a string, JSON, image, or whatever else the business problem demands. Examples of KV databases include Redis (*https://redis.io*) and Oracle NoSQL (*https://oreil.ly/pYcfy*).

Document

> A document database builds on the KV model, again with each document in the database requiring a unique key. The value associated with the key is not

opaque to the database. Rather it is encoded, typically in JSON, making it possible to reference individual elements in a document in queries and for the database to build indexes on document fields. Documents are usually organized into logical collections analogous to relational tables, but there is no requirement for all documents in the collection to have the same format. Leading document databases are MongoDB (*https://www.mongodb.com*) and Couchbase (*https://www.couchbase.com*).

Wide column

A wide column database extends the KV model by organizing data associated with a key in named columns. It's essentially a two-dimensional hash map, enabling columns within a row to be uniquely identified and sorted using the column name. Like a document database, each row in a collection can have different columns. Apache Cassandra (*https://oreil.ly/hgvAg*) and Google Bigtable (*https://oreil.ly/rvR9n*) are examples of wide column databases.

Graph

Graphs are well understood data structures for storing and querying highly connected data. Think of your friends on Facebook, or the routes flown by an airline between airports. Graphs treat relationships between database objects as first-class citizens, and hence enable a wide range of graph-based algorithms to be efficiently implemented. Conceptually closest to relational databases, prominent examples are Neo4j (*https://neo4j.com*) and Amazon Neptune (*https://oreil.ly/n1sCR*).

Regardless of data model, NoSQL databases are usually termed as *schemaless* databases. Unlike relational databases, the format of every object you write into the database does not have to be defined up front. This makes it possible to easily evolve data object formats as there is no need for every object in a logical collection to have the same format.

The inevitable trade-off for this flexibility is that it becomes the responsibility of the application to discover the structure of the data it reads. This requires data objects to be stored in the database along with metadata (basically field names) that make structure discovery possible. You'll often see these two approaches called schema-on-write (defined schema) and schema-on-read (schemaless).

Query Languages

NoSQL database query languages are nearly always proprietary to a specific database, and vary between explicit API-based capabilities and SQL-like declarative languages. Client libraries in various languages, implemented by the vendor as well as third parties, are available for utilization in applications. For example, MongoDB officially supports twelve client libraries (*https://oreil.ly/1xJfN*) for different languages and has third-party offerings for many more (*https://oreil.ly/GxWb2*).

KV databases may offer little more than APIs that support CRUD operations based on individual key values. Document databases normally support indexing of individual document fields. This enables efficient implementations of queries that retrieve results sets and apply updates to documents that satisfy various search criteria. For example, the following is a MongoDB query that retrieves all the documents from the *skiers* database collection for individuals older than 16 who have not renewed their ski pass:

```
db.skiers.find( {
    age: { $gt:  16},
    renew: { $exists: false }}
)
```

Wide column databases have a variety of query capabilities. HBase supports a Java CRUD API (*https://oreil.ly/VwMCo*) with the ability to retrieve result sets using filters. Cassandra Query Language (CQL) is modeled on SQL and provides a declarative language for accessing the underlying wide column store. If you are familiar with SQL, CQL will look very familiar. CQL by no means implements the full set of SQL features. For example, the CQL SELECT statement can only apply to a single table and doesn't support joins or subqueries.

Graph databases support much richer query capabilities. OrientDB uses SQL as the basic query language and implements extensions to support graph queries (*https://oreil.ly/3E5zK*). Another example is Cypher, originally designed for the Neo4j graph database, and open sourced through the openCypher project (*https://opencypher.org*). Cypher provides capabilities to match patterns of nodes and relationships in the graph, with powerful query and insert statements analogous to SQL. The following example returns the emails of everyone who has a *visited* relationship to the ski resort node with a name property of *Mission Ridge*:

```
MATCH (p:Person)-[rel:VISITED]->(c:Skiresort)
WHERE c.name = 'Mission Ridge'
RETURN p.email
```

Data Distribution

NoSQL databases are in general designed to natively scale horizontally across distributed compute nodes equipped with local storage. This is a *shared nothing* architecture, as opposed to the *shared everything* approach I described with Oracle RAC. With no shared state, bottlenecks and single points of failure are eliminated,[5] and performance, scalability, and availability enhanced. There's one notable exception to this rule, and that is graph databases, as I describe in the following sidebar.

---

5 Again, this is in fact database implementation dependent. Shared-nothing architecture theoretically removes single points of failure and bottlenecks, but some implementations add them back!

Distributing Graph Databases

Graph databases are commonly included in the NoSQL database categorization. They are, however, a little bit of an outsider. Graph data structures, as implemented by graph databases, explicitly represent relationships between nodes in the graph. This means that, just like with relational databases, how to partition the data is not obvious.

The core of the problem is: how can a graph be partitioned into subgraphs that can then be distributed across multiple nodes and support efficient query processing? This is both theoretically and practically a challenging problem, especially at the scale of contemporary graphs with billions of nodes and relationships. A solution would have to take into account, for example, access patterns to try and ensure queries don't constantly follow relationships that point to remote data.

For these reasons, partitioning a graph database can benefit from human guidance. For example, Neo4j's Fabric extension (*https://oreil.ly/dw5zd*) allows a graph to be manually partitioned. Fabric creates what is essentially a proxy database to support queries that traverse relationships between nodes on different servers.

In summary, graph databases are nontrivial to scale out to improve performance. But give one enough compute resources, memory, and disk in a single big server, and graph database engines can do some remarkable things.

Partitioning, commonly known as sharding, requires an algorithm to distribute the data objects in a logical database collection across multiple server nodes. Ideally, a sharding algorithm should evenly distribute data across the available resources. Namely, if you have one hundred million objects and ten identical database servers, each shard will have ten million objects resident locally.

Sharding requires a shard or partition key that is used to allocate a given data object to a specific partition. When a new object is created, the shard key maps the object to a specific partition that resides on a server. When a query needs to access an object, it supplies the shard key so the database engine can locate the object on the server it resides. This is illustrated in Figure 10-7.

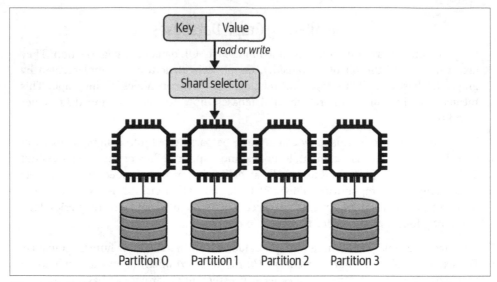

Figure 10-7. Data partitioning

Three main techniques exist for sharding, and all distributed databases will implement one or more of these approaches:

Hash key

The partition for any given data object is chosen as the result of applying a hash function to the shard key. The result of the hash is then mapped to a partition. There are two main ways of doing this, using a modulus approach or an algorithm known as consistent hashing.

Value-based

The partition is chosen based on the value of the shard key. For example, you might want to partition your data on customers based on their country of residence. Choosing the country field as the shard key would ensure all data objects for customers who live in China reside in the same partition, all Finland customers are allocated to the same partition, and so on.

Range-based

Partitions host data objects where the shard key resides within a specific range of the shard key value. For example, you might use zip code/post code ranges to allocate all customer objects who reside in the same geographical area to the same partition.

Partitioning makes it possible to scale out a database by adding processing and disk capacity and distributing data across these additional resources. However, if one of the partitions is unavailable due to a network error or disk crash, then a chunk of the database cannot be accessed.

Solving this availability problem requires the introduction of replication. The data objects in each partition are replicated to typically two or more nodes. If one node becomes unavailable, the application can continue to execute by accessing one of the replicas. This partitioned, replicated architecture is shown in Figure 10-8. Each partition has three replicas, with each replica hosted on a different node.

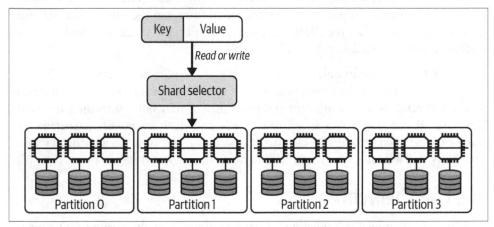

Figure 10-8. Data partitioning and replication with three replicas per partition

Replication enhances both availability and scalability. The additional resources that store replicas can be used to handle both read and write requests from applications.

There is however, as always with distributed systems, a complication to address. When a data update request occurs, the database needs to update all replicas. This ensures the replicas are consistent and all clients will read the same value regardless of the replica they access.

There are two basic architectures for managing distributed database replication. These are:

Leader-follower
> One replica is designated the leader and it always holds the latest value of any data object. All writes are directed to the leader, which is responsible for propagating updates to the replicas. The followers are read-only replicas. Application reads can be load balanced across the followers to scale out read performance.

Leaderless
> Any replica can handle both reads and updates. When an update is sent to a replica, it becomes the request coordinator for that update and is responsible for ensuring the other replicas get correctly updated. As writes can be handled by any replica, the leaderless approach tends to be more scalable for write-heavy applications.

Replica consistency turns out to be a thorny distributed systems issue. The core of the problem revolves around how and when updates are propagated to replicas to ensure they have the same values. The usual issues of varying latencies and network and hardware failures make this totally nontrivial.

If a database can ensure all replicas always have the same value, then it is said to provide *strong consistency*, as all client accesses will return the same value for every data object. This implies the client must wait until all replicas are modified before an update is acknowledged as successful.

In contrast, a client may only want to wait for one replica to be updated, and trust the database to update the others as soon as it can. This means you have a window of time when replicas are inconsistent and reads may or may not return the latest value. Databases that allow replica inconsistency are known as *eventually consistent*. The trade-offs between strong and eventual consistency and how design choices affect scalability and availability are dealt with in detail in the next three chapters.

The CAP Theorem

Eric Brewer's famous CAP theorem[6] elegantly encapsulates the options you have for replica consistency and availability when utilizing distributed databases. It describes the choices a database system has if there is a network partition, namely when the network drops or delays messages sent between the nodes in the database.

Basically, if the network is operating correctly, a system can be both consistent and available. If a network partition occurs, a system can be either consistent (CP) or available (AP).

This situation arises because a network partition means some nodes in the database are not accessible to others—the partition splits the database into two groups of nodes. If an update occurs and the replicas for the updated data object reside on both sides of the partition, then the database can either:

- Return an error as it cannot ensure replica consistency (CP).
- Apply the update to the subset of replicas that are visible (AP). This means there is replica inconsistency until the partition heals and the database can make all replicas consistent. Until the inconsistency is resolved, clients may see different values for the same data object.

You'll see the AP or CP categorization used for different NoSQL databases. It's useful but not totally meaningful as most databases, as I'll explain in Chapter 13, make it

---

6 Eric Brewer, "CAP Twelve Years Later: How the 'Rules' Have Changed," *Computer*, Volume 45, Issue 2 (2012), 23–29.

possible to tune configuration parameters to achieve AP or CP to meet application requirements.

In the Wild: Internet-Scale Database Examples

Facebook is well known for using MySQL to manage petabytes of social-related activities such as user comments and likes. The basic architecture is based on replica sets, with a single primary that handles all writes. Updates are replicated asynchronously to geographically distributed read-only replicas. Facebook engineering has made multiple updates to the MySQL code base, including building their own storage technology, MyRocks (*https://oreil.ly/kicaw*), to replace MySQL's InnoDB default storage engine. MyRocks improves write performance and uses 50% less storage than a compressed InnoDB database. At Facebook scale, this provides a major storage saving. Porting to MyRocks for MySQL version 8.0 took two years and 1,500 code patches.[7]

MongoDB has many large-scale deployments. One of the highest-profile ones is Baidu, China's largest internet services company. It has utilized MongoDB since 2012 and now uses MongoDB to manage data for multiple services including maps, messaging, and photo sharing. Collectively, this amounts to 200 billion documents and more than 1 petabyte of data. This is managed by 600 nodes and is distributed across multiple locations for availability.[8]

Summary and Further Reading

As the scale of systems has grown, a revolution has taken place in the database realm. Databases must store massive volumes of data, provide rapid query response times for globally distributed clients and be available 24/7. This has required database technologies to become distributed and adopt new data models that are more amenable to the unstructured, ever changing data types necessitated by modern applications.

In this chapter, I've explained why relational databases and SQL can become problematic at scale. In contrast, NoSQL databases adopt simple data models that can be replicated and partitioned to support massive data sets and request volumes. As always, there are trade-offs. NoSQL databases do not support the rich query features of SQL, placing a greater burden on the application. Distributed database designers also need to be aware of the consistency and availability trade-offs that are enumerated by the CAP theorem.

---

7 The story (*https://oreil.ly/JALXm*) of the move to MyRocks and MySQL version 8.0 is well worth a few minutes' reading.

8 MongoDB's usage at Baidu is briefly described here (*https://oreil.ly/ZOM0C*), and links to an excellent presentation with more details.

With these foundations, the following three chapters focus on the complexities of the trade-offs inferred by the CAP theorem. I'll explain the approaches that have been devised and implemented in various databases to enable applications to balance consistency, availability, and performance to meet their requirements.

For an excellent introduction to NoSQL databases, it's still hard to beat *NoSQL Distilled: A Brief Guide to the Emerging World of Polyglot Persistence* by Pramod Sadalage and Martin Fowler (Addison-Wesley Professional, 2013). For broader coverage of the database landscape, including both SQL and NoSQL, *SQL and NoSQL Databases: Models, Languages, Consistency Options and Architectures for Big Data Management* by Andreas Meier and Michael Kaufmann (Springer, 2019) is well worth a read. Finally, if this chapter has whetted your appetite for learning about how databases work in depth, Alex Petrov's *Database Internals* (O'Reilly, 2019) is highly recommended.

CHAPTER 11

Eventual Consistency

Eventual consistency has risen in prominence with the emergence of distributed, NoSQL databases. It's still a concept that has been and remains heretical to some, raised in the era of transactions with relational databases. In some application domains, with banking and finance usually cited, eventual consistency simply isn't appropriate. So goes the argument, anyway.

In fact, eventual consistency has been used in the banking industry for many years. Anyone remember writing checks? Checks take days to be reconciled on your account, and you can easily write checks for more money than you have in your account. When the checks get processed, and consistency is established, you might see some consequences, however.

It is similar with ATM transactions. If an ATM is partitioned from the network and cannot check your balance, you will still usually be able to get cash, albeit limited to a small amount. At this stage your account balance is inconsistent. When the partition heals, the ATM will send the transactions to be processed by the backend systems and the correct value for your account will be calculated.

In the era of scalable internet systems, eventual consistency has found many suitable use cases. In this chapter, I'll delve into the major issues that you need to be aware of when building eventually consistent systems with distributed databases at scale.

What Is Eventual Consistency?

In the good old days, when systems had a single source of truth for all data items—the database—replica consistency was not a problem. There simply were no replicas. But as I explained in Chapter 10, many systems need to scale out their databases across multiple nodes to provide the necessary processing and storage capacity. In addition, to ensure the data for each node is highly available, you also need to replicate the contents of each node to eliminate single points of failure.

Suddenly your database has become a distributed system. When the database nodes and networks are fast and working reliably, your users have no idea they are interacting with a distributed system. Replicas are updated seemingly instantaneously, and user requests are processed with low response times. Inconsistent reads are rare.

But as you know by now, distributed systems need to be able to handle various failure modes. This means the database has to deal with all the issues inherent with highly variable network latencies, and communication and machine failures. These failures mean your database replicas may remain inconsistent for longer periods than your application may wish to tolerate. This creates issues you need to understand and be able to address.

Inconsistency Window

The inconsistency window in an eventually consistent system is the duration it takes for an update to a data object to propagate to all replicas. In a leader-based system, the leader coordinates the updating of other replicas. In a leaderless system, any replica (or potentially any database node—this is implementation dependent) coordinates the update. The inconsistency window ends when all replicas have the same value.

Several factors affect the duration of the inconsistency window. These are outlined in the following:

The number of replicas
> The more replicas you have, the more replica updates need to be coordinated. The inconsistency window only closes when all replicas are identical. If you have three replicas, then only three updates are needed. The more replicas you have, the chances of one of your replicas responding slowly and elongating the inconsistency window increases.

Operational environment
> Any instantaneous operational glitches, such as a transient network failure or lost packets, can extend the inconsistency window. Probably the main cause for replica update delays is a heavy read/write workload at a node. This causes replicas to become overloaded and introduces additional data propagation latency. Hence the more load your database is experiencing, the longer the inconsistency window is likely to be.

Distance between replicas
> If all replicas are on the same local area network subnet, communications latencies can be submillisecond. If one of your replicas is across the continent or across the world, the minimum value of the inconsistency window will be the

round-trip time between replicas. With geographical distribution, this could be relatively large, several tens of milliseconds, in fact.[1] It all depends on the distance as I explained in Chapter 3.

All these issues mean that you don't have control over the duration of the inconsistency window. You can't provide or know an upper bound. With eventually consistent systems that communicate state changes asynchronously, this is a fact of life you have to live with.

Read Your Own Writes

Not too long ago, while booking a flight, I had to update my credit card information as a new one had been issued due to a hack at a major store. I duly added my new card information, saved it, and continued the checkout process to pay for my flight. To my surprise, the payment was rejected because I hadn't updated my credit card information. Wait a minute, I thought, and checked my profile. The new card details were in my profile marked as the default card. So, I tried the transaction again, and everything worked fine.

I don't know exactly how this system was implemented, but I'm betting it uses an eventually consistent database and does not support *read your own writes (RYOWs)*. RYOWs is a property of a system that ensures if a client makes a persistent change to data, the updated data value is guaranteed to be returned by any subsequent reads from the same client.

In an eventually consistent system, the inconsistency window makes it possible for a client to:

- Issue an update to a database object key.
- Issue a subsequent read for the same database object key and see the old value as it accesses a replica that has not yet persisted the prior update.

This is illustrated in Figure 11-1. The client request to update their credit card details is coordinated by *Replica 1*, which sends the new card details asynchronously to the other replicas. The update to *Replica 3* incurs a delay however. Before the update is applied, the same client issues a read which is directed to *Replica 3*. The result is a stale read.

---

1 The quantum communications systems of the future may well overcome distance-induced latencies (*https://oreil.ly/Zje4h*).

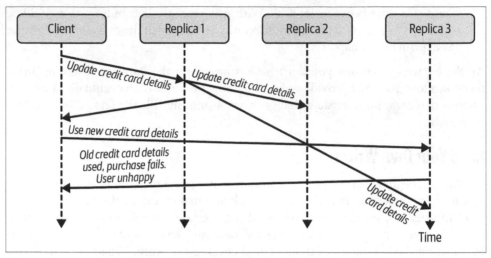

Figure 11-1. Eventual consistency leads to stale reads

To avoid this situation, a system needs to provide RYOWs consistency.[2] This guarantees, for an individual user, that any updates made by the user will be visible in subsequent reads. The guarantee doesn't hold for other users. If I add a comment to an online article, when I reload the page, I will see my comment. Other users who load the page at the same time may or may not see my comments immediately. They will see it eventually.

With leader-follower replication, implementing read your writes consistency is straightforward. For use cases that require RYOWs, you simply ensure the subsequent read is handled by the leader replica. This is guaranteed to hold the latest data object value.

The implementation of RYOWs, if supported, varies by database platform. With MongoDB, a database I'll describe in more detail in Chapter 13, this is the default behavior achieved by accessing the master replica.[3] In Neo4j clusters (*https://oreil.ly/ f7yXy*), all writes are handled by the leader, which asynchronously updates read-only followers. Reads, however, may be handled by replicas. To implement RYOWs consistency, any write transaction can request that a *bookmark* is returned that uniquely identifies that update. A subsequent read request passes the bookmark to Neo4j, enabling the cluster to ensure that only replicas that have received the bookmarked transaction process the read.

---

2 For an excellent description of eventual consistency models, see *https://oreil.ly/2qUQh*.

3 MongoDB enables you to tune which replica handles reads (*https://oreil.ly/2hsiW*).

Tunable Consistency

Many eventually consistent databases provide configuration options and API parameters to enable you to tailor the database's eventually consistent behavior. This makes it possible to trade off the performance of individual read and write operations based on the level of eventual replica consistency a use case can tolerate. The basic approach is known as tunable consistency.

Tunable consistency is based on specifying the number of replicas that a request must access to complete a database request. To explain how this works, let's define the following:

N

Total number of replicas

W

Number of replicas to update before confirming the update to the client

R

Number or replicas to read from before returning a value

As an example, assume $N = 3$, and there is a leaderless database in which any individual request can be handled by any one of the replicas. The replica handling the request is called the coordinator. You can tune write operation performance and the extent of the inconsistency window by specifying the W value as shown in the following examples:

$W = 3$

The request coordinator will wait until all three replicas are updated before returning success to the client.

$W = 1$

The request coordinator will confirm the update locally and return success to the client. The other two replicas will be updated asynchronously.

This means if $W = 3$, all replicas will be consistent after the write completes. This is sometimes called immediate consistency. In this case, clients can issue reads with a value of $R = 1$ (or quorum—see next section) and they should receive the latest value, as long as reads are not concurrent with the replica updates. Reads that occur while the replicas are being updated may still see different values depending on the replicas they access. Only once the replica values have converged will all reads see the same value. Hence immediate consistency is not the same as strong consistency (see Chapter 12) as stale reads are still possible.[4]

If $W = 1$, then you have an inconsistency window as only one replica, the request coordinator in our example, is guaranteed to have the latest value. If you issue a read with $R = 1$, the result may or may not be the latest value.

Remember the CAP theorem from Chapter 10? There are some consistency-availability trade-offs to consider here. If we set $W = N$, then there are two consequences:

- All replicas are consistent. This option favors replica consistency. Note that writes will be slower. The client must wait for updates to be acknowledged by all replicas, and this will add latency to writes, especially if one replica is slow to respond.

- Writes may fail if a replica is not accessible. This would make it impossible for the request coordinator to update all replicas, and hence the request will throw an exception. This negatively affects availability (see discussion of hinted handoffs later in this chapter).

This option is *CP* in CAP terminology.

Alternatively, if we set $W = 1$, writes succeed if any replica is available. There will be an inconsistency window that will last until all replicas are updated. The write will succeed even if one or more replicas are partitioned or have failed. This option therefore favors availability over replica consistency, or *AP* in CAP parlance.

To combat this inconsistency window, a client can specify how many replicas should be read before a result is returned. If we set $R = N$, then the request coordinator will read from all replicas, determine which is the latest update, and return that value to the client (I'll return to precisely how the coordinator determines which replica holds the latest value later in this chapter. For now just assume it is possible). The result is that by reading from all replicas, you are guaranteed to access the one that holds the latest updated value.

Another way to look at the trade-offs involved is *read optimized* versus *write optimized*. The $(W = N, R = 1)$ setting favors both consistency and read latencies, as only one replica needs to be accessed. The trade-off is longer write times. The $(W = 1, R = N)$ option favors both availability and write latencies, as writes succeed after any replica is updated. The trade-off is slower reads.

---

4 Immediate consistency should not be confused with strong consistency, as described in the next chapter. Databases that favor availability over consistency and use $W = N$ for writes still have an inconsistency window. Also, writes may not be completed on every replica if one or more is unreachable. To understand why, see discussion of hinted handoffs later in this chapter.

These settings enable you to tune individual database requests to match your requirements. If inconsistent reads are not desirable, choose either $W = N$ and $R = 1$, which will add latency to writes but make reads as fast as possible, or $W = 1$ and $R = N$, to optimize writes at the expense of reads. If your use cases can tolerate inconsistency, set $W = R = 1$ and benefit from fast reads and writes. Or, if you want to balance performance and consistency, there's another option, as I'll explain in the next section.

Quorum Reads and Writes

There's an option that lies between the alternatives discussed in the previous section. These are known as *quorum* reads and writes. Quorum simply means the majority, which is $(N / 2) + 1$.[5] For our three replicas, the majority is two. For five replicas, the majority is three, and so on.

If we configure both the W and R value to be the quorum, we can balance the performance of reads and writes and still provide access to the latest updated value of a data object. Figure 11-2 illustrates how quorums work. With three replicas, a quorum means a write must succeed at two replicas, and a read must access two replicas. Initially all three replicas have a data object K with value *v1*, and the following sequence of actions takes place:

1. *Client 1* updates the object to hold value *v2* and the write is acknowledged as successful once a quorum—in this case *Replica 1* and *Replica 2*—are updated.
2. The command to update to *Replica 3* is delayed (slow network? busy node?).
3. *Client 2* issues a read on object *K*.
4. *Replica 2* acts as the request coordinator and sends a read request to the other two replicas for their value for *K*. *Replica 3* is first to respond with $K = v1$.
5. *Replica 2* compares its value for *K* with that returned from *Replica 3* and determines that *v2* is the most recently updated value. It returns value *v2* to *Client 2*.

The basic intuition of quorums is that by always reading and writing from the majority of replicas, read requests will see the latest version of a database object. This is because the majority that is written to and the majority that are read from must overlap. In Figure 11-2, even though *Replica 3* is not updated before the read takes place, the read accesses *Replica 2*, which does hold the updated value. The request coordinator can then ensure the latest value is returned to the client.

---

5 This formula uses integer division, such that the fractional part is discarded. For example, 5 / 2 = 2.

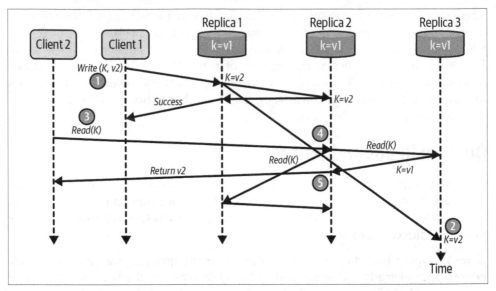

Figure 11-2. Quorum reads and writes

So, what's the inevitable trade-off here? Simply, writes and reads will fail if a quorum of nodes is not available. A network failure that partitions a group of replicas such that the partition visible to a client does not contain a quorum will cause that client's requests to fail.

In some database systems designed to favor availability over consistency, the concept of a *sloppy quorum* is supported. Sloppy quorums were first described in Amazon's original Dynamo paper,[6] and are implemented in several databases including DynamoDB, Cassandra, Riak, and Voldemort.

The idea is simple. If a given write cannot achieve quorum due to the unavailability of replicas nodes, the update can be stored temporarily on another reachable node. When the home node(s) for the replica(s) become available again, the node storing the update performs what is called a *hinted handoff*. A hinted handoff sends the latest value of the replica to the home nodes from its temporary location.

This scheme is depicted in Figure 11-3. The client sends an update to *Replica 1*. *Replica 1* attempts to update *Replica 2* and *Replica 3*, but *Replica 3* is unavailable due to a transient network partition. *Replica 1* therefore sends the update to another database node, *Node N*, which temporarily stores the update. Sometime later, *Node N* sends the update to *Replica 3*, and the value for the updated object becomes consistent across all replicas.

---

6 Giuseppe DeCandia et al., "Dynamo: Amazon's Highly Available Key-Value Store," in the Proceedings of the 21st ACM Symposium on Operating Systems Principles, Stevenson, WA, October 2007.

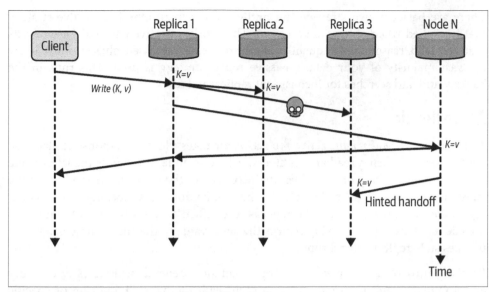

Figure 11-3. Sloppy quorum and hinted handoff

Sloppy quorums have two main implications. First, a write that has achieved a sloppy quorum guarantees durability on W nodes, but the W nodes are not all nodes that hold replica values of the updated data object. This means a client may still read a stale value, even with quorums configured (i.e., $R + W > N$), as it may access R nodes that have not been updated by the previous write operation.

Second, sloppy quorums increase write availability for a system. The trade-off is the potential for stale reads until the hinted handoff has occurred. Databases that support these features typically allow the system designer to turn these capabilities on or off to suit application needs.

Replica Repair

In a distributed, replicated database, you expect every replica will be consistent. Replication may take a while, but consistency is always the ultimate outcome. Unfortunately, in operational databases, replica drift occurs. Network failures, node stalls, disk crashes, or (heaven forbid!) a bug in the database code can cause replicas to become inconsistent over time.

A term from thermodynamics, entropy, is used to describe this situation. Basically, systems tend to entropy (disorder) over time. Because of entropy, databases need to take active measures to ensure replicas remain consistent. These measures are known collectively as anti-entropy repair.

There are basically two strategies for anti-entropy repair. One is an active strategy that is applied when objects are accessed. This works effectively for database objects that are read reasonably frequently. For infrequently accessed objects, most likely the vast majority of your data, a passive repair strategy is used. This runs in the background and searches for inconsistent replicas to fix.

Active Repair

Also known as *read repair*, active replica repair takes place in response to database read requests. When a read arrives at a coordinator node, it requests the latest value for each replica. If any of the values are inconsistent, the coordinator sends back the latest value to update the stale replicas. This can be done in a blocking or nonblocking mode. Blocking waits for the replicas to confirm updates before responding to the client, whereas nonblocking returns the latest value to the client immediately and updates stale replicas asynchronously.

Precisely how read repair works is implementation dependent. Factors to consider are how many replicas are accessed on each read—perhaps all, quorum or specific R value—and how replica divergence is detected and fixed. For detection, instead of requesting and comparing a complete, potentially large object with a complex structure, a hash value of the object can be used. If replica hashes match, then there is no need to perform a repair operation. Reading hashes, known as digest reads, reduces network traffic and latency. You'll find digest read implementations in several NoSQL databases, for example, ScyllaDB (*https://oreil.ly/HNSvp*) and Cassandra.

Passive Repair

Passive anti-entropy repair is a process that typically runs periodically and is targeted at fixing replicas that are infrequently accessed. Essentially, the approach builds a hash value that represents each replicated collection of objects and compares the hashes of each collection. If the hashes match, no repair is needed. If they don't, you know some replicas in the collection are inconsistent and further action is needed.

To create an efficient hash representation of a potentially very large collection of data objects, a data structure called a Merkle tree[7] is typically utilized. A Merkle tree is a binary hash tree whose leaf nodes are hashes of individual data objects. Each parent node in the tree stores a hash of its pair of children nodes, such that the root node hash provides a compact representation of the entire data collection. Figure 11-4 shows a representation of a simple Merkle tree.

---

[7] Merkle trees are useful in many use cases (*https://oreil.ly/rr8Yh*), including Bitcoin/blockchain transaction verifications.

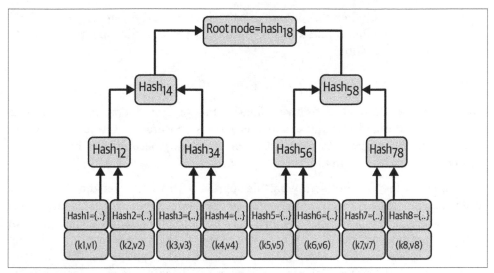

Figure 11-4. Merkle tree example

Once a Merkle tree for a collection of objects has been constructed, it can be efficiently utilized to compare Merkle trees for each replica collection. Two nodes can exchange the root node hash, and if the root node values are equal, then the objects stored in the partitions are consistent. If they are not, the two child nodes of the root must be compared. One (or maybe both) of the child node hashes must be different as the root node hashes were different. The traversal and data exchange algorithm basically continues down the tree, following branches where hashes are not equal between replica trees, until leaf nodes are identified. Once identified, the stale data objects can be updated on the appropriate replica node.

Merkle tree construction is a CPU- and memory-intensive operation. For these reasons, the process is either initiated on demand, initiated by an administration tool, or scheduled periodically. This enables anti-entropy repair to occur when the database is experiencing a low request load, and hence doesn't cause increased latencies on database accesses during production. Examples of NoSQL databases that implement anti-entropy repair are Riak (*https://oreil.ly/1ZKIt*) and Cassandra.

Handling Conflicts

Up until now in this chapter, I've assumed that a database has some mechanism to discern the latest value for any given replicated database object. For example, when reading from three replicas, the database will somehow be able to decide which replica is the most recently updated and return that value as the query result.

In a leaderless system, writes can be handled by any replica. This makes it possible for two clients to concurrently apply independent updates to the same database key on different replicas. When this occurs, in what order should the updates be applied? What should be the final value that all replicas hold? You need some mechanism to make this decision possible.

Last Writer Wins

One way to decide final, definitive values is to use timestamps. A timestamp is generated for the update request and the database ensures that when concurrent writes occur, the update with the most recent timestamp becomes the final version. This is simple and fast from the database perspective.

Unfortunately, there's a problem with this approach. In what order did the updates really happen? As I described in Chapter 3, clocks on machines drift. This means one node's clock may be ahead of others, making comparing timestamps meaningless. In reality, we can't determine the order of the events. They are executed on different replicas of the same data object by two or more independent processes. These updates must be considered as simultaneous, or concurrent. The timestamps attached to the updates simply impose an arbitrary order on the updates for conflict resolution.

The consequence of this is when concurrent updates occur using last writer wins, updates will be silently discarded. Figure 11-5 depicts one scenario where updates are lost using a shared playlist as an example. *Client 1* writes the first entry to the playlist, and this entry is subsequently read at some time later by both *Client 1* and *Client 2*. Both clients then write a new entry to the playlist, but as *Client 2*'s update is timestamped later than *Client 1*'s, the updates made by *Client 1* are lost.

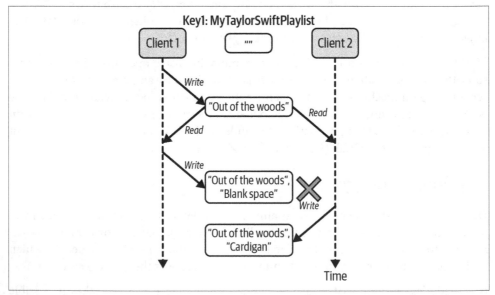

Figure 11-5. Concurrent writes cause lost updates with last writer wins

Data loss with a last writer wins conflict resolution policy is inevitable. There are mitigation strategies such as timestamps on individual fields and conditional writes (which I'll discuss in Chapter 13) that can minimize or mitigate the likelihood of data loss. However, the only way to safely utilize a database that employs purely a last writer wins policy is to ensure all writes store data objects with a unique key, and objects are subsequently immutable. Any changes to data in the database require the existing data object to be read and the new contents written to the database with a new key.

Version Vectors

To handle concurrent updates and not lose data, we need a way to identify and resolve conflicts. Figure 11-6 shows an approach to achieving this for a single replica using versioning. Each unique database object is stored along with a version number.

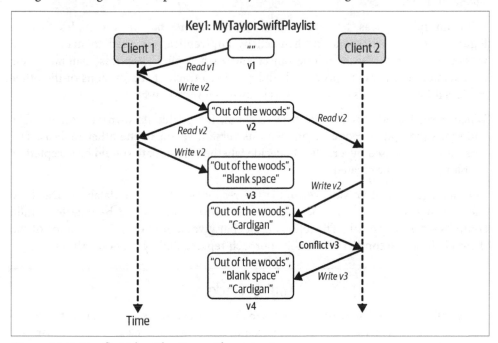

Figure 11-6. Conflict identification with versioning

Reading and writing data from the database proceeds as follows:

- When a client reads a database object, the object and its version are returned.
- When a client updates a database object, it writes the new data values and the version of the object that was received from the previous read.

- The database checks that the version in the write request is the same as the object's version in the database, and if it is, it accepts the write and increments the version number.

- If the version number accompanying a write does not match the database object version, a conflict has occurred, and the database must take remedial action to ensure data is not lost. It may return an error to the client and make it reread the new version. Alternatively, it may store both updates and inform the client that a conflict has occurred.

In Figure 11-6, the remedial action depicted is based on the Riak database (*https://oreil.ly/RRLQu*). When a conflict occurs in Riak, the database stores both versions of the database object and returns the conflicts to the client. In this example, the resolution is for the client to simply merge the two updates, which are known as *siblings* in Riak.

With multiple replicas, however, the situation is somewhat more complex than in Figure 11-6. As writes may be handled by any replica, we need to maintain the version number for each unique object and each replica. Replicas maintain their own version as writes are processed, and also keep track of the versions of the other replicas it has seen. This creates what is known as a *version vector*.

When a replica accepts a write from a client, it updates its own version number and sends the update request along with its version vector to the other replicas. The version vector is used by a replica to decide whether the update should be accepted or if siblings should be created.

The management of version vectors is the responsibility of the database. Database clients just need to present the latest version with updates and be able to handle conflicts when they occur. The following sidebar gives a brief overview of some of the theory behind the conflict resolution approach represented by version vectors.

Logical Clocks

Physical, CPU-measured time is not a reliable source of reference in distributed systems (see Chapter 3). Consequently, you need another approach to make sense of the order that database accesses occur. This is where logical clocks enter the scene.

Logical clocks were first described by Leslie Lamport in his seminal paper.[8] The essence of the work is the definition of a *happens-before* relationship. This means:

---

8 Leslie Lamport, "Time, Clocks, and the Ordering of Events in a Distributed System," *Communications of the ACM* 21, no. 7 (1978): 558–65. *https://doi.org/10.1145/359545.359563*.

- If a process issues operation a (e.g., a database request), and after it completes, issues operation b, then a *happens-before* b. This is denoted by $a \rightarrow b$.

- If a process sends a message m to another process, the send *happens-before* the receipt.

- If two independent processes perform operations $a \rightarrow b$ and $c \rightarrow d$, then it is not possible to define an order between the $\{a, b\}$ and $\{c, d\}$. In this case, the operations are concurrent.

- The *happens-before* relationship is transitive, such that if $a \rightarrow b$ and $b \rightarrow c$, then $a \rightarrow c$.

Systems can capture the *happens-before* relationship using a logical clock. This is done using a simple counter and algorithm. Each process has a local clock, which it initializes to zero on startup. The following shows pseudocode for when a process sends a message to another:

```
# increment local clock
local_clock ++;
# send message to another process
send(msg, local_clock);
```

When the receiving process accepts the message, it sets its own local clock as follows:

```
(msg, clock_msg) = receive();
local_clock = max(clock_msg, local_clock) + 1;
```

This ensures the value of `local_clock` in the receiving process is greater than the value sent in the message. This reflects that the send operation *happens-before* the receive operation. Whenever there is a cause and effect, or causal relationship between two events, such that $a \rightarrow b$, then *clock(a) < clock(b)*.

Lamport clocks define a partial order between events as they cannot discern between concurrent requests with no causal relationship. Hence, they cannot be used to detect database conflicts. This is where version vectors enter the scene. Version vectors define an array of logical clocks, with one element for each database object replica. This is shown in the following for a newly created object with three replicas:

```
r1, r2, r3 = [ [r1,0], [r2,0], [r3,0] ]
```

When an update is processed by a coordinator node, in the following this is $r2$, it increments its own clock in the vector, and sends the updated vector to the other replicas:

```
r2 = [ [r1,0], [r2,1], [r3,0] ]
```

When a replica receives an update and version vector from the coordinator, it compares the vector with its local copy. If every clock value for the updated object version vector is greater than or equal to the clock values stored by the replicas, the write is accepted. All replicas synchronize and will have identical version vectors.

If concurrent updates occur at replicas two and three, as shown in the following, each replica will update its own clock:

```
r2 = [ [r1,0], [r2,2], [r3,0] ]
r3 = [ [r1,0], [r2,1], [r3,1] ]
```

When the version vectors are exchanged and compared by *r2* and *r3*, the conflict is detected as all the clock values do not obey the *greater than or equal to* rule. This is how version vectors enable conflict detection in replicated databases.

As Figure 11-6 illustrates, when a database detects a conflict, the client typically needs to do some work to resolve it. If the database throws an error, the client can reread the latest version of the database object and attempt the update again. If siblings are returned, the client must perform some form of merge. These situations are very use case–specific and hence impossible to generalize.

Luckily, there are circumstances when a database can automatically resolve conflicts. Some databases, including Redis, Cosmos DB, and Riak, are leveraging recent results from the research community to support a collection of data types known as conflict-free replicated data types (CRDTs). CRDTs have semantics such that they can be concurrently updated and any conflicts can be resolved sensibly by the database. The value of a CRDT will always converge to a final state that is consistent on all replicas.

A simple example of a CRDT is a counter that could be used to maintain the number of followers for a user on a social media site. Increments and decrements to a counter can be applied in any order on different replicas, and the resulting value should eventually converge on all replicas.

Common CRDTs include sets, hash tables, lists and logs. These data structures behave identically to their nondistributed counterparts, with minor caveats.[9] Importantly, they alleviate the application from the burden of conflict handling. This simplifies application logic, saving you time and money, and will probably make your applications less error prone.

In the Wild: Eventual Consistency

Eventually consistent databases are widely used in large-scale systems. For example, at Netflix, the Cassandra database underpins the user experience when viewing content. In 2019, Netflix reported over six petabytes of subscriber related content in Cassandra, stored in tens of thousands of database instances and hundreds of globally distributed clusters.[10] Cassandra's low write latencies provide an excellent solution for

---

9 For example, if one process removes an element from a set concurrently with another node adding the same elements, the "add wins."

use cases that have a 9:1 write-to-read ratio. Netflix also exploits Cassandra's tunable consistency and global data replication to support its most time-critical use cases for its more than 100 million subscribers.[11]

Netflix benchmarks results from Cassandra testing are really useful for quantifying the latencies that are achievable with eventually consistent technologies.[12] For example, one benchmark test achieved 1 million writes per second with an average latency of 6 milliseconds and a P95 of 17 milliseconds. These results were produced using a Cassandra cluster with 285 nodes. Like all benchmark studies, you need to delve into the details on the Netflix technical blog to make full sense of the results.

The online betting and gaming industry relies on high availability and low latencies. It's not hard to imagine the effect of downtime and slow responses when huge amounts of bets are being placed on high-profile events such as a world championship boxing match or the soccer world cup. bet365 is one of the largest online gambling sites and built its site based on the Riak KV database.[13] bet365 calculates odds, takes bets, and manages account and transaction data for millions of concurrent users, generating gigabytes of data for processing every second. Odds change constantly and must be recalculated with low latencies to capture the effect of in-game variables. Data written to Riak KV is automatically written to multiple replicas across globally distributed clusters with tunable consistency. This provides high availability and low latencies through enabling users to access replicas that are physically close to their location.

Summary and Further Reading

Eventually consistent databases have become an established part of the landscape of scalable distributed systems. Simple, evolvable data models that are naturally partitioned and replicated for scalability and availability provide an excellent solution for many internet-scale systems.

Eventual consistency inevitably creates opportunities for systems to deliver stale reads. As a consequence, most databases provide tunable consistency. This allows the system designer to balance latencies for read and writes, and trade off availability and consistency to meet application needs.

---

10 For more details on how Netflix's cloud data engineering team uses Cassandra to manage data at petabyte scale, check out this excellent presentation (*https://oreil.ly/qVSYB*).

11 This Netflix technical blog entry (*https://oreil.ly/tUaqS*) explains how the Cassandra-based solution for scaling the user viewing history database evolved over time.

12 Cassandra benchmarks are indicative of the capabilities of eventually consistent data stores (*https://oreil.ly/HkFmB*).

13 bet365 relies so heavily on Riak KV, it actually bought the technology! An overview of its business challenges is described here (*https://oreil.ly/NGOUW*).

Concurrent writes to different replicas of the same database object can cause conflicts. These cause the database to have inconsistent replicas and to silently lose updates, neither of which are desirable in most systems. To address this problem, conflict resolution mechanisms are required. These often need application logic (and/or users) to resolve conflicts and ensure updates are not lost. This can cause additional application complexity. New research is coming to the rescue, however, and some databases support data types that have semantics to automatically resolve conflicts.

The classic reference for eventually consistent databases and the inspiration for many of today's implementations is the original Dynamo paper (*https://oreil.ly/xmR5O*). It is still a great read over a decade after its 2007 publication.

If you want to know more about how eventually consistent databases—and massive data stores in general—are built, I can think of no better source than *Designing Data-Intensive Applications* by Martin Kleppman (O'Reilly, 2017). I also enjoy *NoSQL for Mere Mortals* by Dan Sullivan (Addison-Wesley Professional, 2015) for solid basic information. And if you want to know more about CRDTs, this review paper (*https://oreil.ly/zbU7G*) is a great place to start.[14]

---

14 Marc Shapiro et al., "Convergent and Commutative Replicated Data Types," *European Association for Theoretical Computer Science*; 1999, 2011, 67–88. ⟨hal-00932833⟩ (*https://oreil.ly/2g2QH*).

CHAPTER 12

Strong Consistency

As I described in Chapter 11, eventually consistent databases are designed to scale by allowing data sets to be partitioned and replicated across multiple machines. Scalability is achieved at the expense of maintaining strong data consistency across replicas, and allowing conflicting writes.

The consequences of these trade-offs are twofold. First, after a data object has been updated, different clients may see either the old or new value for the object until all replicas converge on the latest value. Second, when multiple clients update an object concurrently, the application is responsible for ensuring data is not lost and the final object state reflects the intent of the concurrent update operations. Depending on your system's requirements, handling inconsistency and conflicts can be straightforward, or add considerable complexity to application code.

Another class of distributed databases provides an alternative model, namely strongly consistent data systems. Also known as NewSQL or, more recently, distributed SQL, strongly consistent systems attempt to ensure all clients see the same, consistent value of a data object once it has been updated. They also deliver the well-known benefits of atomicity, consistency, isolation, durability (ACID) database transactions to handle conflicting updates.

Transactions and data consistency, the characteristics everyone is familiar with in existing single-node relational databases, eliminate many of the complexities inherent in eventually consistent systems. Together they can significantly simplify application logic. As stated in Google's original Spanner distributed database paper: "We believe it is better to have application programmers deal with performance problems due to overuse of transactions as bottlenecks arise, rather than always coding around the lack of transactions."[1]

For internet-scale systems, the trick of course is to provide the benefits of strongly consistent databases, along with the performance and availability that eventually consistent systems can achieve. This is the challenge that distributed SQL databases are tackling. In this chapter, I'll explain the characteristics of these strongly consistent systems and the algorithms required to make it possible for consistent data systems to be partitioned and replicated for scalability and availability.

Introduction to Strong Consistency

In sequential programs, once you write a value (x) to a variable, you expect all subsequent reads will return (x). If this guarantee didn't hold, as it doesn't for concurrent programs without careful thread synchronization, writing software systems would be a lot more fraught.

This, however, is the case when you use an eventually consistent database system. A client may think it has written a new value to a data object, but other clients may access the same object and receive a stale value until the inconsistency window closes and all replica values have converged. In fact, as I described in Chapter 11, a client may even access an object it successfully updated and receive a stale value unless RYOWs consistency is supported.

In systems based on eventually consistent databases, applications must be aware of the precise consistency guarantees of the underlying data store, and be designed to deal with these accordingly. Handling inconsistent reads and concurrent write conflicts can add considerable complexity to code bases and test cases. If you do not take appropriate care, difficult-to-reproduce errors can creep into applications. Following Murphy's law, these will inevitably only become apparent when the system experiences high load or unexpected failures.

In contrast, strongly consistent databases aim to deliver the same consistency guarantees as single-node systems. With strong consistency, you can write applications with assurances that once an update has been confirmed by the database, all subsequent reads by all clients will see the new value. And if concurrent clients attempt to update the same object, the updates behave as if one happens before the other. They do not occur concurrently and cause data loss or corruption.

Slightly confusingly, the technical community uses strong consistency to describe two subtly different concepts in distributed databases. These are:

---

1 James C. Corbett et al., "Spanner: Google's Globally Distributed Database." ACM Transactions on Computer Systems (TOCS) 31.3 (2013), 1–22. *https://oreil.ly/QYX8y*.

Transactional consistency

This is the "C" in ACID transactions (see "ACID Transactions" on page 225) as supported by relational databases. In a distributed database that supports ACID transactions, you need an algorithm that makes it possible to maintain consistency when data objects from different physical data partitions and nodes are updated within a single transaction. Consistency in this case is defined by the semantics of the business logic executed within the transaction.

Replica consistency

Strong replica consistency implies that clients all see the same value for a data object after it has been updated, regardless of which replica they access. Basically, this eliminates the inconsistency window I covered in Chapter 11 in eventually consistent systems. There are various subtleties inherent in supporting strong replica consistency that I will explore later in this chapter.

The algorithms used for transactional and replica consistency are known as *consensus algorithms*. These algorithms enable nodes in a distributed system to reach consensus, or agreement, on the value of some shared state. For transactional consistency, all participants in the transaction must agree to commit or abort the changes executed within the transaction. For replica consistency, all replicas need to agree on the same order of updates for replicated data objects.

Solutions for transactional and replica consistency were developed by different technical communities at different times. For transactional consistency, the two-phase commit algorithm originated from work by Jim Gray, one of the pioneers of database systems, in 1978.[2] The classic replica consistency algorithm, Paxos, was first described in 1998 by Leslie Lamport.[3] I'll spend the rest of this chapter exploring transaction and replica consistency and how these algorithms are used in distributed SQL databases.

ACID Transactions

Transactions in database systems may modify multiple database objects. Such transactions support ACID properties, namely:

Atomicity

All changes to the database must be executed as if they are a single operation. This means all updates must succeed (commit), or all must fail (roll back). For example, for a purchase I make online, if my credit card is successfully charged,

---

2 Jim Gray, "Notes on Database Operating Systems." In R. Bayer et al. *Operating Systems: An Advanced Course.* Vol. 60. Lecture Notes in Computer Science. Berlin: Springer, 1978.

3 Leslie Lamport, "The Part-Time Parliament." *ACM Transactions on Computer Systems* 16, no. 2 (1998), 133–69. *https://doi.org/10.1145/279227.279229.*

my order details are recorded and sent for processing. If I have no credit, my purchase is refused.

Consistency
> Transactions will leave the database in a consistent state. If my online purchase succeeds, the number of items in stock for the products I have purchased is decreased by the number of items I selected. This property is defined by the specific business logic the transaction executes.

Isolation
> While a transaction is in progress, any data modified by the transaction is invisible to other concurrent transactions. Transactions that compete for resources are isolated from each other, and the results of a transaction are not accessible to other concurrent transactions until the transaction completes. A database achieves this by acquiring locks on the data objects that a transaction accesses, and releasing the locks when the transaction completes.

Durability
> If a transaction commits, the changes are permanent and recoverable in the event of a system failure.

The isolation property in ACID requires transactions to execute as if they were serialized (*https://oreil.ly/0dnJQ*). Serializability guarantees that concurrent transactions appear to execute in some sequential, or total, order.

Consistency Models

The database and distributed systems communities have studied consistency for more than four decades. Each has developed several different consistency models that have subtly different semantics and guarantees. This has led to a somewhat confusing and complex landscape of definitions and overloaded terminology. If you are interested in the full details, there is an excellent depiction of the different models and their relationships organized as a hierarchy on the Jepsen website (*https://oreil.ly/Z3zu7*). I'll just focus on the strongest consistency model in this chapter. This is known variously as strict consistency, strict serializability or external consistency, and implies the combination of the two most restrictive consistency models defined by the database and distributed systems communities. These are serializability and linearizability respectively, as explained in the following:

Serializability
> This is commonly referred to as *transactional* consistency, the "C" in ACID. Transactions perform one or more reads and writes on multiple data objects. Serializability guarantees that the execution of a set of concurrent transactions over multiple items is equivalent to some sequential execution order of the transactions.

Linearizability

> This is concerned with reads and writes to single data objects. Basically, it says that all clients should always see the most recent value of a data object. Once a write to a data object succeeds, all subsequent reads that occur after the write must return the value of that write, until the object is modified again. Linearizability defines the order of operations using wall clock time, such that an operation with a more recent wall clock time occurs after any operations with lower wall clock times. In distributed databases with multiple data object replicas, linearizable consistency is concerned with *replica* consistency, essentially the "C" in the CAP theorem.

Combining these two models gives the strongest possible data consistency. The basic effect is that transactions execute in a serial order (serializability), and that order is defined by the wall clock times of the transactions (linearizability). For simplicity, I'll refer to this as *strong consistency*.

Anyway, that's a summary of the theory. To support these consistency models in distributed SQL databases, we require consensus algorithms, as I explain in the rest of this chapter.

Distributed Transactions

From an application developer's perspective, the simplest way to think of transactions is as a tool to simplify failure scenarios in distributed systems. The application simply defines which operations must be carried out with ACID properties, and the database does the rest. This greatly reduces the application complexity, as you can ignore the subtle and numerous failure possibilities. Your code simply waits for the database to inform it of the transaction outcome (commit or abort) and behaves accordingly.

Example 12-1 shows a simple example of a purchasing transaction using the SQL variant of YugabyteDB.[4] The transaction modifies the `stock` table to reflect the number of items ordered by the customer, and inserts a new row in the `purchases` table to represent the customer's order. These operations are defined with a transaction boundary, marked by the `BEGIN/END TRANSACTION` syntax.

Example 12-1. An example YugabyteDB transaction

```
BEGIN TRANSACTION
UPDATE stock SET in_stock = in_stock - purchase_amount
WHERE stock_id = purchase_stock_id;
    INSERT INTO purchases (cust_id, stock_id, amount)
```

---

4 YugabyteDB (*https://oreil.ly/YKoYw*) is a distributed relational database.

```
                VALUES (customer, purchase_stock_id, purchase_amount);
    END TRANSACTION;
```

Transactional semantics ensure that both operations either succeed or fail. If a database does not support transactions, as in most NoSQL databases, the application programmer would effectively have to break the transaction down into two individual updates and define potentially complex exception handling. Basically, this would mean:

- Performing each update separately, and checking that each succeeds.

- If the INSERT fails after the UPDATE succeeds, the stock table updates must be undone using another SQL statement. This is known as a compensating action.

- If the compensating action fails, or the service executing the code fails, you need to take remedial actions. This is where things start to get really complicated!

In a single node database, committing a transaction is relatively straightforward. The database engine ensures transaction modifications and state are persisted to disk in a transaction log file. Should the database engine fail, the transaction log can be utilized on restart to restore the database to a consistent state. However, if the purchases and stock tables from Example 12-1 reside in different databases or different partitions in a distributed database, the process is somewhat more complex. You need an algorithm to ensure that both nodes agree on the transaction outcome.

Two-Phase Commit

Two-phase commit (2PC) is the classic distributed transaction consensus algorithm. It is widely implemented in established relational databases like SQL Server and Oracle, as well as contemporary distributed SQL platforms including VoltDB and Cloud Spanner. 2PC is also supported by external middleware platforms such as the Java Enterprise Edition, which includes the Java Transaction API (JTA) and Java Transaction Service (JTS) (*https://oreil.ly/BaYmu*). These external coordinators can drive distributed transactions across heterogeneous databases using the XA protocol.[5]

Figure 12-1 illustrates an example of the basic 2PC protocol based on Example 12-1. The protocol is driven by a coordinator, or leader. The coordinator can be an external service, for example the JTS, or an internal database service. In a distributed SQL database, the coordinator can be one of the partitions that is being updated as part of a multipartition transactional update.

---

5 Support for XA is mixed across platforms, and it is rarely used in large-scale systems. If you want to learn more, yours truly wrote a book on it: Ian Gorton, *Enterprise Transaction Processing Systems: Putting the Corba OTS, Encina++ and OrbixOTM to Work* (Addison-Wesley, 2000).

When a database client starts a transaction (e.g., the BEGIN TRANSACTION statement in Example 12-1), a coordinator is selected. The coordinator allocates a globally unique transaction identifier (*tid*) and returns this to the client. The *tid* identifies a data structure maintained by the coordinator known as the transaction context. The transaction context records the database partitions, or participants, that take part in the transaction and the state of their communications. The context is persisted by the coordinator, so that it durably maintains the state of the transaction.

The client then executes the operations defined by the transaction, passing the *tid* to each participant that performs the database operations. Each participant acquires locks on mutated objects and executes the operations locally. It also durably associates the *tid* with the updates in a local transaction log. These database updates are not completed at this stage—this only occurs if the transaction commits.

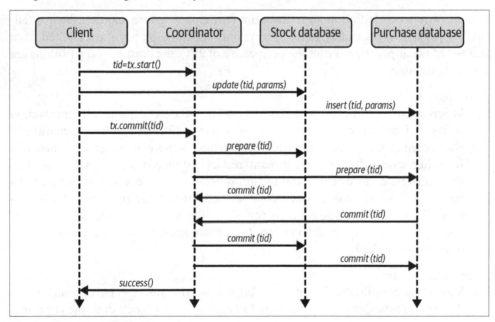

Figure 12-1. Two-phase commit

Once all the operations in the transaction are completed successfully, the client tries to commit the transaction. This is when the 2PC algorithm commences on the coordinator, which drives two rounds of votes with the participants:

Prepare phase

The coordinator sends a message to all participants to tell them to prepare to commit the transaction. When a participant successfully prepares, it guarantees that it can commit the transaction and make it durable. After this, it can no longer unilaterally decide to abort the transaction. If a participant cannot prepare, that is, if it cannot guarantee to commit the transaction, it must abort. Each participant then informs the coordinator about its decision to commit or abort by returning a message that contains its decision.

Resolve phase

When all the participants have replied to the *prepare* phase, the coordinator examines the results. If all the participants can commit, the whole transaction can commit, and the coordinator sends a commit message to each participant. If any participant has decided that it must abort the transaction, or doesn't reply to the coordinator within a specified time period, the coordinator sends an abort message to each participant.

2PC Failure Modes

2PC has two main failure modes. These are participant failure and coordinator failure. As usual, failures can be caused by systems crashing, or being partitioned from the rest of the application. From the perspective of 2PC, the crashes and partitions are indistinguishable:

Participant failure

When a participant crashes before the *prepare* phase completes, the transaction is aborted by the coordinator. This is a straightforward failure scenario. It's also possible for a participant to reply to the *prepare* message and then fail. In either case, when the participant restarts, it needs to communicate with the coordinator to discover transaction outcomes. The coordinator can use its transaction log to look up the outcomes and inform the recovered participant accordingly. The participant then completes the transaction locally. Essentially then, participant failure doesn't threaten consistency, as the correct transaction outcome is reached.

Coordinator failure

Should the coordinator fail after sending the *prepare* message, participants have a dilemma. Participants that have voted to commit must block until the coordinator informs them of the transaction outcome. If the coordinator crashes before or during sending out the commit messages, participants cannot proceed, as the coordinator has failed and will not send the transaction outcome until it recovers. This is illustrated in Figure 12-2, where the coordinator crashes after receiving the participant responses from the *prepare* phase.

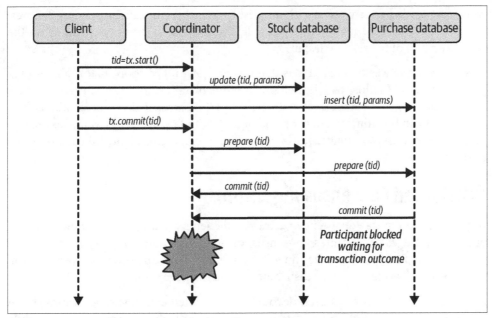

Figure 12-2. Coordinator failures causes transaction outcome to be uncertain and participants to block

There is no simple resolution to this problem. A participant cannot autonomously decide to commit as it does not know how other participants voted. If one participant has voted to roll back, and others to commit, this would violate transaction semantics. The only practical resolution is for participants to wait until the coordinator recovers and examines its transaction log.[6] The log enables the coordinator to resolve all incomplete transactions. If it has logged a commit entry for an incomplete transaction, it will inform the participants to commit. Otherwise, it will roll back the transaction.

Transaction coordinator recovery and the transaction log make it possible to finalize incomplete transactions and ensure the system maintains consistency. The downside is that participants must block while the coordinator recovers. How long this takes is implementation dependent, but is likely to be at least a few seconds. This negatively impacts availability.

In addition, during this time, participants must hold locks on the data objects mutated by the transaction. The locks are necessary to ensure transaction isolation. If other concurrent transactions try to access these locked data items, they will be blocked. This results in increased response times and may cause requests to time out.

---

6 It is possible to introduce another phase of voting to get around the problem of 2PC blocking when the coordinator fails. This is known as a three-phase commit. However, it adds even more overheads to those already inherent in 2PC, and is hence rarely used in practice.

In heavily loaded systems or during request spikes, this can cause cascading failures, circuit breakers to open, and other generally undesirable outcomes depending on the characteristics of the system design.

In summary, the weakness of 2PC is that it is not tolerant of coordinator failure. One possible way to fix this, as with all single point of failure problems, is to replicate the coordinator and transaction state across participants. If the coordinator fails, a participant can be promoted to coordinator and complete the transaction. Taking this path leads to a solution that requires a distributed consensus algorithm, as I describe in the next section.

Distributed Consensus Algorithms

Implementing replica consistency such that all clients see a consistent view of a data object's replica values requires consensus, or agreement, on every replica value. All updates to replicas for an object must be applied in the same order at every replica. Making this possible requires a distributed consensus algorithm.

Much intellectual effort has been devoted to distributed consensus algorithms in the last 40 years or so. While consensus is simple conceptually, it turns out many subtle problems arise because messages between participants can be lost or delayed, and participants can crash at inconvenient times.

As an example of the need for consensus, imagine what could happen at the end of an online auction when multiple last second bids are submitted. This is equivalent to multiple clients sending update requests that can be handled by different replicas of the same *auction* data object. In an eventually consistent system, this could lead to replicas with different bid values and potentially the loss of the highest bid.

A consensus algorithm makes sure such problems cannot occur. More specifically:

- All replicas must agree on the same winning bid. This is a correctness (or safety) property. Safety properties ensure *nothing bad happens*. In this case, two winning bids would be bad.

- A single winning bid is eventually selected. This is a liveness property. Liveness ensures *something good happens* and the system makes progress. In this case consensus is eventually reached on a single winning bid. Consensus algorithms that guarantee liveness are known as fault-tolerant consensus algorithms.

- The winning bid is one of the bids that was submitted. This ensures the algorithm can't simply be hardcoded to agree on a predetermined value.

The basis of fault-tolerant consensus approaches are a class of algorithms called atomic broadcast, total order broadcast, or replicated state machines.[7] These guarantee that a set of values, or states, are delivered to multiple nodes exactly once, and in the same order. 2PC is also a consensus algorithm. However, as I explained earlier in this chapter, it is not fault tolerant as it cannot make progress when the transaction coordinator, or leader, fails.

A number of well-known consensus algorithms exist. For example, Raft (*https:// oreil.ly/xqDOj*) is a leader-based atomic broadcast algorithm.[8] A single leader receives clients requests, establishes their order, and performs an atomic broadcast to the followers to ensure a consistent order of updates.

In contrast, Leslie Lamport's Paxos, probably the best known consensus algorithm, is leaderless. This, along with other complexities, make it notoriously tricky to implement.[9] As a consequence, a variant known as Multi-Paxos[10] was developed. Multi-Paxos has much in common with leader-based approaches like Raft and is the basis of implementations in distributed relational databases like Google Cloud Spanner.

To be fault tolerant, a consensus algorithm must make progress in the event of both leader and follower failures. When a leader fails, a single new leader must be elected and all followers must agree on the same leader. New leader election approaches vary across algorithms, but at their core they require:

- Detection of the failed leader
- One or more followers to nominate themselves as leaders
- Voting, with potentially multiple rounds, to select a new leader
- A recovery protocol to ensure all replicas attain a consistent state after a new leader is elected

Of course, followers may also be unavailable. Fault-tolerant consensus algorithms are therefore designed to operate with just a quorum, or majority, of participants. Quorums are used both for acknowledging atomic broadcasts and for leader election. As

---

7 The elements replicated are the commands which cause transitions in the replicated state machines to execute in the same order at each replica.

8 Diego Ongaro and John Ousterhout, "In Search of an Understandable Consensus Algorithm." In Proceedings of the 2014 USENIX conference on USENIX Annual Technical Conference (USENIX ATC'14), 305–320. USA: USENIX Association.

9 Tushar D. Chandra et al., "Paxos Made Live: An Engineering Perspective." In *Proceedings of the Twenty-Sixth Annual ACM Symposium on Principles of Distributed Computing (PODC '07)*, 398–407. New York, NY, USA: Association for Computing Machinery.

10 Robbert Van Renesse and Deniz Altinbuken, "Paxos Made Moderately Complex," ACM Computing Surveys 47, no. 3 (2015), 1–36. *https://doi.org/10.1145/2673577*.

long as a quorum of the participating nodes are available and agree, the algorithm can make progress. I'll explore these issues in more detail in the following subsections, which use the Raft algorithm as an example.

Raft

Raft was designed as a direct response to the complexity inherent in the Paxos algorithm. Termed "an understandable consensus algorithm," it was first published in 2013.[11] Importantly, a reference implementation was also published. This provides a concrete description of the concepts in Raft, and acts as a basis for implementers to leverage in their own systems.

Raft is a leader-based algorithm. The leader accepts all updates and defines an order for their execution. It then takes responsibility for sending these updates to all replicas in the defined order, such that all replicas maintain identical committed states. The updates are maintained as a log, and Raft essentially replicates this log to all members of the system.

A Raft cluster has an odd number of nodes, for example, three or five. This enables consensus to proceed based on quorums. At any instant, each node is either a leader, a follower, or a candidate for leader if a leader failure has been detected. The leader sends periodic heartbeat messages to followers to signal that it is still alive. The message flow in a basic Raft cluster architecture is shown in Figure 12-3. The time period for leader heartbeats is typically around 300–500 milliseconds.

Each leader is associated with a monotonically increasing value known as a *term*. The term is a logical clock, and each valid term value is associated with a single leader. The current term value is persisted locally by every node in the cluster, and is essential for leader election, as I'll soon explain. Each heartbeat message contains the current term value and leader identity and is delivered using an `AppendEntries()` message. `AppendEntries()` is also utilized to deliver new entries to commit on the log. During idle periods when the leader has no new requests from clients, an empty `AppendEntries()` simply suffices as the heartbeat.

---

11 Diego Ongaro and John Ousterhout, "In Search of an Understandable Consensus Algorithm." In Proceedings of the 2014 USENIX conference on USENIX Annual Technical Conference (USENIX ATC'14), 305–320. USA: USENIX Association.

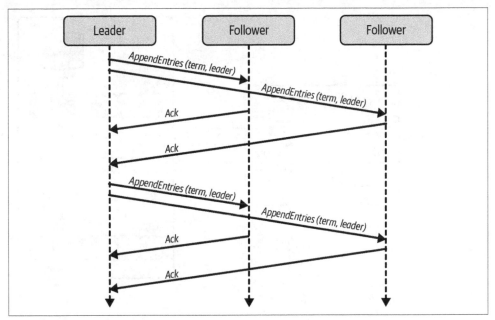

Figure 12-3. Message exchange in a Raft cluster, with one leader and two followers

During normal operations, all client updates are sent to the leader. The leader orders the updates and appends them to a local log. Initially, all log entries are marked as uncommitted. The leader then sends the updates to all followers using an `AppendEn tries` message, which also identifies the term and the position of the updates in the log. When a follower receives this message, it persists the update to its local log as uncommitted and sends an acknowledgment to the leader. Once the leader has received positive acknowledgments from a majority of followers, it marks the update as committed and communicates the decision to all followers.

This protocol is depicted in Figure 12-4. Log entries 1 and 2 are committed on all three replicas, and the corresponding mutations are applied to the database partitions to become visible to clients. Log entry 3 is only committed on the leader and one follower. *Follower 1* will eventually commit this update.

Clients also have sent updates to the leader represented by log entries 4 and 5. The leader writes these to its local log and marks them as uncommitted. It will then send `AppendEntries()` messages to the followers and if no exceptions occur, followers will acknowledge these updates and they will be committed at all the replicas.

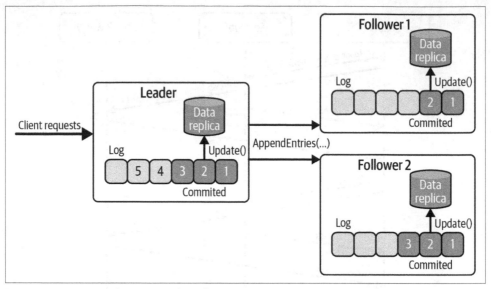

Figure 12-4. Log replication with Raft

Only a majority of followers are required to commit an entry on the log. This means the committed log entries may not be identical at every follower at any instant. If a follower falls behind or is partitioned, and is not acknowledging `AppendEntries` requests, the leader continues to resend messages until the follower responds. Duplicated messages to followers can be recognized using the term and sequence numbers in the messages and safely discarded.

Leader Election

The leader in Raft sends periodic heartbeat messages to followers. Each follower maintains an election timer, which it starts after receiving a heartbeat message. If the timer expires before another heartbeat is received, the follower starts an election. Election timers are randomized to minimize the likelihood that multiple followers time out simultaneously and call an election.

If a follower's election timeout expires, it changes its state to candidate, increments the election term value, and sends a `RequestVote` message to all nodes. It also votes for itself. The `RequestVote` message contains the candidate's identifier, the new term value, and information about the state of the committed entries in the candidate's log. The candidate then waits until it receives replies. If it receives a majority of positive votes, it will transition to leader, and start sending out heartbeats to inform the other nodes in the cluster about its newly acquired status. If a majority of votes are not received, it remains a candidate and resets its election timer.

When followers receive a `RequestVote` message, they perform one of the following actions:

- If the term in the incoming message is greater than the locally persisted term, and the candidate's log is at least as up to date as the follower's, it votes for the candidate.
- If the term is less than or equal to the local term, or the follower's log has committed log entries that are not present in the candidate's log, it denies the leadership request.

For example, *Follower 1* in Figure 12-4 could not become leader as its committed log entries are not up to date. *Follower 2* does have all committed log entries and could become leader. To illustrate this, Figure 12-5 shows how *Follower-2* can transition to leader when its election timer expires.

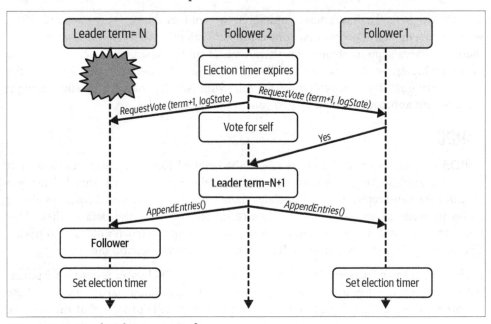

Figure 12-5. Leader election in Raft

These conditions on Raft's leader election ensure that any elected leader has all the committed entries from previous terms in its log. If a candidate does not have all committed entries in its log, it cannot receive a positive vote from more up-to-date followers. The candidate will then back down, another election will be started, and eventually a candidate with the most up-to-date log entries will win.

It's also possible for the election timers of two or more followers to expire simultaneously. When this happens, each follower will transition to a candidate, increment the term, and send `RequestVote` messages. Raft enforces a rule whereby any node can only vote once within a single term. Hence, when multiple candidates start an election:

- One may receive a majority of votes and win an election.
- None may receive a majority. In this case, candidates reset their election timers and another election will be initiated. Eventually a leader will be elected.

Raft has attracted considerable interest due to its relative simplicity. It is implemented in multiple production systems that require consensus. These include databases such as the Neo4j and YugabyteDB databases, the etcd key-value store, and Hazelcast, a distributed in-memory object store.

Strong Consistency in Practice

Distributed SQL databases have undergone a rapid evolution since around 2011, when the term NewSQL was first coined (*https://oreil.ly/62Aji*). The manner in which these databases support strong consistency varies quite considerably across this class of technologies, so it pays to dig into the often-murky details to understand the consistency guarantees provided. In the following two sections, I'll briefly highlight the different approaches taken by two contemporary examples.

VoltDB

VoltDB (*https://www.voltdb.com*) is one of the original NewSQL databases. It is built upon a shared-nothing architecture, in which relational tables are sharded using a partition key and replicated across nodes. Low latencies are achieved by maintaining tables in memory and asynchronously writing snapshots of the data to disk. This limits the database size to the total memory available in the cluster of VoltDB nodes. The primary deployments of VoltDB are in the telecommunication industry.

Each VoltDB table partition is associated with a single CPU core. A core is responsible for executing all read and write requests at its associated partitions, and these are ordered sequentially by a Single Partition Initiator (SPI) process that runs on the core. This means each core executes database requests on its associated partitions in a strict single-threaded manner. Single-threaded execution alleviates contention concerns and the overheads of locking, and is an important mechanism that facilitates VoltDB's ACID consistency support. The SPI for a partition also ensures write requests are executed in the same order for each partition replica.

Clients submit requests as SQL stored procedures. A stored procedure is regarded as a transactional unit. When a client request arrives at VoltDB, the SQL query analyzer generates an execution plan based on the database schema and the partition keys and indexes available for the tables. Based on this execution plan, VoltDB sends requests to the partition or partitions that the query needs to access.

Importantly, VoltDB delivers queries to each partition replica for execution in exactly the same order. The SPI associated with a partition simply accepts requests into a local command log and executes them one at a time, as illustrated in Figure 12-6. The query analyzer determines which table a stored procedure wishes to access. It then dispatches the stored procedures to be executed serially by the CPU core that is associated with the table partitions necessary to execute the transaction.

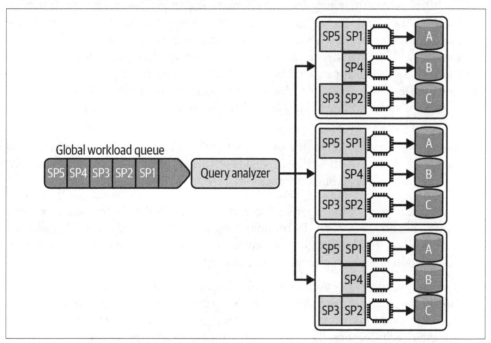

Figure 12-6. VoltDB single partition transaction execution architecture

This has important implications for write transactions, based on whether the transaction mutates data in one or multiple partitions. If a transaction only modifies data in a single partition, as in Figure 12-6, it can execute at each SPI and commit unimpeded at each replica. As VoltDB sends transactions to execute at each partition replica in exactly the same order, this guarantees serializability without the need for data object locking and 2PC. Simply, you don't have isolation concerns in a single-threaded system. Hence, single partition transactions can execute with extremely low latency.

However, if the query planner determines a transaction mutates data in two or more partitions, VoltDB sends the request for coordination across multiple cores. A cluster-wide Multi-Partition Initiator (MPI) acts as the coordinator and drives a 2PC algorithm to ensure the transaction commits or aborts atomically at all partitions. This introduces higher overheads and hence lower performance for multipartition transactions.

As VoltDB is an in-memory database, it must take additional measures to provide data safety and durability. You can configure two mechanisms, periodic command logging and partition snapshots, to meet application performance and safety requirements as described in the following:

- Each SPI writes the entries in its command log to persistent storage. If a node fails, VoltDB can restore the partition by reading the latest snapshot of the partition and sequentially executing the commands in the command log. Command log durability hence facilitates recoverability. The frequency with which the command log is persisted is controlled by a system-defined interval value. The shorter the interval (on the scale of a few milliseconds), the lower risk of losing updates if a node should crash. There's an inherent trade-off here between performance and safety.
- Each partition also defines a snapshot interval. This defines how often the local partition's data is written to disk. Typically, this is configured in the seconds-to-minutes range, depending on transaction load.

These two settings have an important interaction. When VoltDB successfully writes a partition to persistent storage, the command log can be truncated. This is because the outcome of all the transactions in the command log are durable in the latest partition snapshot, and hence the commands can be discarded.

Finally, since version 6.4, VoltDB supports linearizability, and hence the strongest consistency level, within the same database cluster. VoltDB achieves linearizability because it reaches consensus on the order of writes at all partitions, and transactions do not interleave because they are executed sequentially. However, up until this version, stale reads were possible as read-only transactions were not strictly ordered with write transactions, and could be served by out-of-date replicas. The root cause of this issue was an optimization that tried to load balance reads across partitions. You can read all about the details of the tests that exposed these problems and the fixes at the Jepsen website.[12]

---

12 Kyle Kingsbury provides distributed database consistency testing using the Jepsen test suite. The results for testing VoltDB 6.3 (*https://oreil.ly/eCj8P*) are a fascinating read.

Google Cloud Spanner

In 2013, Google published the Spanner database paper.[13] Spanner is designed as a strongly consistent, globally distributed SQL database. Google refers to this strong consistency as *external consistency*. Essentially, from the programmer's perspective, Spanner behaves indistinguishably from a single machine database. Spanner is exposed to Google clients through the Cloud Spanner service. Cloud Spanner is a cloud-based database as a service (DBaaS) platform.

To scale out, Cloud Spanner partitions database tables into splits (shards). Splits contain a contiguous key range for a table, and one machine can host multiple splits. Splits are also replicated across multiple availability zones to provide fault tolerance. Cloud Spanner keeps replicas consistent using the Paxos consensus algorithm. Like Raft, Paxos enables a set of replicas to agree on the order of a sequence of updates. The Cloud Spanner Paxos implementation has long-lived elected leaders and commits replica updates upon a majority vote from the replica set.

Cloud Spanner hides the details of table partitioning from the programmer. It will dynamically repartition data across machines as data volumes grow or shrink and migrate data to new locations to balance load. An *API layer* processes user requests. This utilizes an optimized, fault tolerant lookup service to find the machines that host the key ranges a query accesses.

Cloud Spanner supports ACID transactions. If a transaction only updates data in a single split, the Paxos leader for the split processes the request. It first acquires locks on the rows that are modified, and communicates the mutations to each replica. When a majority of replicas vote to commit, in parallel the leader responds to the client and tells the replicas to apply the changes to the persistent storage.

Transactions that modify data in multiple splits are more complex, and incur more overhead. When the client attempts to commit the transaction, it selects the leader of one of the modified splits as the transaction coordinator to drive a 2PC algorithm. The other split leaders become participants in the transaction. This architecture is depicted in Figure 12-7. The *Purchases* table leader is selected as the 2PC coordinator, and it communicates with the leaders from the modified *Stock West* and *Stock East* table splits as 2PC participants. Cloud Spanner uses Paxos to ensure consensus on the order of replica updates within each replica group.

---

13 James C. Corbett et al., "Spanner: Google's Globally Distributed Database." ACM Transactions on Computer Systems (TOCS) 31.3 (2013), 1–22. *https://dl.acm.org/doi/10.1145/2491245.*

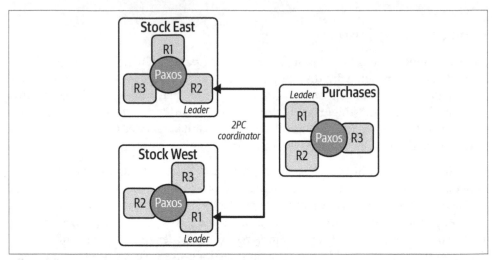

Figure 12-7. Cloud Spanner 2PC

The coordinator communicates the client request to each participant. As each participant is the Paxos leader for the split, it acquires locks for the rows modified on a majority of split replicas. When all participants confirm they have acquired the necessary locks, the coordinator chooses a commit timestamp and tells the participants to commit. The participants subsequently communicate the commit decision and timestamp to each of their replicas, and all replicas apply the updates to the database. Should a participant be unable to prepare to commit, the coordinator directs all participants to abort the transaction.

Importantly, the 2PC implementation behaves as a Paxos group. The coordinator replicates the state of the transaction to the participants using Paxos. Should the coordinator fail, one of the participants can take over as leader and complete the transaction. This eliminates the problem I described earlier in this chapter of coordinator failure leading to blocked transactions, at the cost of additional coordination using Paxos.

Cloud Spanner also supports linearizability of transactions. This basically means that if transaction T1 commits before transaction T2, then transaction T2 can only commit at a later time, enforcing real-time ordering. T2 can also observe the results of T1 after it commits.

Figure 12-8 demonstrates how this works in Spanner. Transaction T1 reads and modifies data object (x). It then successfully commits, and the commit occurs at time t1. Transaction T2 starts after T1 but before T1 commits. T2 reads and modifies data object (y), then reads and modifies (x), and finally commits at time t2. When T2 reads (x), it sees the effects of T1 on (x) as the read occurs after T1 commits.

Cloud Spanner uses the commit time for a transaction to timestamp all the objects modified within the transaction scope. This means all the effects of a transaction appear to have occurred at exactly the same instant in time. In addition, the order of the transactions is reflected in the commit timestamps, as t1 < t2.

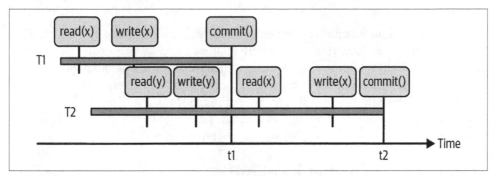

Figure 12-8. Linearizability of transactions in Cloud Spanner

Achieving linearizability requires a reliable time source across all nodes.[14] This is not possible using the NTP-style time services, as clock skew across nodes can be of the order of a few hundred milliseconds. From Figure 12-8, transaction T2 may commit at an earlier time than transaction T1 if T2 is using a time source that is behind that of T1.

Cloud Spanner implements a unique solution to this problem, namely the TrueTime service. TrueTime equips Google data centers with satellite connected GPS and atomic clocks, and provides closely synchronized clocks with a known upper bound clock skew, reportedly around 7 milliseconds. All data objects in Spanner are associated with a TrueTime timestamp that represents the commit time of the transaction that last mutated the object.

As TrueTime still has an inherent, albeit small, clock skew, Cloud Spanner introduces a *commit wait* period. A commit timestamp is generated from TrueTime and the coordinator then waits for a period that is equal to the known upper bound clock skew. By introducing this wait period, all transaction locks are held and the data mutated by the transaction is not visible to other transactions until TrueTime is guaranteed to report a higher timestamp at all nodes. This ensures any concurrent transactions will be blocked on the locks and hence must use a higher commit timestamp, and all clients will always see commit timestamps that are in the past.

There's one more ingredient needed for strong consistency in Cloud Spanner. As updates are replicated by Paxos and committed when a majority of nodes agree, it is possible for a client read request to access a replica that has not received the

---

14 Or serialized execution of transactions based on a globally agreed order—see "VoltDB" on page 238.

latest update for a data object. By default, Cloud Spanner provides strongly consistent reads. When a replica receives a read, it communicates with the Paxos leader for its replica split and checks it has the most up-to-date value for all objects accessed by the read. Again, this mechanism introduces overheads to guarantee clients do not see stale data.

Cloud Spanner is an integral component of GCP. Its customer base spans industries such as financial services, retail, and gaming, all attracted by the strong consistency guarantees as well as high availability and globally distributed deployment capabilities. Interestingly, Cloud Spanner has inspired open source implementations based on the Spanner architecture, but which do not require custom TrueTime-style hardware. The trade-off, of course, is lower consistency guarantees.[15] Notable examples are CockroachDB (*https://oreil.ly/jIQlw*) and YugabyteDB (*https://oreil.ly/QtOgO*).

Summary and Further Reading

For many application areas, a scalable and highly available distributed database with the consistency guarantees and ease of programming of a single machine is the holy grail of data management systems. Building such a database turns out to be rather difficult. Additional coordination and consensus mechanisms need to be incorporated to provide the data consistency expected of a sequential system. These database platforms are complex to build correctly and even more complex to make highly available and provide low response times.

Consistency in general is a complex topic, with overloaded terminology generated separately by the database and distributed systems communities. In this chapter, I've focused on the two strongest consistency guarantees from each community, serializability and linearizability, and explained consensus algorithms that are fundamental to achieving these levels of consistency. Using VoltDB and Cloud Spanner as examples, I've shown how distributed databases at scale utilize these algorithms along with innovative design approaches to achieve strong consistency.

Distributed systems consistency remains a topic of active research and innovation. A unique approach for a strongly consistent database is embodied in the Calvin database system.[16] Calvin preprocesses and sequences transactions so that they are executed by replicas in the same order. This is known as deterministic transaction execution. It essentially reduces the coordination overheads of transaction execution as every replica sees the same inputs and hence will produce the same outputs.

---

15 This blog post (*https://oreil.ly/lUUSp*) by Spencer Kimball and Irhan Sharif is an excellent analysis of how distributed SQL databases can approach the highest consistency guarantees with NTP-based clocks.

16 Alexander Thompson et al, 2012. "Calvin: Fast Distributed Transactions for Partitioned Database Systems." In Proceedings of the 2012 ACM SIGMOD International Conference on Management of Data (SIGMOD '12), 1–12. New York, NY, USA: Association for Computing Machinery.

Fauna (*https://fauna.com*) is the most notable database implementation of the Calvin architecture.

If you really want to deep dive into the world of consistency, the Jepsen website (*https://jepsen.io*) is a wonderful resource. There are around 30 detailed analyses of adherence to promised consistency levels for multiple distributed databases. These analyses are often extremely revealing and expose areas where promises don't always meet reality.

CHAPTER 13

Distributed Database Implementations

In the previous three chapters, I've described the various distributed system principles and architectures that are widely employed in scalable distributed databases. These make it possible to partition and replicate data over multiple storage nodes, and support different consistency and availability models for replicated data objects.

Precisely how specific databases build on these principles is highly database dependent. Different database providers pick and choose among well-understood approaches, as well as designing their own proprietary mechanisms, to implement the software architecture quality attributes they wish to promote in their products. This means databases that are superficially similar in their architectures and features will likely behave very differently. Even implementations of the same feature—for example, primary election—can vary significantly in terms of their performance and robustness across databases.

Evaluating a database technology for a specific use case therefore requires both knowledge and diligence. You need to understand how the basic architecture and data model of a candidate technology match your requirements in terms of scalability, availability, consistency, and of course other qualities such as security that are beyond the scope of this book. To do this effectively, you need to delve under the hood and gain insights into precisely how high-priority features for your application work. I don't think I'd surprise anyone by telling you about the dangers of faithfully believing marketing materials. With apologies to George Orwell, all databases are scalable, but some are more scalable than others.

In this chapter I'll briefly review the salient features of three widely deployed distributed databases, namely Redis, MongoDB, and DynamoDB. Each of these implementations support different data models and make very different trade-offs on the consistency-versus-availability continuum. These design decisions percolate through to the performance and scalability each system offers.

The approach I take can work as a blueprint for carrying out your own database platform comparisons. You'll see many of the concepts already discussed in this book raising their heads here again. You'll also see product-specific approaches to solving some of the problems faced in distributed databases. As always, the devil lurks deeply in the details.

Redis

Since its initial release in 2009, Redis (*https://redis.io*) has grown in popularity to become one of the most widely deployed distributed databases. The main attraction of Redis is its ability to act as both a distributed cache and data store. Redis maintains an in-memory data store, known as a *data structure store*. Clients send commands to a Redis server to manipulate the data structures it holds.

Redis is implemented in C and uses a single-threaded event loop to process client requests. In version 6.0, this event loop was augmented with additional threads to handle network operations in order to provide more bandwidth for the event loop to process client requests. This enables a Redis server to better exploit multicore nodes and provide higher throughput.

To provide data safety, the in-memory data structure maintained by a single Redis server can be made durable using two approaches. In one, you can configure a periodic background thread to dump the memory contents to disk. This snapshot process uses the fork() system call, and hence can be expensive if the memory contents are large. In high-throughput systems, snapshots are typically configured at intervals of tens of seconds. Snapshots can also be triggered after a configurable number of writes to provide a known bound of potential data loss.

The other approach is to configure Redis to log every command to an append-only file (AOF). This is essentially an operation log, and is persisted by default every second. Using both approaches, namely snapshots and operation logging, provides the greatest data safety guarantees. In the event of a server crash, the AOF can be replayed against the latest snapshot to recreate the server data contents in memory.

Data Model and API

Redis is a key-value store. It offers a small collection of data structures that applications can use to create data objects associated with unique keys. Each data structure has a set of defined commands that applications use to create, manipulate, and delete data objects. Commands are simple and operate on a single object identified by the key.

The core Redis structures are:

Strings

Strings are versatile in Redis and are able to store both text and binary data with a maximum of 512 MB in length. For example, you can use strings as a random access vector using `get()` and `set()` operations on specified subranges. Strings can also be used to represent and manipulate counters.

Linked lists

These are lists of strings, with operations to manipulate elements at the head, tail, and in the body of the list.

Sets and sorted sets

Sets represent a collection of unique strings. Sorted sets associate a *score* value with each element and maintain the strings in ascending score order. This makes it possible to efficiently access elements in the set by score or rank order.

Hashes

Like a Python map, a Redis hash maps a key value represented as a string to one or more string values. Hashes are the primary Redis structure for representing application data objects such as user profiles or stock inventory.

Operations on a single key are atomic. You can also specify a group of operations as requiring atomic execution using the `multi` and `exec` commands. All commands you place between `multi` and `exec` are called Redis transactions, and are serialized and executed in order. An example of a Redis transaction is in the code example below, which defines a transaction with two operations. The first adds a string representing a new customer order to a `neworders` list. The second modifies the value of the key `lastorder` in the hashmap for the user. A Redis server queues these commands until it receives the `exec` command, and then executes them in sequence:

```
multi
lpush neworders "orderid 600066 customer 89788 item 788990 amount 11 date
12/24/21"
hmset user:89788 lastorder 600066
exec
```

Transactions are essentially the only way to perform operations that move or compute data across multiple types. They are limited, however, in that they only provide atomicity when all commands succeed. If a command fails, there are no rollback capabilities. This means that even if one command fails, the remaining commands in the transaction will still be executed. Similarly, if a crash occurs while the server is executing the transaction, the server is left in an unknown state. Using the AOF durability mechanism, you can fix the state administratively on restart. In reality, Redis transactions are somewhat of a misnomer; they certainly aren't ACID.

Distribution and Replication

In its original version, Redis was a single server data store, which somewhat limited its scalability. In 2015, Redis Cluster (*https://oreil.ly/Ut17g*) was released to facilitate partitioning and replication of a Redis data store across multiple nodes. Redis Cluster defines 16,384 hash slots for a cluster. Every key is hashed modulo 16,384 to a specific slot, which is configured to reside on a host in the cluster. This is illustrated in Figure 13-1, in which four nodes with unique identifiers comprise the cluster and an equal range of hash slots is assigned to each.

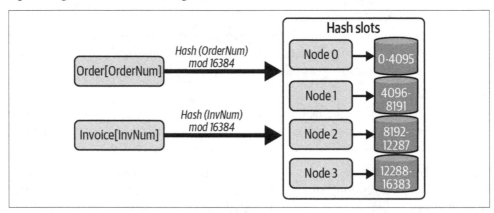

Figure 13-1. Sharding in Redis using hash slots

Each node in the cluster runs a Redis server and an additional component that handles internode communications in the cluster. Redis uses a protocol known as the *Cluster bus* to enable direct TCP communications between every node in the cluster. Nodes maintain state information about all other nodes in the cluster, including the hash slots that each node serves. Redis implements this capability using a gossip protocol that efficiently enables nodes to track the state of all the nodes in the cluster.

Clients can connect to any node in the cluster and submit commands to manipulate specified keys. If a command arrives at a node that does not manage the hash slot for a given object, it looks up the address of the server that hosts the required hash slot. It then responds to the client with a MOVED error and the address of the node where the keys in the hash slot reside. The client must then resend the command to the correct node. Typically, Redis client drivers will maintain an internal directory that maps hash slots to server nodes so that redirections do not occur when the cluster is stable.

Another implication of this architecture is that commands in transactions must access keys that reside in the same hash slot. Redis does not have capabilities to execute commands on objects that reside in different hash slots and different nodes. This requires careful data modeling to work around this limitation. Redis does provide support for a workaround using a concept known as hash tags which force keys into the same hash slot based on a substring of the key which is identical for different objects.

You can resize a Redis Cluster to add new nodes or remove nodes from the cluster. When this occurs, hash slots must be assigned to the new nodes or moved from the deleted nodes to existing nodes. You perform this action using the CLUSTER administrative command that modifies a node's cluster configuration information. Once hash slots are reassigned to a different node, Redis migrates the objects in the migrated hash slots automatically. Objects are serialized and sent from their existing home node to the new home node. When an object is successfully acknowledged, it is removed from the original home node and becomes visible to clients at its new location.

You can also replicate every node in a cluster using a primary-replica architecture. The primary updates replicas asynchronously to provide data safety. To scale out read workloads, you can configure replicas to handle read commands. By default, the primary does not wait until replicas acknowledge an update before returning success to the client.

Optionally, the client can issue a WAIT command after an update. This specifies the number of replicas that should acknowledge the update and a timeout period after which the WAIT should return. A timeout period of zero specifies that the client should block indefinitely. In the following example, the client blocks until two replicas have acknowledged updates, or a 500 milliseconds timeout expires. In either case, Redis returns the number of replicas that have been updated:

```
WAIT 2 500
```

In the event of a primary failure, a replica is promoted to primary. Redis uses a custom primary election algorithm. A replica that detects its primary has failed starts an election and attempts to obtain a vote from a majority of primary nodes in the cluster. If it obtains a majority, it promotes itself to primary and informs the nodes in the cluster. The election algorithm enables replicas to exchange information to try and determine which replica is most up to date. There is no guarantee, however, that the most up-to-date replica will eventually be promoted to primary. Hence some data loss is possible if an out-of-date replica becomes primary.

Strengths and Weaknesses

One way to think about Redis, and in fact most in-memory databases, is that it is essentially a disk-backed cache with trailing persistence. This architecture has an inherent performance versus data safety trade-off. I'll dig into how this manifests in Redis in the following subsections.

Performance

Redis is designed for low latency responses and high throughput. The primary data store is main memory, making for fast data object access. The limited collection of data structures and operations also make it possible for Redis to optimize requests and use space-efficient data object representations. As long as you can design your data model within the constraints of the Redis data types, you should see some very impressive performance.

Data safety

Redis trades off data safety for performance. In the default configuration, there is a 1-second window between AOF writes during which a crash can cause data loss. You can improve data safety by persisting the AOF on every write. Unfortunately, the performance hit of this configuration is substantial under heavy write loads.

Redis also uses a proprietary replication and primary election algorithm. A replica that is not up to date can be elected as leader, and hence data persisted at the previous leader may be lost.

The bottom line is that you probably don't want to use Redis (or any in-memory database) as your primary data store if data loss is not an option.[1] But if you can tolerate occasional data loss, Redis can provide very impressive throughput indeed.

Scalability

Redis Cluster is the primary scalability mechanism for Redis. It allows up to 1,000 nodes to host sharded databases distributed across 16,384 hash slots. Replicas for each primary can also serve read requests, enabling scaling of read workloads. If you need more than 1,000 primary nodes, then you must design your data store accordingly.

Consistency

Redis replication provides eventual consistency by default based on asynchronous replication. Stale reads from replicas are therefore possible. Using the WAIT command, the replication approach becomes effectively synchronous, as the primary does not respond to the client until the requested number of replicas have acknowledged the update. The trade-off of WAIT is longer latencies. In addition, it only guarantees data resides in memory in replicas. A replica crash before the next snapshot of AOF write could lead to the update being lost.

---

1 Emil Koutanov goes into more detail with an excellent analysis of data safety in Redis (*https://oreil.ly/MOBIq*).

Availability

Redis Cluster implements a tried-and-tested primary-replica architecture for individual database shards. Write availability is inevitably impacted by leader failure. Writes will be unavailable for a given shard until a replica is promoted to leader.

Network faults can split a Redis Cluster deployment into majority and minority partitions. This has implications for both availability and data safety. Client writes can continue to all leader nodes in both partitions as long as they have at least one replica available. If a leader is split from its replicas in a minority partition, writes are still initially available for clients that also reside in the minority partition. After a timeout period, the partitioned leader will stop accepting writes as it cannot send updates to its replicas. Concurrently, a leader election will occur in the majority partition and a replica will be promoted to primary. When the partition heals, the write modifications made to the previous leader while partitioned will be lost.

MongoDB

MongoDB has been at the forefront of the NoSQL database movement since its first release in 2009. It directly addressed the well-known object-relational impedance mismatch by essentially harmonizing the database model with object models. The resulting document database can be best thought of as a JSON database. You can transform your business objects to JSON and store, query, and manipulate your data directly as a document. No elaborate object-relational mapper is needed. The result is intuitive and simpler business logic.

The initial popularity of MongoDB was driven by its ease of programming and use. The underlying storage engine in the early releases, known as MMAPv1,[2] left something to be desired. MMAPv1 implements memory-mapped files using the `mmap()` system call. Documents in the same logical groupings, known as *collections*, are allocated contiguously on disk. This is great for sequential read performance. But if an object grows in size, new space has to be allocated and all document indexes updated. This can be a costly operation, and leads to disk fragmentation.

To minimize this cost, MMAPv1 initially allocates documents with additional space to accommodate growth. A solution indeed, but perhaps not the most space efficient and scalable. In addition, document locks for updates are obtained at very coarse grain levels (e.g., in various releases, server, database, collection), causing less than spectacular write performance.

Around 2015, the development team reengineered MongoDB to support a pluggable storage engine architecture. Soon after, a new storage engine, WiredTiger, became

---

2 MMAPv1 was deprecated in MongoDB version 4.0. You can find its documentation at *https://oreil.ly/uWiNx*.

default in MongoDB v3.2. WiredTiger addresses many of the shortcomings of MMAPv1.[3] It introduces optimistic concurrency control and document-level locking, compression, operational journaling and checkpointing for crash recovery, and its own internal cache for improved performance.

Data Model and API

MongoDB documents are basically JSON objects with a set of extended types defined in the Binary JSON (BSON) specification. Documents are stored in BSON format and organized in databases comprising one or more collections. Collections are equivalent to a relational database table, but without a defined schema. This means MongoDB collections do not enforce a structure on documents. Documents with different structures can be stored in the same collection. This is a schemaless, or schema-on-read approach that requires the application to interpret a document structure on access.

MongoDB documents are composed of name-value pairs. The value of a field may be any BSON data type. Documents can also incorporate other documents, known as embedded or nested documents, and arrays of values or documents. Every document has an _id field which acts as the primary key. Applications can set this key value on document creation, or allow the MongoDB client to automatically allocate a unique value. You can also define secondary indexes on any field, subfield or on multiple fields—a compound key—in a collection.

An example document that you might find in a skier management system is shown in the code below. The field `skiresorts` is represented as an array of strings, and each different ski day is represented by an element in an array of nested documents:

```
{
    _id: 6788321471
    name: { first: "Ian", last: "Gorton" }
    location: "USA-WA-Seattle",
    skiresorts: ["Crystal Mountain", "Mission Ridge"]
    numdays: 2
    season21 {
        {
            day: 1
            resort: "Crystal Mountain",
            vertical: 30701
            lifts: 27
            date: "12/1/2021"
        }
        {
            day: 2
            resort: "Mission Ridge",
```

---

3 A good comparison of the two file systems can be found on the Percona blog (*https://oreil.ly/NVLTb*).

```
                    vertical: 17021
                    lifts: 10
                    date: "12/8/2021"
            }
        }
    }
```

As there is no uniform document structure in a collection, the storage engine needs to persist field names and values for every document. For small documents, long field names may end up representing the majority of the document size. Shorter field names can reduce the size of the document on disk, and at scale, in a collection with many millions of documents, this saving will become significant.[4] Optimized document sizes reduce disk usage, memory and cache consumption, and network bandwidth. As usual, at scale, small optimizations can pay back many times in minimizing resource utilization.

To manipulate documents, MongoDB provides APIs for basic CRUD operations. There is a `.find()` method with an extensive set of conditions and operators that emulate an SQL `SELECT` statement for documents in a single collection. MongoDB supports aggregate queries with the `$match` and `$group` operators, and the `$lookup` operator provides SQL `JOIN`-like behavior across collections in the same database. A simple example of querying a collection is shown in the following. The `.find()` operation returns all documents for skiers who have registered more than 20 ski days from the `skiers2021` collection:

```
db.skiers2021.find({ numdays: { $gt: 20 } })
```

Write operations to a single document in MongoDB are atomic. For this reason, if you denormalize your data model to make extensive use of nested documents, you can avoid the complexities of updating multiple documents and distributed transactions in your application code. Before MongoDB version 4.0, this was essentially the only way to ensure consistency for multidocument updates without complex application logic to handle failures.

Since version 4.0, support for ACID, multidocument transactions has been implemented. MongoDB transactions use two-phase commit (*https://oreil.ly/3K2XG*) and leverage the underlying WiredTiger storage engine's snapshot isolation capabilities. Snapshot isolation is a weaker guarantee than the serialization implied by the ACID semantics. This enables higher performance than serialization and avoids most, but not all, of the concurrency anomalies that serializability avoids. Snapshot isolation is actually the default in many relational databases, including Oracle and PostgreSQL.

---

4 This blog post (*https://oreil.ly/SFe45*) by David Murphy illustrates how a 25% reduction in document size can be achieved with shorter field names.

Distribution and Replication

To scale horizontally, you can choose between two data partitioning or sharding strategies with MongoDB. These are hash-based and range-based sharding, respectively. You define a shard key for each document based on one or more field values. Upon document creation, MongoDB then chooses a database shard to store the document based on either:

- The result of a hash function applied to the shard key
- The shard that is defined to store the shard key range within which the key resides

Sharded deployments in MongoDB require you to deploy several distinct database components. The *mongod* process is the MongoDB database daemon that must run on every shard. The *mongos* process is responsible for processing database client queries by routing requests to the targeted shard(s) and returning the results to the client. Clients issue MongoDB API calls using a MongoDB driver. *Config servers* store database cluster configuration metadata, which the *mongos* uses to route queries to the correct shards based on shard key values. This architecture is depicted in Figure 13-2.

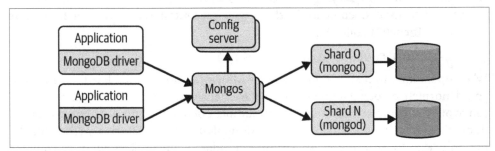

Figure 13-2. MongoDB database partitioning architecture

The *mongos* process acts as a proxy between the client's MongoDB driver and the database shards. All client requests must pass through a *mongos* instance. A *mongos* has no persistent state, and simply caches the cluster configuration information it obtains from the *config servers*.

The *mongos* process is the client's only query interface. It is therefore critical for performance and scalability that sufficient *mongos* processing capacity is available. Precisely how you configure *mongos* deployments is highly dependent on your applications needs, and MongoDB provides you with flexibility to design your system to satisfy the required workload. There are three basic alternatives, as depicted in Figure 13-3:

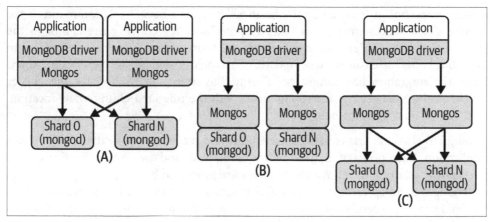

Figure 13-3. MongoDB database deployment alternatives

Configuration (A)
> Deploy a *mongos* on each application server that acts as a MongoDB client. This reduces latency by making every client request to *mongos* a local call.

Configuration (B)
> Deploy a *mongos* on every database shard. In this configuration, a *mongos* can communicate with the shard locally.

Configuration (C)
> Deploy a collection of *mongos* on their own dedicated hardware. You incur additional network latency communicating with the client and database shards. The trade-off is that the *mongos* load is eliminated from the application server and database nodes, and the *mongos* processes are allocated more exclusive processing capacity.

Within each shard, MongoDB stores documents in storage units known as chunks. By default a chunk is a maximum of 64 MB. When a chunk grows beyond its maximum configured size, MongoDB automatically splits the chunk into two or more new chunks. Chunk splitting is a metadata change, triggered by inserts or updates, and does not involve any data movement.

As the data grows across the cluster, the data distribution across shards can become unbalanced. This creates uneven loads on shards and can produce hotspots—shards that are heavily loaded with requests for commonly accessed keys. Hotspots impair query performance. For this reason, MongoDB runs a cluster balancer process on the primary *config server*. The cluster balancer monitors the data distribution across shards and if it detects that a (configurable) migration threshold has been reached, it triggers a chunk migration. Migration thresholds are based on the difference between the number of data chunks between the shard with the most chunks and the shard with the least chunks for a collection.

Chunk migration is initiated by the balancer. It sends a `moveChunk` command to the source shard. The source shard takes responsibility for copying the chunk to the destination. While migration is occurring, the source shard handles any updates to the chunk, and it ensures these updates are synchronized to the destination shard after the migration has completed. Finally, the source shard updates the cluster configuration metadata at the *config server* with the migrated chunk's new location, and deletes its copy of the chunk.

MongoDB also supports enhanced availability and read query capacity through shard replication. Each primary shard can have multiple secondaries, and collectively these are known as a replica set. All client writes are processed by the primary, and it logs all changes to an *operations log (oplog)* data structure. Periodically, the primary ships its oplog to the secondaries, which in turn apply the modifications in the oplog to their local database copy. This approach is illustrated in Figure 13-4.

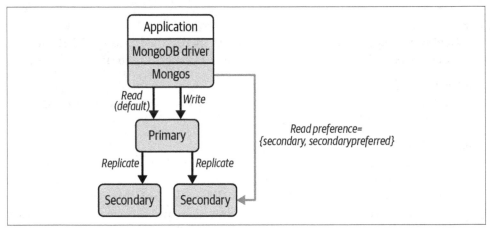

Figure 13-4. MongoDB replica sets

Nodes in a replica set send periodic heartbeat messages, by default every two seconds, to confirm member availability. If a secondary node does not receive a heartbeat message from a primary in a (by default) 10-second period, it commences a leader election. The leader election algorithm is based on Raft (*https://oreil.ly/ymXl5*). In addition, if a leader is partitioned in a minority partition, it will step down as leader. A new leader will subsequently be elected from the majority partition or when the partition heals. In either case, writes are not available to the replica set while the new leader is elected.

MongoDB supports tunable consistency. You can control replica consistency for writes using MongoDB *write concerns*. In version 5.0, the default is *majority*, which ensures writes are durable at the majority of nodes in a replica set before success is acknowledged. In earlier versions, the default setting only waited for the primary to make a write durable, trading off performance against data safety.

Similarly, *read preferences* make it possible to configure which nodes in a replica set may handle reads. By default, requests are sent to primaries, ensuring consistent reads. You can modify this to trade off read performance and consistency. For example, you can specify reads may be handled by any replica (see Figure 13-4) or the nearest replica as measured by shortest round-trip time. In either case, stale reads are possible. Reading from the nearest replica is especially useful in widely geographically distributed deployments. You can locate the primary in one data center and place replicas in other data center locations that are closer to the origins of client read requests. This reduces network latency costs for replica reads.

Strengths and Weaknesses

MongoDB has matured massively since its initial releases. The attractive programming model drove initial popularity, and the core platform has been evolved by MongoDB engineers over more than a decade to improve performance, availability, scalability, and consistency. This has resulted in a powerful distributed database platform that applications can configure and tune to meet their requirements.

Performance

Initial MongoDB releases suffered from poor write performance. This has improved dramatically over the last decade, fueled to a large extent by the WiredTiger storage layer. Like most databases, each node's performance benefits greatly from large local memory space allocated for internal caching. You can also choose read preferences and write concerns that favor raw performance over consistency if application requirements allow.

Data safety

The default *majority* write concern ensures updates are durable on a quorum of nodes in the replica set. You can achieve greater write performance by specifying that updates must only be made durable on the primary. This creates the potential for data loss if the primary crashes before updates are replicated. The Raft-based leader election algorithm ensures that only an up-to-date secondary can be promoted to leader, again guarding against data loss.

Scalability

You can scale data collections horizontally using sharding and by deploying multiple *mongos* query router processes. Automatic data rebalancing across nodes helps spread requests evenly across the cluster, utilizing cluster capacity. You can add new and retire existing nodes, and the MongoDB cluster balancer automatically moves chunks across the cluster to utilize capacity. You can scale read loads by enabling reads to secondaries in a replica set.

Consistency

The availability of ACID transactions across multiple sharded collections provides developers with transaction consistency capabilities. You can also achieve replica consistency using appropriate write concerns settings. Session-based causal consistency provides RYOWs capabilities. You can also ensure linearizable reads and writes for single documents. This requires a read concern setting of *linearizable* and a write concern value of *majority*.[5]

Availability

Replica sets are the primary mechanism to ensure data availability. You should configure *config servers* as a replica set to ensure the cluster metadata remains available in the face of node failures and partitions. Your configurations also need to deploy sufficient *mongos* query router processes, as clients cannot query the database if a *mongos* process is not reachable.

Amazon DynamoDB

Amazon's DynamoDB is a core service offering in the AWS Cloud. Its origins go back to the original research published by Werner Vogels and his team on the Dynamo database.[6] Dynamo was built for usage on Amazon's website. Lessons learned internally, especially about the need for ease of management, led to the evolution of Dynamo to become the publicly available, fully managed DynamoDB database service in 2012.

As a fully managed database, DynamoDB minimizes the database administration effort required for applications. Replicated database partitions are automatically managed by DynamoDB, and data is repartitioned to satisfy size and performance requirements. Data items are hashed across partitions based on a user-defined partition key. Individual data items comprise nested, key-value pairs, and are replicated three times for data safety. The point-in-time recovery feature automatically performs incremental backups and stores them for a rolling 35-day period. Full backups can be run at any time with minimal effect on production systems.

As part of AWS, you are charged based on both the amount of storage used and the application's DynamoDB usage. Storage charges are straightforward. You basically pay for each GB of data storage. Charging for application usage is more complex, and affects both performance and scalability. Basically you pay for every read and write

---

5 A slightly out-of-date but still fascinating analysis of MongoDB consistency is provided by this Jepsen report (*https://oreil.ly/Elw1M*).

6 G. Decandia et al. "Dynamo: Amazon's Highly Available Key-Value Store.". In Proceedings of Twenty-First ACM SIGOPS Symposium on Operating Systems Principles—SOSP '07, p. 205. New York, NY, USA: ACM.

you make to your database. You can choose between two modes, known as capacity modes. The on-demand capacity mode is intended for applications that experience unpredictable traffic profiles with rapid spikes and troughs. DynamoDB employs its adaptive capacity capabilities to attempt to ensure the database deployment is able to satisfy performance and scalability requirements. You are charged for every operation (*https://oreil.ly/vqtqw*).

For applications with more predictable load profiles, you can choose *provisioned* capacity mode. You specify the number of reads and writes per second that your DynamoDB database should provide in terms of read and write capacity units. Should your application exceed this read/write capacity, requests may be throttled. DynamoDB provides burst capacity, based on recently unused provisioned capacity, to try to avoid throttling. You can also define a database to utilize autoscaling based on minimum and maximum provisioned capacity limits. Autoscaling dynamically adjusts the provisioned capacity on your behalf, within the specified limits, in response to observed traffic load.

DynamoDB has many optional features that either make it easier for you to write applications or provide your applications with higher levels of management automation. In general, the rule of thumb is that the more you ask DynamoDB to do for you, the more you pay. For example, if you enable point-in-time backups, then you pay per GB per month. If you disable this feature, you pay nothing. This is pretty much the way the world works with all cloud-based managed services. Caution is needed in how prolifically you use these options, especially at scale. But in most cases, your costs are reduced considerably due to the reduction in administrative and management effort.

Data Model and API

DynamoDB organizes data items in logical collections known as tables. Tables contain multiple items, which are uniquely identified by a primary key. Each item has a collection of uniquely identified attributes, which can optionally be nested. An individual item is restricted to 400 KB in size. DynamoDB is schemaless—items in the same table can have a different set of attributes.

In terms of data types, DynamoDB is fairly limited. Scalar types supported include strings, binary, numbers, and Booleans. You can build documents using list and map data types, and these can be nested up to 32 levels deep. You can also use sets to create a named attribute containing unique values. The code below depicts a DynamoDB item as an example. The primary key is `skierID`. The `skiresorts` field is represented by a list, and `season21` is a map containing nested documents representing each of the skier's visits to a resort:

```
{
  "skierID": "6788321471",
```

```
    "Name": {
            "last": "Gorton",
            "first": "Ian"
    },
 "location": "USA-WA-Seattle",
 "skiresorts": [
            "Crystal Mountain",
            "Mission Ridge"
 ],
 "numdays": "2",
 "season21": {
    "day1": {
            "date": "12/1/2021",
            "vertical ": 30701,
            "lifts": 27,
            "resort": "Crystal Mountain"
    },
    "day2": {
            "date": "12/8/2021",
            "vertical": "17021",
            "lifts": 10,
            "resort": "Mission Ridge"
    }
 }
}
```

The primary key value for an item acts as the partition key, which is hashed to map each item to a distinct database partition. You can also create composite primary keys by defining a sort key using items in the table. This creates the ability to group logically related items in the same partition by using the same primary key and a unique sort key; DynamoDB still hashes the primary key to locate the partition, and it then stores all items with the same partition key value together, in sorted order by sort key value.[7]

As a simple example using the skier item in the code above, you could create a unique composite key using the location as the primary key and the skierID as the sort key. This would group together all skiers in the same location in the same partition, and store them in sorted order.

To support alternative efficient query paths, you can create multiple secondary indexes on a table, referred to as the base table. There are two types of secondary indexes, local and global.

A local secondary index must have the same partition key as the base table, and a different sort key. Local indexes are built and maintained on the same partition as the

---

7 For more examples of the power of sort keys, see *https://oreil.ly/5G5le*.

items to which they refer. Local index reads and writes consume the capacity units allocated to the base table.

Global secondary indexes can have different primary and sort keys to the base table. This means index entries can span all partitions for the table, hence the global terminology. A global secondary index is created and maintained in its own partition, and requires capacity to be provisioned separately from the base table.

For data access, you have two choices for APIs in DynamoDB. The so-called *classic* API provides single- and multiple-item CRUD capabilities using variations of four core operations, namely `PutItem`, `GetItem`, `DeleteItem`, and `UpdateItem` operations. The following Java example shows a `GetItem` API. It retrieves the complete document identified by the `skierID` primary key value specified in the API:

```
Table table = dynamoDB.getTable("Skiers");
Item item = table.getItem("skierID", "6788321471");
```

If you want to read or write to multiple items at the same time, you can use the `Batch GetItem` and `BatchWriteItem` operations. These are essentially wrappers around individual `GetItem` and `PutItem/DeleteItem/UpdateItem` APIs. The advantage of using these batch versions is that all the requests are submitted in a single API call. This reduces the number of network round trips from your client to DynamoDB. Your performance also benefits because DynamoDB executes each individual read or write operation in parallel.

The more recently available alternative API, known as PartiQL, is an SQL-derived dialect. You submit SQL statements using the `ExecuteStatement` and `BatchExecuteStatement` APIs. DynamoDB translates your SQL statements into individual API calls as defined in the classic API.

You also have ACID transaction capabilities using the `ExecuteTransaction` API. This enables you to group multiple CRUD operations to multiple items both within and across tables, with guarantees that all will succeed, or none will. Under the hood, DynamoDB uses the 2PC algorithm to coordinate transactions across distributed partitions.

Transactions have an impact (*https://oreil.ly/adQml*) on capacity provisioning. In provisioned mode, each transaction will incur two reads or writes to each data item accessed in the transaction. This means you have to plan your read and write capacity units accordingly. If sufficient provisioned capacity is not available for any of the tables accessed in the transaction, the transactions may fail.

Distribution and Replication

As a managed service, DynamoDB simplifies data distribution and replication from the application's perspective. You define a partition key for items, and DynamoDB hashes the key to store three copies of every item. To enhance availability, the nodes that host each partition are in different availability zones within a single AWS region. Availability zones are designed to fail independently of others within each AWS region.

Each partition has a leader and two followers. When you issue an update request to an item, you receive an HTTP 200 response code when the update is made durable on the leader. Updates then propagate asynchronously to replicas.

By default, read operations can access any replica, leading to the potential for stale reads. If you want to ensure you read the latest value of an item, you can set the ConsistentRead parameter in read APIs to true. This directs writes to the leader node, which has the latest value. Strongly consistent reads consume more capacity units than eventually consistent reads, and may fail if the leader partition is unavailable.

DynamoDB manages your partitions, and its adaptive capacity capabilities will automatically repartition data, while maintaining availability, under the following circumstances:

- A partition exceeds the size limits for partitions, which is approximately 10 GB.
- You increase the provisioned throughput capacity for a table, requiring performance that is higher than the existing partitions can support.
- A table configured to use on-demand capacity experiences a spike in requests that exceeds the throughput it is able to sustain.

By default, DynamoDB tables reside in a single AWS region. AWS regions are tied to physical resources known as data centers that are located in different places around the world. For applications that serve large-scale, globally distributed user populations, latencies can be potentially prohibitive if requests must travel long distances to the region where your DynamoDB database resides.

As an example, imagine the skier management system from earlier in this chapter has ski resorts all over the globe, and uses a DynamoDB database located in the US west coast region (e.g., us-west-1). Skiers at European and Australian resorts would experience considerably longer latencies to access the system than those located in North America.

You can address these latencies by deploying your tables across multiple regions using DynamoDB global tables. Global tables maintain additional replicas in multiple AWS regions, and replicate all items across all the regions you wish to locate the table. Updates made in one region propagate to other replicas asynchronously. You also pay storage charges at each region, increasing the overall application costs. This scheme is shown in Figure 13-5, with global tables located in the US, India, and Italy.

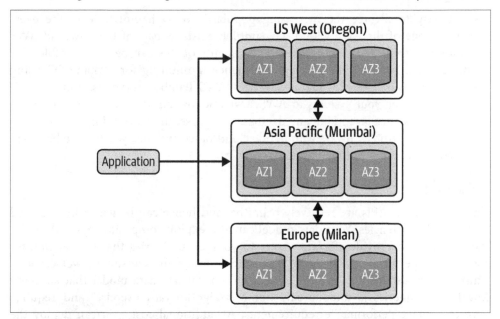

Figure 13-5. DynamoDB global tables

Importantly, global tables are multileader, meaning you can update the leader replica in any region. This creates the potential for conflicts if the same item is concurrently updated in two regions. In this case, DynamoDB uses a last writer wins conflict resolution strategy to converge replicas on a single value.

Global tables have some subtle restrictions you need to be aware of. These concern strongly consistent reads and transactions, which both operate at the scope of a single region:

- A strongly consistent read returns the latest value for an item within the region that the read takes place. If the same item key has been more recently updated in another region, this value will not be returned. It may take several seconds for the latest version to be replicated across regions.

- The ACID properties of transactions are only guaranteed within the region that processes the transaction. Once the transaction has been committed in this source region, DynamoDB replicates the resulting updates to the other regions. The updates flow using the standard replication protocol, meaning you may see partial updates in destination regions while all the updates from the transaction are applied.

Strengths and Weaknesses

It's not easy to divorce the increasing popularity of DynamoDB from the ever-growing usage of the AWS Cloud. DynamoDB exists as part of the powerful AWS ecosystem of tools and technologies. The benefits of this can be considerable. For example, AWS provides integrated performance monitoring for DynamoDB using CloudWatch, and integrates seamlessly with AWS Lambda serverless functions. If you are deploying your systems to AWS, DynamoDB can be an excellent candidate for your persistence layer. Like any database of course, there are things you need to carefully assess. And as always with public cloud-based systems, you have to be aware of the costs your applications accrue.

Performance

The DynamoDB APIs are relatively primitive and hence can be generally executed with very low latencies. Your data model can also exploit composite keys and secondary indexes to provide efficient access to your data. Queries that exploit indexes rather than performing table scans will execute faster and consume fewer capacity units, which also reduces costs. Crafting an appropriate data model that supports low latency queries is undoubtedly not a straightforward exercise[8] and requires care to achieve performance requirements. At additional cost, you can deploy the DynamoDB Accelerator (DAX) in-memory cache (*https://oreil.ly/N2Q9K*) that can further reduce query latencies.

Data safety

Updates are acknowledged when the leader partition makes the modification durable, and all items in tables are replicated across three partitions in the local region. Using global tables increases the replication factor, but does introduce the potential for data loss if the same item is concurrently updated in two different regions. Point-in-time and on-demand backups are fully integrated with the AWS environment.

Scalability

DynamoDB's adaptive capacity is designed to rebalance large databases to provide sufficient partitions to match observed demand. This provides excellent scalability for workloads that exert relatively even loads across partitions.

---

8 Best practices for data modeling are described in the AWS documentation (*https://oreil.ly/Dr1eb*).

A well-known problem revolves around hotkeys. Provisioned capacity is allocated on a per-table basis. This means if your application has 10 partitions, each partition receives a tenth of the overall table capacity. If requests disproportionately access a small number of *hot keys*, the partitions that host those items can consume the provisioned capacity for the table. This can cause requests to be rejected due to a lack of provisioned capacity.

Adaptive capacity (*https://oreil.ly/gHIuz*) in extreme cases may create a partition that holds a single item with a hotkey. In this case, requests to the item are limited to the maximum throughput a single partition can deliver of 3,000 read capacity units or 1,000 write capacity units per second.

Consistency

Replicas are eventually consistent, so stale reads from nonleader replicas are possible. You can obtain the latest replica value using strongly consistent reads at the cost of additional capacity unit usage and latency. Reads from global indexes are always eventually consistent. You can also use ACID transactions to perform multi-item updates.[9] Both strongly consistent reads and transactions are scoped to a region and hence do not provide consistency guarantees with global tables.

Availability

DynamoDB provides users with a service-level agreement (SLA). This basically guarantees 99.999% availability for global tables and 99.99% availability for single-region tables. AWS outages do occur occasionally; for example, a major one brought down many applications in December 2021 (*https://oreil.ly/Wc58e*) and it's possible a failure in a part of the AWS ecosystem could make your data unavailable. It's basically a risk you take when you adopt a cloud-based service, and the reason that deployment strategies like hybrid and multicloud are becoming more and more popular.

Summary and Further Reading

In this chapter, I've described some of the major architectural features of three prominent NoSQL databases, namely Redis, MongoDB, and DynamoDB. Each is a powerful distributed platform in its own right, with large user communities. Underneath the hood, the implementations vary considerably. This affects the performance, scalability, availability, and consistency you can expect from applications built on each platform.

Redis favors raw performance and simplicity over data safety and consistency. MongoDB has a richer feature set and is suited to a broad range of business applications

---

9 An explanation of transaction isolation levels is at *https://oreil.ly/kDRnC*.

that require future growth. DynamoDB is a fully managed service and supports low-latency key-value lookups. It is deeply integrated into the AWS Cloud infrastructure, providing automatic scalability and availability guarantees. Similarly, you can use cloud-hosted implementations of both MongoDB and Redis (and several other databases) that are supported by major cloud vendors to simplify your operations and management.

In reality, there's no perfect solution or approach for choosing a distributed database to match your application needs. There are simply too many dimensions and features to thoroughly evaluate even for a small number of candidate platforms. The best you can do most of the time is serious due diligence, and ideally build a proof-of-technology prototype that lets you test-drive one or two platforms. There will always be unexpected roadblocks that make you curse your chosen platform. Software engineering at scale is an imperfect practice, I'm afraid, but with deep knowledge of the issues involved, you can usually avoid most disasters!

For a book with excellent coverage (both breadth and depth) of distributed database systems, *Principles of Distributed Database Systems*, 4th ed. (Springer, 2020) by M. Tamer Özsu and Patrick Valduriez is one to have on your bookshelf.

An excellent place for gaining insights into how some of the largest systems on the internet operate is *highscalability.com*. For example, recent posts describe the design of Tinder (*https://oreil.ly/h12rc*), which uses DynamoDB among a whole collection of technologies, and Instagram (*https://oreil.ly/4tPfh*), built upon Cassandra and Neo4j.

Finally, the complexity of managing distributed databases at scale is driving many businesses to use managed services such as DynamoDB. Platforms providing equivalent "serverless database" capabilities are emerging for many popular databases. Examples are MongoDB Atlas, Astra DB for Cassandra, and Yugabyte Cloud.

Event and Stream Processing

Part IV switches gears and describes architectures and technologies for processing streaming events at scale. Event-based systems pose their own unique challenges. They require technologies for reliably and efficiently capturing and persisting high-volume event streams. You also need tools to support calculating partial results from the most recent snapshots of the event stream (think trending topics in Twitter), with real-time capabilities and tolerance of processing node failures. I'll explain the architectural approaches required and illustrate solutions using the widely deployed Apache Kafka and Flink open source technologies.

CHAPTER 14
Scalable Event-Driven Processing

In Chapter 7, I described the benefits and basic primitives of asynchronous messaging systems. By utilizing a messaging system for communications, you can create loosely coupled architectures. Message producers simply store a message on a queue, without concern about how it is processed by consumers. There can be one or many consumers, and the collection of producers and consumers can evolve over time. This buys you immense architectural flexibility and has benefits in improving service responsiveness, smoothing out request arrival spikes through buffering, and maintaining system processing in the face of unavailable consumers.

Traditionally, the message broker technologies used to implement asynchronous systems focus on message transit. A broker platform such as RabbitMQ or ActiveMQ supports collections of queues that are used as temporary FIFO-based memory or disk-based storage. When a consumer accesses a message from a queue, the message is removed from the broker. This is known as *destructive consumer semantics*. If publish-subscribe messaging is used, brokers implement mechanisms to maintain messages in queues until all active subscribers have consumed each message. New subscribers do not see old messages. Brokers also typically implement some additional features for message filtering and routing.

In this chapter I'm going to revisit asynchronous systems through the lens of event-driven architectures. Event-driven systems have some attractive features for scalable distributed applications. I'll briefly explain these attractions, and then focus on the Apache Kafka platform. Kafka is designed to support event-driven systems at scale, utilizing a simple persistent message log data structure and nondestructive consumer semantics.

Event-Driven Architectures

Events represent that *something interesting* has happened in the application context. This might be an external event that is captured by the system, or an internally generated event due to some state change. For example, in a package shipping application, when a package arrives at a new location, a barcode scan generates an event containing the package identifier, location, and time. A microservice in a car hire system that manages driver details could emit an event when it detects a driver's license has expired. Both these examples demonstrate using events for notifications. The event source simply emits the event and has no expectations on how the event might be processed by other components in the system.

Events are typically published to a messaging system. Interested parties can register to receive events and process them accordingly. A package shipping barcode scan might be consumed by a microservice that sends a text to the customer awaiting the package. Another microservice might update the package's delivery state, noting its current location. The expired license event may be utilized to send the driver an email to remind them to update their information. The important thing is that the event source is oblivious to the actions that are triggered by event generation. The resulting architecture is loosely coupled and affords high levels of flexibility for incorporating new consumers of events.

You can implement an event-based architecture using messaging systems like RabbitMQ's publish/subscribe features. Once every subscriber has consumed an event, the event is removed from the broker. This frees up broker resources, but also has the effect of destroying any explicit record of the event.

It turns out that keeping a permanent record of immutable events in a simple log data structure has some useful characteristics. In contrast to FIFO queues managed by most message brokers, an event log is an append-only data structure, as shown in Figure 14-1. Records are appended to the end of the log and each log entry has a unique entry number. The sequence numbers explicitly capture the order of events in the system. Events with a lower sequence number are defined to have occurred before entries with a higher sequence number. This order is especially useful in distributed systems and can be exploited to produce useful application insights and behaviors.

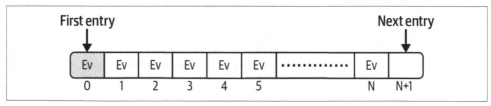

Figure 14-1. A log data structure

For example, in the package shipping example, you could process the log to discover the number of packages at each location at any instant, and the duration that packages reside at locations before being loaded onto the next stage of delivery. If a package gets misplaced or delayed, you can generate another event to trigger some remedial action to get a package moving again. These analyses become straightforward to implement as the log is the single source of truth about where every package is (and was) at any instant.

Another common use case for event-based systems is keeping replicated data synchronized across microservices. For example, a manufacturer might change the name of a product by sending an update request to the *Catalog* microservice. Internally, this microservice updates the product name in its local data store and emits an event to an event log shared with other microservices in the application. Any microservice that stores product details can read the event and update its own copy of the product name. As shown in Figure 14-2, the event log is essentially being used for replication across microservices to implement state transfer.

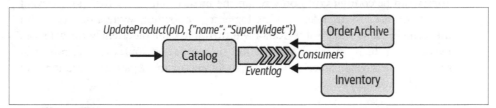

Figure 14-2. Using an event log to replicate state changes across microservices

The persistent nature of the event log has some key advantages:

- You can introduce new event consumers at any time. The log stores a permanent, immutable record of events and a new consumer has access to this complete history of events. It can process both existing and new events.

- You can modify existing event-processing logic, either to add new features or fix bugs. You can then execute the new logic on the complete log to enrich results or fix errors.

- If a server or disk failure occurs, you can restore the last known state and replay events from the log to restore the data set. This is analogous to the role of the transaction log in database systems.

As with all things, there are downsides to immutable, append-only logs. I briefly describe one of these, deleting events, and Apache Kafka's related capabilities in the following sidebar. You can read an awful lot more about designing event-driven architectures and patterns such as event collaboration and event sourcing. I'll point you to several excellent sources in "Summary and Further Reading" on page 284. For the remainder of this chapter, however, I want to explore the features of the Apache Kafka platform.

Deleting Events from a Log

Some use cases require log entries to be deleted. A prominent one is the *right to be forgotten* regulatory requirements of the European Union's General Data Protection Regulation (GDPR) laws. Append-only immutable logs are not designed for deletion of entries, which can make deleting entries problematic.

Apache Kafka provides two main mechanisms for log entry deletion. There are:

Time to live
Log entries are deleted after a default period of two weeks. You can adjust this to meet your requirements for log entry retention and deletion.

Compacted topics
Topics can be configured to only retain the most recent entry for a given event key. If you need to delete an existing log entry, you simply write a new one with the same key and a null value. Kafka will then mark the older entry for deletion. Events are actually marked for deletion in compacted topics and removed at some time later when a period log compaction task runs. Again, the frequency of this task is configurable.

Apache Kafka

At its core, Kafka is a distributed persistent log store. Kafka employs what is often called a *dumb broker/smart clients* architecture. The broker's main capabilities revolve around efficiently appending new events to persistent logs, delivering events to consumers, and managing log partitioning and replication for scalability and availability. Log entries are stored durably and can be read multiple times by multiple consumers. Consumers simply specify the log offset, or index, of the entries they wish to read. This frees the broker from maintaining any complex consumer-related state.

The resulting architecture has proven to be incredibly scalable and to provide very high throughput. For these reasons, Kafka has become one of the most widely used open source messaging platforms in use in modern systems.

Kafka originated at LinkedIn from efforts to streamline their system integration efforts.[1] It migrated to become an Apache project (*https://oreil.ly/Z4RvD*) in 2012. The

---

[1] Jay Kreps, one of the inventors of Kafka, wrote this excellent article (*https://oreil.ly/LwseT*) going into detail about logs and the project's development.

Kafka broker, which is the focus of the following subsections, sits at the core of a suite of related technologies. These are:

Kafka Connect

This is a framework designed for building connectors to link external data systems to the Kafka broker. You can use the framework to build high-performance connectors that produce or consume Kafka messages from your own systems. Multiple vendors also provide prefabricated connectors for pretty much any data management system most of you can probably think of![2]

Kafka Streams

This is a lightweight client library for building streaming applications from events stored in the Kafka broker. A data stream represents an unbounded, continuously updating data set. Streaming applications provide useful real-time insights by processing data in batches or time windows. For example, a supermarket may process a stream of incoming item purchases to discover the highest selling items in the last hour. This could be used to trigger reordering or restocking of items that are unexpectedly selling quickly. Streaming applications and platforms are the topic I cover in depth in Chapter 15, so I won't return to Kafka Streams here.

Kafka supports highly distributed cluster deployments in which brokers communicate to distribute and replicate event logs. This requires management of cluster metadata, which essentially specifies where the multiple event logs live in the cluster, and various other elements of cluster state. Kafka delegates this metadata management to Apache ZooKeeper (*https://oreil.ly/OOsna*).

ZooKeeper is a highly available service that is used by many distributed platforms to manage configuration information and support group coordination. ZooKeeper provides a hierarchical namespace similar to a normal filesystem that Kafka uses to maintain the cluster state externally, making it available to all brokers. This means you must create a ZooKeeper cluster (for availability) and make this accessible to the brokers in your Kafka cluster.[3] After that, Kafka's use of ZooKeeper is transparent to your application.

Topics

Kafka topics are the equivalent of queues in general messaging technologies. In Kafka, topics are managed by a broker and are always persistent, or durable. One or more producers send events to a topic. Topics are implemented as append-only logs, meaning new events are always written to the end of the log. Consumers read events

---

2 Confluent is a major provider of Kafka connectors (*https://oreil.ly/buaM9*).

3 The ZooKeeper dependency is likely to be removed in a future version (*https://oreil.ly/EhtIv*).

by specifying the name of the topic they wish to access and the index, or offset, of the message they want to read.

Reading an event from a topic is nondestructive. Each topic persists all events until a topic-specific configurable event retention period expires. When events have been stored for longer than this retention period, they are automatically removed from the topic.

Brokers take advantage of the append-only nature of logs to exploit the linear read and write performance capabilities of disks. Operating systems are heavily optimized for these data access patterns, and use techniques such as prefetching and caching of data. This enables Kafka to provide constant access times regardless of the number of events stored in a topic.

Returning to the skier management system example from Chapter 13, Figure 14-3 shows a Kafka broker that supports three topics used to capture ski lift ride events from three different ski resorts. Each time a skier rides a lift, an event is generated and written to the corresponding topic for that resort by a Kafka producer. Consumers can read events from the topic to update the skier's profile, send alerts for high-traffic lifts, and various other useful analytical functions related to the ski resort management business.

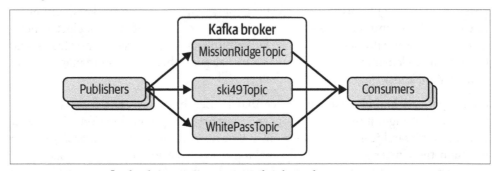

Figure 14-3. A Kafka broker managing topics for three ski resorts

Producers and Consumers

Kafka provides APIs for both producers to write events and consumers to read events from a topic. An event has an application-defined key and an associated value, and a publisher-supplied timestamp. For a lift ride event, the key might be the *skierID* and the value would embed the *skiLiftID* and a timestamp for when the skier rode the lift. The publisher would then send the event to the topic for the appropriate resort.

Kafka producers send events to brokers asynchronously. Calling the `producer.send()` operation causes the event to be written to a local buffer in the producer. Producers create batches of pending events until one of a configurable pair of parameters is triggered. The whole event batch is then sent in one network request. You can, for example, use these parameters to send the batch to the broker as soon as the batch size exceeds a specified value (e.g., 256 K) or some latency bound (e.g., 5 ms) expires. This is illustrated in Figure 14-4 along with how to set these configuration parameter values using a `Properties` object. Producers build independent batches in local buffers for each topic they deliver events to. Batches are maintained in the buffer until they are successfully acknowledged by the broker.

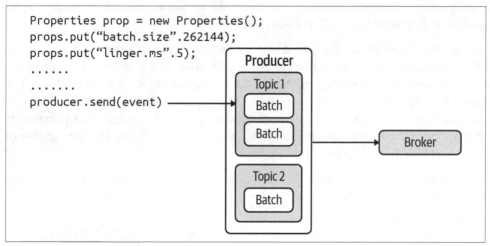

Figure 14-4. Kafka producer

Accumulating events in batches enables Kafka to incur less network round trips to the broker to deliver events. It also enables the broker to perform fewer, larger writes when appending event batches to the topic. Together, these efficiency measures are responsible for much of the high throughput that a Kafka system can achieve. Buffering events on producers allows you to trade off the additional latency that is incurred while batches are accumulated (the `linger.ms` value) for improved system throughput.

The following code snippet shows a simple method that sends a ski lift ride event to a topic that represents the resort on the broker. The `send()` method returns a `Future` of type `RecordMetaData`. Calls to `Future.get()` will block until the broker has appended the event to the topic and returns a `RecordMetaData` object. This contains information about the event in the log such as its timestamp and offset:

```
public Future<RecordMetadata> sendToBroker(final String skierID, final String
                                            liftRideEvent) {

    // initialization of producer and resortTopic omitted for brevity
    final ProducerRecord<String, String> producerRecord = new
        ProducerRecord<>(resortTopic, skierID, liftRideEvent);
    return producer.send(producerRecord);
}
```

Kafka supports different event delivery guarantees for producers through the `acks` configuration parameter. A value of zero provides no delivery guarantee. This is a "fire-and-forget" option—events can be lost. A value of one means an event will be acknowledged by the broker once it has been persisted to the destination topic. Transient network failures may cause the producer to retry failed events, leading to duplicates. If you can't accept duplicates, you can set the `enable-idempotence` configuration parameter to `true`. This causes the broker to filter out duplicate events and provide exactly-once delivery semantics.

Kafka consumers utilize the pull model to retrieve events in batches from a topic. When a consumer first subscribes to a topic, its offset is set to the first event in the log. You then call the `poll()` method of the consumer object in an event loop. The `poll()` method returns one or more events starting from the current offset. Similarly to producers, you can tune consumer throughput using configuration parameters that specify how long a consumer waits for events to be available and the number of events returned on each call to `poll()`.

The following simple consumer code example shows an event loop that retrieves and processes a batch of events:

```
while (alive) {
  ConsumerRecords<K, V> liftRideEvents = consumer.poll(LIFT_TOPIC_TIMEOUT);
  analyze(liftRideEvents);
  consumer.commitSync();
}
```

Kafka increments the consumer's offset in the topic automatically to point to the next unprocessed event in the topic. By default Kafka will automatically commit this value such that the next request to fetch events will commence at the new offset. The commit message is actually sent as part of the `poll()` method, and this commits the offset returned by the previous `poll()` request. Should your consumer fail while processing the batch of events, the offset is not committed as `poll()` is not called. This gives your consumer at-least-once delivery guarantees, as the next fetch will start at the same offset as the previous one.

You can also choose to manually commit the offset in consumers. You do this by calling the `consumer.commitSync()` API, as shown in the example. If you call `commit Sync()` before you process the events in a batch, the new offset will be committed. This means if the consumer fails while processing the event batch, the batch will not be redelivered. Your consumers now have at-most-once delivery guarantees.

Calling `commitSync()` after you have processed all the events in a batch, as in the example, gives your consumers at-least-once delivery guarantees. If your consumer crashes while processing a batch of events, the offset will not be committed and when the consumer restarts the events will be redelivered. Consumers can also at any time explicitly set the offset for the topic using the `consumer.seek(topic, offset)` API.

Note the Kafka consumer API is not thread safe. All network interactions with the broker occur in the same client thread that retrieves events. To process events concurrently, the consumer needs to implement a threading scheme. A common approach is a thread-per-consumer model, which provides a simple solution at the cost of managing more TCP connections and fetch requests at the broker. An alternative is to have a single thread fetch events and offload event processing to a pool of processing threads. This potentially provides greater scalability, but makes manually committing events more complex as the threads somehow need to coordinate to ensure all events are processed for a topic before a commit is issued.

Scalability

The primary scalability mechanism in Kafka is topic partitioning. When you create a topic, you specify the number of partitions that should be used for storing events and Kafka distributes partitions across the brokers in a cluster. This provides horizontal scalability, as producers and consumers respectively can write to and read from different partitions in parallel.

When a producer starts, you specify a list of host/port pairs to connect to the cluster using the Properties object, as shown in the following Java snippet:

```
Properties props = new Properties();
props.put("bootstrap.servers", "IPbroker1,IPBroker2");
```

The producer connects to these servers to discover the cluster configuration in terms of broker IP addresses and which partitions are allocated to which brokers.

In tune with the "dumb broker" architecture that Kafka implements, producers, not the broker, are responsible for choosing the partition that an event is allocated to. This enables the broker to focus on its primary purpose of receiving, storing, and delivering events. By default, your producers use the DefaultPartitioner class provided by the Kafka API.

If you do not specify an event key (i.e., the key is null), the DefaultPartitioner sends batches of messages to topic partitions in a round-robin fashion. When you specify an event key, the partitioner uses a hash function on the key value to choose a partition. This directs events with the same key to the same partition, which can be useful for consumers that process events in aggregates. For example, in the ski resort system, you could use a liftID as a key to ensure all lift ride events on the same lift at the same resort are sent to the same partition. Or you could use skierID to ensure all lift rides for the same skier are sent to the same partition. This is commonly called semantic partitioning.

Partitioning a topic has an implication for event ordering. Kafka will write events to a single partition in the order they are generated by a producer, and events will be consumed from the partition in the order they are written. This means events in each partition are ordered by time, and provide a partial ordering of the event stream.[4]

However, there is no total order of events across partitions. You have to design your applications to be cognizant of this restriction. In Figure 14-5, consumers will see lift ride events for each lift hashed to a partition in order, but determining the lift ride event order across partitions is not possible.

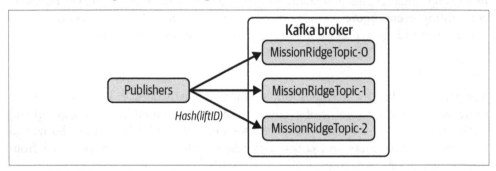

Figure 14-5. Distributing events to topic partitions using hashing

You can also increase—but not decrease—the number of topic partitions after initial deployment. Existing events in the partitions remain in place, but new events with the same keys may potentially be hashed to a different partition. In the example, suddenly lift rides with the key value liftID = 2 could be hashed to a different partition. You must therefore design your consumers so that they do not expect to process the same set of key values indefinitely from a partition.[5]

Partitions also enable concurrent event delivery to multiple consumers. To achieve this, Kafka introduces the concept of consumer groups for a topic. A consumer group comprises one or more consumers for a topic, up to a maximum of the number of partitions configured for a topic. There are basically three consumer allocation alternatives depending on the number of topic partitions and the number of subscribers in the group:

- If the number of consumers in the group is equal to the number of partitions, Kafka allocates each consumer in the group to exactly one partition.
- If the number of consumers in the group is less than the number of partitions, some consumers will be allocated to consume messages from multiple partitions.

---

4 Kafka producers will retry sending events that are not acknowledged by the broker. This may lead to events being stored in a different order from that in which they were originally produced.

5 To avoid this complexity completely, it is common for systems to slightly overprovision (e.g., 20%) the number of partitions for a topic so you can accommodate growth without increasing partitions post-deployment.

- If the number of consumers in the group exceeds the number of partitions, some consumers will not be allocated a partition and remain idle.

Figure 14-6 illustrates these allocation possibilities when (a) the consumer group size is equal to the number of partitions and (b) the consumer group size is less than the number of partitions.

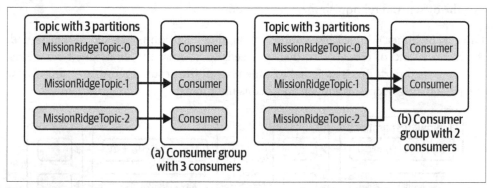

Figure 14-6. Kafka consumer groups where (a) group size = number of partitions, and (b) group size < number of partitions

Kafka implements a rebalancing mechanism for consumer groups.[6] This is triggered when a new consumer joins or an existing consumer leaves the group, or new partitions are added to a topic. For each consumer group, Kafka allocates one broker as the group coordinator. The coordinator tracks the partitions of topics and the members and subscriptions in the consumer group. If the number of topic partitions or group membership changes, the coordinator commences a rebalance. The rebalance must ensure that all topic partitions are allocated to a consumer from the group and all consumer group members are allocated one or more partitions.

To perform a rebalance, Kafka chooses one consumer from a group chosen as the group leader. When the rebalance is invoked, the group coordinator on the broker informs the consumer group leader of the existing partition assignments to the group members and the configuration changes needed. The consumer group leader decides how to allocate new partitions and group members, and may need to reassign existing partitions across group members. Moving a partition between consumers requires the current owner to first relinquish its subscription. To trigger this change, the group leader simply removes these subscriptions from the consumer's allocations and sends the new partition assignments to each consumer.

Each consumer processes the new allocation from the leader:

---

6 Kafka rebalancing is a complex process; this blog post (*https://oreil.ly/Of3nG*) by Konstantine Karantasis gives a good description of how it works.

- For partitions that are not moved between consumers, event processing can continue with no downtime.

- New partitions that are allocated to the consumer are simply added.

- For any of the consumer's existing partitions that do not appear in their new allocation, consumers complete processing the current batch of messages, commit the offset, and relinquish their subscription.

Once a consumer relinquishes a subscription, that partition is marked as unassigned. A second round of rebalancing then proceeds to allocate the unassigned partitions, ensuring each partition is assigned to a member of the group. Figure 14-7 shows how the rebalancing occurs when you add a consumer to a group.

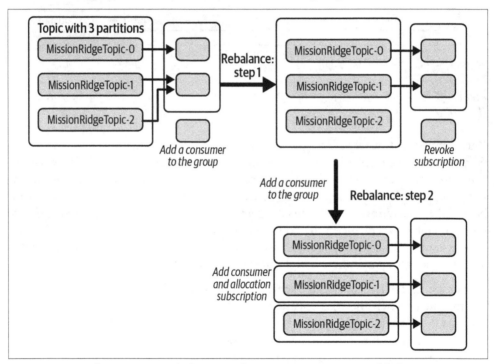

Figure 14-7. Kafka partition rebalancing when a new consumer is added to a group

In reality, most rebalances require very few partition reassignments. Kafka's rebalancing approach exploits this fact and enables consumers to keep processing messages while the rebalance proceeds. The group coordinator on the broker also has minimal involvement, basically just orchestrating the rebalances. The group leader is responsible for making partition reassignments. This simplifies the broker—dumb broker architecture, remember—and makes it possible to inject custom partition allocation algorithms for groups through a pluggable client framework. Kafka provides a `CooperativeStickyAssignor` out of the box, which maintains as many existing partition assignments as possible during a rebalance.

Availability

When you create a topic in Kafka, you can specify a replication factor of N. This causes Kafka to replicate every partition in the topic N times using a leader-follower architecture. Kafka attempts to allocate leaders to different brokers and deploy replicas to different broker instances to provide crash resilience. An example of a replicated partition for the skier management system topics with $N = 3$ is shown in Figure 14-8.

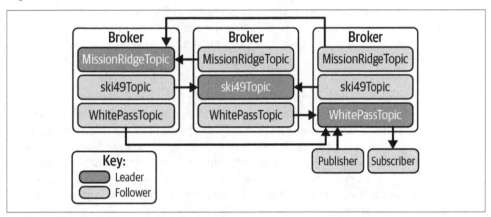

Figure 14-8. Kafka topic replication

Producers and consumers always write and read from the leader partitions, as shown just for the `WhitePassTopic` in Figure 14-8. Followers also behave as consumers from their associated leader, fetching messages at a period specified by the `replica.fetch.wait.max.ms` configuration parameter (default 500 ms).

If a leader fails, Kafka can automatically failover to one of the followers so that the partition remains available. The leader broker dynamically maintains a list of replicas that are up to date with the leader. This list, known as the in-sync replica (ISR) list, is persisted in ZooKeeper so that it is available in the event of leader failure. Kafka's custom leader election algorithm ensures that only members of the ISR can become leaders.

In a replicated deployment, producers can specify `acks=all` for data safety when publishing events. With this setting, the leader will not acknowledge a batch of events until they have been persisted by all ISRs. A topic can specify the minimum ISRs (`min.insync.replicas`) required to acknowledge a successful write. If the number of ISRs falls below this value, writes will fail. For example, you can create a topic with a replication factor of 3, and set `min.insync.replicas` to 2. Send operations will succeed as long as the majority, namely the leader and one follower, have received the write. Applications can therefore trade off data safety and latency versus availability by tuning the minimum ISRs value to meet requirements.

In the Wild: Event-Processing Systems

Kafka is widely deployed as the underlying messaging fabric for event-processing systems across multiple business verticals. Here are two prominent examples:

- Big Fish Games is a leading producer of consumer games. Big Fish uses Kafka (*https://oreil.ly/uELcV*) for high throughput event capture from game usage. This data is known as game telemetry, and includes a diverse set of events such as game device and session information, in-app purchases and responses to marketing campaigns, and game-specific events. This stream of events is fed into a series of downstream analytics to provide Big Fish with real-time insights into game feature usage and patterns of user behavior.

- Slack utilizes Kafka to capture events from their web clients that are too expensive to process synchronously. A custom web-facing gateway writes events to Kafka partitions and consumers retrieve these events and relay them to the appropriate processing logic. When an event surge occurs, and events cannot be processed as quickly as they arrive, Kafka topic partitions act as a buffer, protecting the downstream processing from overload until the arrival rate drops and processing can catch up. The 2018 iteration of this system (*https://oreil.ly/bbFWi*) was able to process more than a billion messages per day on 16 brokers deployed on AWS, with 32 partitions per topic.

Summary and Further Reading

Event-driven architectures are suitable for many use cases in the modern business landscape. You can use events to capture external activities and stream these into analytical systems to give real-time insights into user and system behaviors. You can also use events to describe state changes that are published to support integration across disparate systems or coupled microservices.

Event-processing systems require a reliable, robust, and scalable platform to capture and disseminate events. In this chapter, I've focused on Apache Kafka because it has been widely adopted in recent years and is suitable for high-throughput, scalable application deployments. In contrast to most messaging systems, Kafka persists events in topics that are processed in a nondestructive manner by consumers. You can partition and replicate topics to provide greater scalability and availability.

There's no better source of Kafka knowledge than *Kafka: The Definitive Guide: Real-Time Data and Stream Processing at Scale*, 2nd ed., by Gwen Shapira, Todd

Palino, Rajini Sivaram, and Krit Petty (O'Reilly, 2021). For more general information on event-based architectures, Adam Bellemare's *Building Event-Driven Microservices: Leveraging Organizational Data at Scale* (O'Reilly, 2020) is full of insights and wisdom.

Kafka is a particularly highly configurable platform. This can be both a blessing and a curse. By changing various configuration parameters, you can tune throughput, scalability, data safety, retention, and topic size. But with so many interdependent parameters at your disposal, the best approach is not always obvious. This is why I recommend looking at some of the studies that have been conducted on Kafka performance and tuning. The list below are really interesting reads, and can help guide you tune Kafka's behavior to meet your needs:

- Paul Brebner's blog post *The Power of Apache Kafka Partitions: How to Get the Most Out of Your Kafka Cluster* (*https://oreil.ly/Bhf3w*) shows results from a series of experiments that explore the various configuration options for topic partitioning.

- Konstantine Karantasis' blog post *Incremental Cooperative Rebalancing in Apache Kafka: Why Stop the World When You Can Change It?* (*https://oreil.ly/Vo7IG*) provides a great overview of rebalancing and explores through experiments the impact of rebalancing on Kafka systems.

- For a performance comparison, Alok Nikhil and Vinoth Chandar's benchmarking study, *Benchmarking Apache Kafka, Apache Pulsar, and RabbitMQ: Which Is the Fastest?* (*https://oreil.ly/w5FrI*), has some pearls of wisdom on Kafka performance tuning. This is an excellent, thorough study, but the usual proviso for benchmarks applies. This study was performed by a Kafka vendor, so results should be viewed through that lens. Remember there are lies, damn lies, and benchmarks!

CHAPTER 15

Stream Processing Systems

Time is money. The faster you can extract insights and knowledge from your data, the more quickly you can respond to the changing state of the world your systems are observing. Think of credit card fraud detection, catching anomalous network traffic for cybersecurity, real-time route planning in GPS-enabled driving applications, and identifying trending topics on social media sites. For all of these use cases, speed is of the essence.

These disparate applications have the common requirement of needing to perform computations on the most recent set of observations. Do you care if there was a minor accident that caused a 3-hour traffic backlog on your usual driving route earlier in the day, or that yesterday a snowstorm closed the road overnight? As long as your driving app tells you the highway is clear, you're on the way. Such computations are time sensitive and need access to recent data to be relevant.

Traditionally, you build such applications by persisting data from external feeds into a database and devising queries that can extract the information you need. As the arrival rate of the information your systems process increases, this becomes progressively harder to do. You need fast, scalable write performance from your database, and indexes to achieve low latency aggregate reads and joins for recent data points. After the database writes and the reads complete, you are finally ready to perform useful analysis. Sometimes, "finally" comes after a long wait, and in today's world, late results—even a few seconds late—are as bad as no results at all.

In the face of an ever-growing number of high-volume data sources from sensors, devices, and users, we've seen the emergence of a new class of technologies known as stream processing systems. These aim to provide you with the capabilities to process data streams in memory, without the need to persist the data to get the required results. This is often called *data-in-motion*, or real-time analytics. Stream processing platforms are becoming common parts of scalable systems. Not surprisingly, there's a highly competitive technology landscape that gives you plenty of choice about how to design and deploy your systems.

In this chapter I'll describe the basic concepts of stream processing platforms, and the common application architectures they enable. I'll then illustrate these concepts using Apache Flink, which is one of the leading open source streaming technologies.

Introduction to Stream Processing

Since the dawn of time in software systems, batch processing has played a major role in the processing of newly available data. In a batch processing system, raw data representing new and updated objects are accumulated into files. Periodically, a software component known as a batch data load job processes this newly available data and inserts it into the application's databases. This is commonly known as an extract, transform, load (ETL) process. ETL means the batch files containing new data are processed, aggregating and transforming the data into a format amenable for insertion into your storage layer.

Once a batch has been processed, the data is available to your analytics and external users. You can fire off queries to your databases that produce useful insights from the newly inserted data. This scheme is shown in Figure 15-1.

A good example of batch processing is a real estate website. All new listings, rentals, and sales are accumulated from various data sources into a batch. This batch is applied periodically to the underlying databases and subsequently becomes visible to users. The new information also feeds analytics like how many new listings are available each day in each region, and how homes have sold in the previous day.

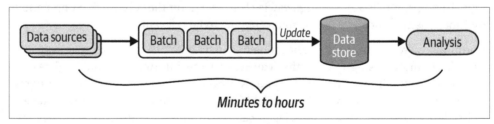

Figure 15-1. Batch processing

Batch processing is reliable, effective, and a vital component of large-scale systems. The downside, however, is the time lag between new data arriving and it being available for querying and analysis. Once you have accumulated a new batch of data, which might take an hour or a day depending on your use case, you must wait until:

- Your ETL job has finished ingesting the new data into your repository
- Your analysis job(s) complete(s)

At scale, it can take anywhere from several minutes to several hours for this whole process to run. This is not a problem for many use cases where absolute data freshness is not required. If you put your home on the market, it's not the end of the world if your listing doesn't appear on your favorite real estate site for a few hours. Even the next day works. But if someone steals your credit card information, waiting up to 24 hours to identify the fraud can cost your credit card provider a lot of money, and everyone a lot of inconvenience. For such use cases, you need streaming analytics.

Streaming systems process new data and events in *real time*. When you make a credit card purchase, the credit provider can utilize streaming analytics to run your transaction through a fraud detection model. This will use a fast statistical model prediction technique such as a support vector machine to evaluate whether a transaction is potentially fraudulent. The system can then flag and deny these transactions instantaneously. In this case, time really is money. "Real time" here is highly application dependent, and can mean processing latencies from less than a second to a few seconds.

Streaming systems can also work on batches, or windows of new data. These are sometimes called microbatches. For example, a public transportation monitoring system wants to update the location of all buses every 30 seconds. Buses send location updates every few seconds, and these are processed as a stream. The stream processor aggregates all the updates from each bus. Every 30 seconds the latest location is used to update the location that is made visible to transportation customers on their app. The series of updates for each bus can also be sent for further processing to calculate speed and predict arrival times at locations on the route. You can see an overview of how such a streaming system looks in Figure 15-2.

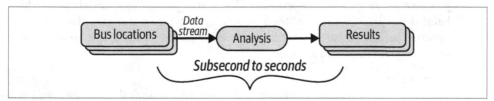

Figure 15-2. Stream processing example

Both batch and stream processing architectures, as well as hybrids like the Lambda architecture (see "The Lambda Architecture" on page 290) have their place in modern scalable systems. Table 15-1 summarizes the batch and streaming approaches, highlighting their essential characteristics.

Table 15-1. Comparing stream and batch processing

Characteristic	Stream processing	Batch processing
Batch size	From individual events to microbatches, typically thousands to tens of thousands in size	Essentially unlimited and commonly millions to billions of records at scale
Latency	Subsecond to seconds	Minutes to hours
Analytics	Relatively simple event detection, event aggregation, and metric calculations over rolling time intervals for newly arrived data	Complex, incorporating both new batch data and existing data

The Lambda Architecture

The Lambda architecture (*https://oreil.ly/JOWCb*) emerged around 2011 as a hybrid incorporating both traditional batch and emerging stream processing approaches. It comprises three layers:

The batch layer

This layer periodically processes massive quantities of new event data and updates the application's databases. At the time Lambda emerged, the dominant technology used for scalable batch processing was Apache Hadoop. As with any batch system, database update frequencies are on the order of minutes to hours depending on how often batches are processed.

The speed layer

This layer complements the batch layer by providing low latency results based on the new arrived events. While a new batch is accumulating for periodic processing, the speed layer processes the events, giving rapid insights into the latest data. You can think of the speed layer as compensating for the time lag between successive batches being processed. Apache Storm was a widely used technology for the speed layer.

The serving layer

This layer is where both the batch and speed layers store their results, and is responsible for handling queries and generating results. Results can be based on the outputs of either the batch or speed layer, or by computing a result that combines the two.

More recently, with new scalable streaming technologies available, the Lambda architecture has become less prominent. New events are stored in immutable log-based storage (e.g., Apache Kafka) and are continually processed as a data stream. You'll see this design referred to as the Kappa architecture (*https://oreil.ly/Qiy3k*).

Stream Processing Platforms

Stream processing platforms have proliferated in recent years. Multiple open source, proprietary, and cloud provider–supplied solutions exist, all with their own pros and cons. The underlying architecture and mechanisms across platforms are similar, however. Figure 15-3 illustrates the basic streaming application anatomy.

Data is made available to the platforms through various data sources. Commonly, these are queues such as a Kafka topic, or files in distributed storage systems such as S3. Stream processing nodes ingest data objects from data sources and perform transformations, aggregations, and application-specific business logic. Nodes are organized as a directed acyclic graph (DAG). Data objects originating from the source are processed as a stream. A data stream is an unbounded sequence of individual data objects. As data objects conceptually are passed, or flow, between processing nodes, streaming applications are also known as dataflow systems.

Stream processing systems provide the capabilities for processing nodes to transform an input stream at one node into a new stream that is processed by one or more downstream nodes. For example, your transport application can produce a new stream of the current bus locations every 30 seconds from a stream of bus location change events.

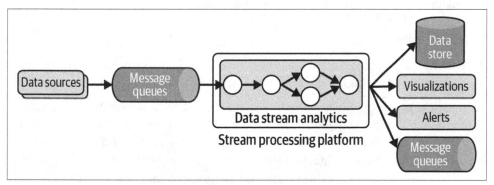

Figure 15-3. Generic stream processing platform architecture

Stream processing applications have two general flavors. The first simply processes and transforms individual events in the stream, without requiring any context, or state, about each event. You might input a stream of the latest data updates from wearable devices and transform the individual data objects into several others representing the user's latest step counts, heart rate, and hourly activity data. The results are written to data sinks such as a database or a queue for downstream asynchronous processing that calculates resting heart rate, calories burned, and so on.

In contrast, some streaming applications need to maintain state that persists across the processing of individual data objects in the stream. The transport monitoring application must know about all the buses in motion and maintain state representing the position updates in the last 30 seconds. A fraud detection application must maintain state representing the current model parameters needed to identify suspicious transactions. A retail store streaming application must maintain information representing the number of each individual item sold in the last hour to identify goods in high demand. This flavor of applications is known as stateful streaming applications.

Finally, stream processing platforms need capabilities to enable applications to scale out their processing and be resilient to failures. This is typically achieved by executing multiple instances of processing nodes across a cluster of computational resources, and implementing a state checkpointing mechanism to support recovery after failure. How this is achieved is extremely platform dependent.

As an example of scaling, the following Apache Storm code creates a stream processing application (called a *topology* in Storm) with a single data source and two processing nodes arranged as a simple pipeline:

```
TopologyBuilder builder = new TopologyBuilder();
builder.setSpout("purchasesSpout", new PurchasesSpout());
builder.setBolt("totalsBolt", new PurchaseTotals(), numTotalsBolts)
        fieldsGrouping("purchasesSpout", new Fields("itemKey"));
builder.setBolt("topSellersBolt", new TopSellers())
        .globalGrouping("totalsBolt");
```

It works as follows.

A PurchasesSpout object emits purchase records as a stream from a data source. A spout in Storm connects the streaming applications to a data source such as a queue.

The stream of purchases is passed from the spout to a processing node object, known as a bolt. This is the PurchaseTotals object. It maintains purchase totals for all items. Multiple instances of the bolt, defined by the numTotalsBolts parameter, are executed by Storm as independent threads. The fieldsGrouping ensures that purchases with the same itemKey value are always sent from the spout to the same bolt instance so that the total for every key is managed by a single bolt.

The PurchaseTotals bolt sends a stream of changed total purchases to the TopSellers bolt. This creates a leaderboard of the best-selling items in the stream. The globalGrouping routes the output of all PurchaseTotals instances to a single TopSellers bolt instance.

The logical Storm topology is depicted in Figure 15-4. Depending on the underlying cluster configuration that the topology is deployed on, Storm will execute the specified number of bolt instances as threads in one or more available JVMs. This enables topologies to take advantage of the computational resources available in the deployment environment.

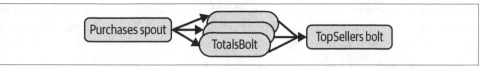

Figure 15-4. Example Apache Storm topology

Apache Storm is a powerful and scalable streaming platform. Its API is relatively simple, however, and places the responsibility for explicit topology definition on the application designer. In the remainder of this chapter, I'll focus instead on the more contemporary Apache Flink, which provides functional programming APIs for building streaming applications.

Case Study: Apache Flink

Apache Flink emerged in 2014 based on original research performed in the European Union Stratosphere project (*https://oreil.ly/JDTQo*). At its core, Flink is a distributed stream processing system designed for high throughput and low latencies. Flink provides a collection of operations for filtering, aggregating, mapping, and joining streams of data from data sources. Unlike explicitly defined Apache Storm topologies, Flink programs are compiled and automatically transformed into data flow programs that can be deployed on a clustered computational environment.

Flink provides a number of distinct APIs. I'll briefly give an example of the Data-Stream API in the following subsection. Flink also supports two APIs based on relational concepts, namely the Table and SQL APIs. You can build streaming applications that perform a subset of SQL SELECT queries on data streams that accumulate in tables with defined schemas.

DataStream API

The Flink DataStream API provides stream processing capabilities for Java and Scala systems. You can utilize a rich collection of stream processing operations for splitting, filtering, aggregating, and transforming streams of events, and creating periodic processing of batches of events in the stream using bounded time windows.

In Flink, a data stream is the logical representation of a stream of typed events, namely DataStream<T> in Java. Each stage in a data stream application applies functions to events and produces a stream of typed output events. Flink can process streams in parallel by replicating the functions in a processing pipeline and distributing events to different replicas.

The first thing you need to do in a Flink system is to create an execution environment. The execution environment for your application can be local, causing execution is a single JVM, or remote, which will invoke execution on a compute cluster.

The Flink environment object gives you the ability to specify various job execution parameters that control the scalability and fault tolerance of your application on a cluster. An example is shown in the following:

```
final StreamExecutionEnvironment env =
            StreamExecutionEnvironment.getExecutionEnvironment();
```

Once you have an execution environment, you can specify a data source. Flink supports a number of native data sources including files, and has connectors for various external technologies. The following example illustrates how to use the Flink Kafka connector to enable your application to ingest data from a Kafka topic using a Flink DataStream:

```
KafkaSource<LiftRide> source = KafkaSource.<LiftRide>builder()
    .setBootstrapServers(brokerList)
    .setTopics("resort-topic")
    .setGroupId("liftConsumers")
    .setStartingOffsets(OffsetsInitializer.earliest())
    .setValueOnlyDeserializer(new LiftRideSchema())
    .build();

DataStream<LiftRide> liftRideStream =
env.fromSource(source, WatermarkStrategy.noWatermarks(),
"Resort Lifts");
```

In this example, Flink:

- Starts reading at the start of the topic - OffsetsInitializer.earliest()

- Uses the Kafka event timestamp as the message time - WatermarkStrategy.noWatermarks()

Next you specify the transformations to perform on events that are received from the source. The following example shows how to count the number of individual lift rides on every ski lift in a resort:

```
DataStream<Tuple2<String, Integer>> liftCounts =
        liftRideStream
        .map(i -> Tuple2.of(i.getLiftID(), 1))
        .returns(Types.TUPLE(Types.STRING, Types.INT))
        .keyBy(value -> value.f0)
        .sum(1)
        .window(SlidingProcessingTimeWindows.of(Time.minutes(10),
                                        Time.minutes(5)));
```

The basic way this code works is as follows:

- Flink extracts each LiftRide event from the source and passes it to a map() function.

- map() generates a new object of type Tuple2. This contains two typed elements, the liftID of type STRING and a value of 1 (of type INT) representing a single lift ride.

- keyBy() partitions the map outputs using the liftID (field 0 in the tuple) as the key, and the sum(1) operator keeps a total of the number of individual lift rides (field 1 in the tuple) for each key.

- A sliding window defines when Flink generates results. Flink maintains a window of all the events it processes in the previous 10 minutes—this is the window size. Flink then generates, every 5 minutes, a set of results of type Tuple2 < String, Integer>. These represent the number of skier lift rides for each lift based on the events processed in the previous 10-minute interval. This is known as the *window slide*.

In general, window operations define the boundaries of finite sets of events and perform operations over this set of events. Sliding windows are extremely useful for performing calculations such as weighted averages. In this example, the results of each 5-minute window would show if the average number of skiers using the lift is increasing, decreasing, or stable. In contrast, a tumbling window defines distinct window boundaries and every event can only belong to a single window.

You also add a destination known as a sink for Flink to write the outputs of processing the messages in the stream:

```
liftRideStream.addSink( … ) // parameters omitted
```

Finally, you can kick off the stream processing. Flink programs are executed lazily. This means nothing happens until your code calls the following:

```
env.execute();
```

Scalability

Your Flink programs are transformed into a logical DAG. Data streams move from sources to sinks through transformations that you define in your code. These are represented as nodes in the DAG. At deployment time, Flink maps your logical graph to physical resources that execute the system. These physical resources can range from your local node to a large cluster running the application across hundreds of computation nodes. This is illustrated in Figure 15-5 for a simple deployment of two nodes.

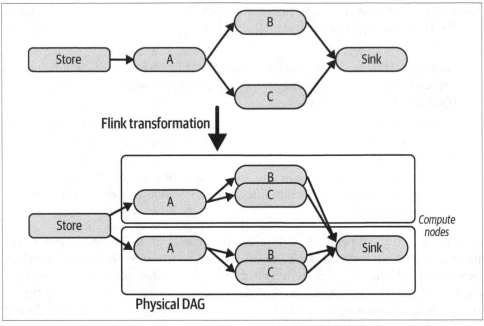

Figure 15-5. Example of mapping a Flink logical data flow to physical resources

You can influence how Flink deploys the logical DAG to physical resources in two main ways. These are by specifying the level of parallelism for various transformations in your program, and configuring the amount of concurrency allowed in the execution environment on each cluster node.

In your code, there are also two ways to inform the Flink runtime of the number of concurrent instances of your operators to execute. The following code example shows one way, which specifies that 10 parallel instances of the .sum transformation should be utilized:

```
.sum(1).setParallelism(10);
```

This results in Flink creating an execution DAG as shown in Figure 15-6. The key-value pairs emitted by the .map() function are hash partitioned across the 10 instances of the .sum() operator.

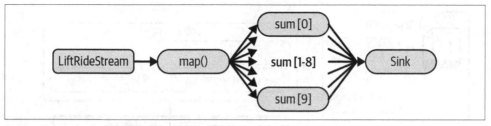

Figure 15-6. Specifying operator parallelism in Flink

You can also specify the default level of parallelism for all operators, data sources, and data sinks in a program using the execution environment object. This is shown in the following example, which sets the default parallelism level to 5:

```
final StreamExecutionEnvironment env =
        StreamExecutionEnvironment.getExecutionEnvironment();
env.setParallelism(5);
```

The default parallelism level is overridden by any operators that you explicitly define a level of parallelism for.

When you submit an application, Flink maps your logical DAG to the physical nodes that are available in your target cluster. Every compute node in the cluster runs a Flink task manager that is responsible for executing components of your streaming system. Each task manager is a JVM that by default can run one parallel task defined in your system. This is known as a task slot.

You can specify how many tasks Flink may deploy to a task manager by defining the `taskmanager.numberOfTaskSlots` configuration parameter in the `flink-conf.yaml` file. The default value for task slots is 1. This means each task manager runs a component of your system in a single thread in the JVM. If you increase the default value to N, the task manager can run N components of your dataflow in different threads, with each thread allocated $1/N$ of the available JVM memory. One common strategy is to allocate the same number of slots as CPU cores available on each task manager node.

The overall architecture is depicted in Figure 15-7. This also depicts the Flink job manager, which is responsible for cluster management, sharing of cluster resources between multiple jobs, monitoring for node failures, and managing recovery. A high availability configuration can be created that has multiple job managers deployed in a leader-follower architecture.

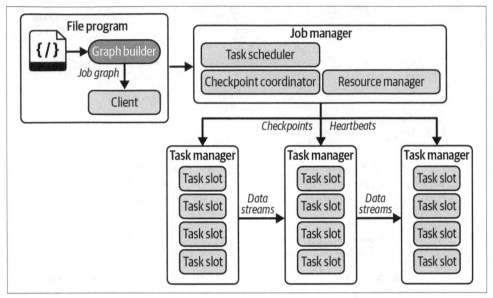

Figure 15-7. Flink runtime architecture

Flink implements a sophisticated transformation algorithm that maps a logical DAG to available physical resources. This includes optimizations, known as operator chaining, to colocate operators in a single task slot to minimize data communication costs. You influence how the physical mapping occurs by specifying parallelism levels, but in general it is not necessary for you to thoroughly understand the specifics of the algorithms employed. I'll point you to excellent resources in "Conclusions and Further Reading" on page 300 that describe the details.

Data Safety

Handling failures is an issue that you need to consider for any streaming systems. If one part of the deployed streaming application fails due to a node crash, network failure, or application exception, any state that is held in memory is lost. In the ski lift rides example, the lift ride counts for the 10-minute window are maintained in memory. If a task manager fails, the local state it manages is lost.

There are two mechanisms necessary in Flink to support data safety. These are persistent state storage and periodically invoking checkpoints for the complete stream.

First, you need to configure stateful operators to periodically persist their state as key-value pairs. By default, Flink supports a RocksDB storage backend (*http:// rocksdb.org*). You can configure this as follows in the flink-conf.yaml file:

```
state.backend: rocksdb
state.checkpoints.dir: file:///checkpt-mystream/
```

The persistent store makes it possible to restore state from snapshots in the case of stream processing failures. In streaming applications, however, the challenge is to ensure that all operators have a consistent checkpoint. Specifically, this means that the snapshots across all operators are based on processing the exact same input event from the stream source.

Flink ensures snapshots are consistent using a concept known as *stream barriers*.[1] The Flink job manager periodically injects events known as barriers into the source stream. These barriers flow strictly in order with events from the source stream. When a stateful operator inputs a barrier event on all its input streams, it writes its local state to the persistent storage. It then echoes the barrier on its outputs so that downstream operators in the stream processing can also persist their state.

This checkpointing mechanism is depicted in Figure 15-8. The barriers contain an identifier that represents their position in the source input stream. For example, if the input source is a Kafka topic, the barrier identifier represents the offset, N, of the event that precedes the barrier in the stream. This ensures all the checkpointed state is based on processing all events from the source up to and including offset N. Once a barrier is delivered on all the inputs to the stream sink, the checkpoint is marked complete. This becomes the latest state that the application can recover, should any failure occur.

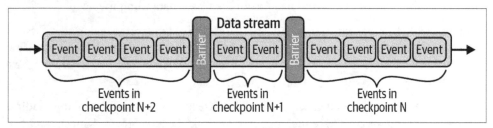

Figure 15-8. Barrier messages for Flink stream checkpointing.

Recovery involves restoring the state of the application after failure across the complete distributed dataflow. Flink achieves this by first stopping and redeploying the entire application. Flink then informs each stateful operator to restore its state from the latest completed snapshot. Finally, Flink informs the stream consumer to resume processing from position $N + 1$ in the data source.

Checkpointing effectively makes Flink applications fault tolerant. The trade-off is the cost of periodic state checkpointing and recovery. If the managed state is small, this

---

1 The approach is based on the paper "Lightweight Asynchronous Snapshots for Distributed Dataflows" (*https://oreil.ly/lAlEe*) by Paris Carbone et al.

will have minimal impact on throughput. However, if operators maintain large state spaces, frequent checkpointing may significantly impact stream throughput.

You can control when checkpoints are triggered through various configuration parameters. A frequently utilized parameter specifies the minimum time that must elapse between checkpoints. Setting this value to, for example, 2 seconds ensures that the next checkpoint will not start until at least 2 seconds after the previous one has completed. By default, checkpointing is not enabled for Flink applications.

Conclusions and Further Reading

The ability of streaming systems to produce relevant and timely results is highly attractive in many application domains. You can transform, aggregate, and analyze incoming data in real time. Your applications can perform analyses on finite batches of data based on time windows or message volumes. This makes it possible to identify trends in data and calculate metrics based on values in the most recent windows of data.

There are numerous streaming platforms that you can utilize to build fault-tolerant, scalable applications. Scalability is achieved by transforming your logical dataflow application architecture into a physical equivalent that distributes and connects processing nodes in the system across computational resources in a cluster. Fault tolerance mechanisms persist processing node state and track which messages have been successfully processed through the complete dataflow application. When failures occur, the streams can be restarted from the first outstanding message.

A great book that covers the broad spectrum of design and development issues for streaming applications is *Streaming Systems: The What, Where, When, and How of Large-Scale Data Processing* by Tyler Akidau, Slava Chernyak, and Reuven Lax (O'Reilly, 2018).

The books below are excellent sources of knowledge for a number of the leading contenders in this space. These include Apache Flink, Apache Storm, Kinesis, Apache Kafka Streams, Apache Spark Streams, and Spring Cloud Data Flow:

- Fabian Hueske and Vasiliki Kalavri, *Stream Processing with Apache Flink: Fundamentals, Implementation, and Operation of Streaming Applications* (O'Reilly, 2019)
- Mitch Seymour, *Mastering Kafka Streams and ksqlDB: Building Real-Time Data Systems by Example* (O'Reilly, 2021)
- Tarik Makota, Brian Maguire, Danny Gagne, and Rajeev Chakrabarti, *Scalable Data Streaming with Amazon Kinesis* (Packt, 2021)
- Sean T. Allen, Matthew Jankowski, and Peter Pathirana, *Storm Applied: Strategies for Real-Time Event Processing* (Manning, 2015)

- Gerard Maas and Francois Garillot, *Stream Processing with Apache Spark: Mastering Structured Streaming and Spark Streaming* (O'Reilly, 2019)
- Felipe Gutierrez, *Spring Cloud Data Flow: Native Cloud Orchestration Services for Microservice Applications on Modern Runtimes* (Apress, 2021)

CHAPTER 16

Final Tips for Success

Let's be blunt. Building scalable distributed systems is hard!

Distributed systems by their very nature are complex, with multiple failure modes that you must take into consideration, and design to handle all eventualities. It gets even trickier when your applications are stressed by high request volumes and rapidly growing data resources.

Applications at scale require numerous, cooperating hardware and software components that collectively create the capacity to achieve low latencies and high throughput. Your challenge is to compose all these moving parts into an application that satisfies requirements and doesn't cost you the earth to run.

In this book I've covered the broad landscape of principles, architectures, mechanisms, and technologies that are foundational to scalable distributed systems. Armed with this knowledge, you can start to design and build large-scale applications.

I suspect that you will not be surprised to hear that this is not the end of the story. We all operate in an ever-changing landscape of new application requirements and new hardware and software technologies. While the underlying principles of distributed systems still hold (for the foreseeable future anyway—quantum physics (*https://oreil.ly/orBDp*) might change things one day), new programming abstractions, platform models, and hardware make it easier for you to build more complex systems with increased performance, scalability, and resilience. The metaphorical train that propels us through this technology landscape will never slow down, and probably only get faster. Be prepared for a wild ride of constantly learning new stuff.

In addition, there are numerous essential ingredients for successful scalable systems that I have not covered in this book. Four of these are depicted in Figure 16-1, and I briefly describe the salient issues of each in the following subsections.

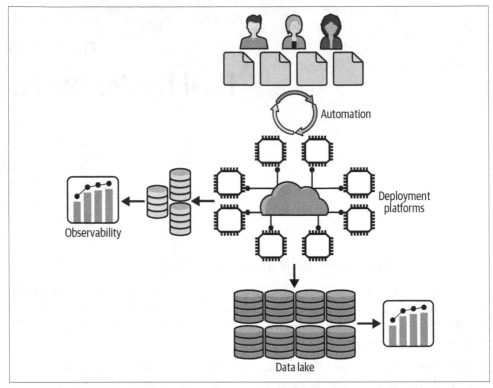

Figure 16-1. Scalable distributed systems

Automation

Engineers are rather expensive but essential resources when building large-scale systems. Any system that needs to be deployed at scale is quickly going to require hundreds of talented engineers. At the scale of the internet giants, this number grows to many thousands. Your engineers then need to be able to rapidly roll out changes, fixes, and new features to growing, complex codebases. The ability to efficiently push hundreds of changes per day to a deployed system without downtime is key at scale. You need to deploy frequent changes to improve the client experience and ensure reliable and scalable operations.

Automation makes it possible for developers to rapidly and reliably make changes to operational systems. The set of tools and practices that facilitate such automation are embodied in the discipline of DevOps. In *DevOps: A Software Architect's Perspective* (O'Reily, 2015), Len Bass et al. define DevOps as "a set of practices intended to reduce the time between committing a change to a system and the change being placed into normal production, while ensuring high quality."

DevOps encompasses a set of practices and tooling that are based on automation at all levels of the development and deployment process. At the heart of DevOps are continuous delivery (CD) practices,[1] supported by sophisticated toolchains for code configuration management, automated testing, deployment, and monitoring. DevOps extends these practices by making the management of the deployment environment the responsibility of the development teams. This typically includes rotating 24-hour on-call responsibilities for team members to respond to incidents or failures in production.

DevOps practices are essential for successful scalable systems. Teams have responsibilities for designing, developing, and operating their own microservices, which interact with the rest of the system through well-defined interfaces. With automated toolchains, they can independently deploy local changes and new features without perturbing the system operations. This reduces coordination overheads, increases productivity, and facilitates fast release cycles. All of which means you get a much bigger bang for your engineering dollars.

Observability

"You can't manage what you can't measure," so goes the saying. In large-scale software systems, this is indeed the truth. With multitudes of moving parts, all operating under variable load conditions and all unpredictably error-prone, you need insights gained through measurements on the health and behavior of your systems. An observability solution encompasses this spectrum of needs, including:

- The infrastructure to capture a system's current state based on constantly generated fine-grained metrics and log data
- The capabilities to analyze and act on aggregated real-time metrics and react to alerts indicating actual or pending failures

The first essential element of observability is an instrumented system that constantly emits system telemetry in the form of metrics and log entries. The sources of this telemetry are many and varied. It can be sourced from operating systems, the foundational platforms (e.g., messaging, databases) you utilize in your applications, and the application code you deploy. Metrics represent resource utilizations and the latencies, response times, and throughput the various parts of your system are delivering.

Code instrumentation is mandatory, and you can use open source frameworks (e.g., OpenTelemetry (*https://oreil.ly/sPiw9*)) or proprietary solutions (e.g., AWS Cloud-Watch) to emit application-specific metrics. These metrics and log entries form

---

1 The classic book in this area is Jez Humble and David Farley's *Continuous Delivery: Reliable Software Releases through Build, Test, and Deployment Automation* (Addison-Wesley Professional, 2010).

a continuous stream of time-series based data that characterizes your application behavior over time.

Capturing raw metrics data is simply a prerequisite for the situational awareness that observability infers. You need to rapidly process this stream of data so that it becomes actionable for systems operations. This includes both continuous monitoring of current state, exploring historical data to understand or diagnose some unexpected system behavior, and sending real-time alerts when thresholds are exceeded or failures occur. You can choose from a number of sophisticated solutions that support monitoring and exploration of time-series data for observability. Prometheus (*https://oreil.ly/IOzGY*), Grafana (*https://oreil.ly/3YIuw*), and Graphite (*https://oreil.ly/LreCj*) are three widely used technologies that provide out-of-the-box solutions for various parts of an observability stack.

Observability is a necessary component of scalable distributed systems. Ignore it at your peril! You'll find a great source for learning more about observability is the book by Charity Majors et al., *Observability Engineering* (O'Reilly).

Deployment Platforms

Scalable systems need extensive, elastic, and reliable compute and data platforms. Modern public clouds and private data centers are packed to the walls and ceilings with hardware you can provision with the click or two of a mouse. Even better, provisioning is invoked automatically using scripting languages designed for operations. This is known as *infrastructure as code (IaC)*, an essential ingredient of DevOps.

Virtual machines were traditionally the unit of deployment for applications. However, the last few years have seen the proliferation of new lighter-weight approaches based on container technologies, with Docker (*http://www.docker.com*) being the preeminent example. Container images enable the packaging of application code and dependencies into a single deployable unit. When deployed on a container engine such as the Docker Engine, containers run as isolated processes that share the host operating systems with other containers. Compared to virtual machines, containers consume considerably fewer resources, and hence make it possible to utilize hardware resources more efficiently by packing multiple containers on a single virtual machine.

Containers are typically utilized in concert with a cluster management platform such as Kubernetes or Apache Mesos. These orchestration platforms provide APIs for you to control how, when, and where your containers execute. They make it possible to automate your deployment of containers to support varying system loads using autoscaling and simplify the management of deploying multiple containers across multiple nodes in a cluster.

Data Lakes

How often do you scroll back in time on your favorite social media feed to look for photos you posted 5, 10, or even more years ago? Not very often, I bet. And I bet your connections do it even less. If you give it a try, you'll probably find, in general, that the further you go back in time, the longer your photos will take to render.

This is an example of the historical data management challenges faced at scale. Your systems will generate many petabytes or more of data over time. Much of this data is rarely, if ever accessed by your users. But for reasons that your application domain dictates (e.g., regulatory, contractual, popularity), you need to keep historical data available for the few occasions it is requested.

Managing, organizing, and storing these historical data repositories is the domain of data warehousing, big data, and (more recently) data lakes. While there are technical and philosophical differences between these approaches, their essence is storage of historical data in a form it can be retrieved, queried, and analyzed.

Data lakes are usually characterized by storing and cataloging data in heterogeneous formats, from native blobs to JSON to relational database extracts. They leverage low-cost object storage such as Apache Hadoop, Amazon S3, or Microsoft Azure Data Lake. Flexible query engines support analysis and transformation of the data. You can also use different storage classes, essentially providing longer retrieval times for lower cost, to optimize your costs.

Further Reading and Conclusions

There's a lot more to designing, building, operating, and evolving software systems at massive scale than can be covered in a single book. This chapter briefly describes four intrinsic elements of scalable systems that you need to be aware of and address in production systems. Add these elements to the ever-expanding palette of knowledge that modern software architects need to possess.

I'll leave you with a couple of recommendations for books I think everyone should have on their (virtual) bookshelf.

First, the classic book *Site Reliability Engineering: How Google Runs Production Systems*, edited by Betsy Beyer et al. (O'Reilly) describes the set of practices and tooling that Google developed to run their production systems. It is an extensive, thorough, and cross-cutting description of the approaches needed to keep massive-scale system infrastructures operating and healthy.

In a similar vein of wide-ranging knowledge, *Software Architecture: The Hard Parts*, by Neal Ford et al. (O'Reilly) is chock-full with insights and examples of how to address the many design conundrums that modern systems present. There's rarely, if ever, simple, correct solutions to these design problems. To this end, the authors describe how to apply contemporary architecture design knowledge and trade off analysis to reach satisfactory solutions.

Happy reading!

Index

producers, 79
    thread pools and, 82
producers, message queues, 128, 129
protocols, stateless, 100
publish-subscribe architecture pattern, 131
publishers, RabbitMQ, 139
pull model, 137

Q

query languages, NoSQL databases, 197-198
queues, RabbitMQ, 133-135
quorum intuition, 211
quorum reads and writes, 211-213
quorums, sloppy, 212

R

RabbitMQ, 128
    AMQP (Advanced Message Queuing Proto-
        col), 133
    availability, performance and, 140
    channel abstraction, 135
    concurrency, 135-138
    consumers, manual acknowledge, 139
    data safety, performance and, 138-140
    distribution, 135-138
    event-based architecture implementation,
        272
    example, 133-140
    exchanges, 133-135
        direct exchanges, 134
    message queues, 139
    messages, 133-135
    persistent messages, 139
    publishers, 139
    queues, 133-135
    TCP/IP and, 135
    throughput increase, 136
race conditions, threads, 69-73
Raft, 234-238
read replicas, 188-188
read your own rights (RYOW), 207-208
read-through caches, 119
reads, quorum reads and writes, 211-213
real-time analytics, 287
Redis, 116, 248
    availability, 253
    Cluster, 250
        resizing, 251
    Cluster bus, 250

consistency, 252
data safety, 252
distribution, 250
hashes, 249
linked lists, 249
performance, 252
scalability, 252
sets, 249
single-key operations, 249
strings, 249
transactions, 249
relational databases
    joins, distributed, 190
    normalization, 195
    Oracle RAC (Real Applications Cluster),
        191
        Cache Fusion, 191
        ClusterWare, 191
        physical storage, 191
    scaling
        scaling out, 188-190
        scaling up, 186-187
remote method invocation, 43-49
replica consistency, 225
    consensus algorithms, 225
replicas, databases
    inconsistency window, 206
        distance between, 206
        tunable consistency, 209
    repairs, 213
        active repair, 214
        passive repair, 214-215
replication
    distributed databases, 201
        CAP theorem, 202-203
        consistency, 202
    DynamoDB, 264-266
    Kafka, 283
    leader-follower, 208
    messages, 132-133
    MongoDB, 256-259
resilience, microservices, 172-180
resolve phase, 2PC (two-phase commit), 230
Resources microservices, 172
REST, 94
right to be forgotten, 274
RMI (Remote Method Invocation), 45
RMI registry, 46
round-robin load distribution, 109

About the Author

Ian Gorton has 30 years' experience as a software architect, author, computer science professor, and consultant. He has focused on distributed technologies since his days in graduate school and has worked on large-scale software systems in areas such as banking, telecommunications, government, health care, and scientific modeling and simulation. During this time, he has seen software systems evolve to the massive scale they routinely operate at today.

Ian has written three books, including *Essential Software Architecture* and *Data Intensive Computing*, and is the author of over 200 scientific and professional publications on software architecture and software engineering. At the Carnegie Mellon Software Engineering Institute, he led R&D projects in big data and massively scalable systems, and he has continued working, writing, and speaking on these topics since joining Northeastern University as a professor of computer science in 2015. He has a PhD from Sheffield Hallam University, UK, and is a senior member of the IEEE Computer Society.

Colophon

The animal on the cover of *Foundations of Scalable Systems* is a dusky grouper (*Epinephelus marginatus*), also known as the yellowbelly rock cod or yellowbelly grouper. It is common in the Mediterranean Sea, and its range stretches from the Iberian Peninsula along the coast of Africa to Mozambique and from Brazil to northern Argentina. Dusky groupers are normally found in rocky marine areas from the surface down to a depth of about 300 meters. They are ambush feeders, hiding among the rocks and then sucking in prey and swallowing it whole.

Like other groupers, they have large, oval bodies and wide mouths with protruding lower jaws. Dusky groupers have dark reddish-brown or grayish heads with yellow bellies and pale blotches on the head and body. They can reach up to five feet long and can weigh over a hundred pounds. All dusky groupers begin adult life as females and begin to breed at around five years of age, but they develop into males between their ninth and sixteenth years. They live up to 50 years in the wild.

The dusky grouper is a popular food fish, leading it to become a victim of overfishing. Although conservation efforts are being taken, the species is classified as vulnerable. Many of the animals on O'Reilly covers are endangered; all of them are important to the world.

The cover illustration is by Karen Montgomery, based on an antique line engraving from *Johnson's Natural History*. The cover fonts are Gilroy Semibold and Guardian Sans. The text font is Adobe Minion Pro; the heading font is Adobe Myriad Condensed; and the code font is Dalton Maag's Ubuntu Mono.

O'REILLY®

Learn from experts.
Become one yourself.

Books | Live online courses
Instant Answers | Virtual events
Videos | Interactive learning

Get started at oreilly.com.

Printed in the USA
CPSIA information can be obtained
at www.ICGtesting.com
JSHW051308241123
52664JS00009B/90